Taxes as Instruments of Public Policy

Taxes as Instruments of Public Policy

MARK SPROULE-JONES

MORLEY GUNDERSON and WAYNE R. THIRSK

ARTHUR DONNER and FRED LAZAR

SHEILA M. BLOCK and ALLAN M. MASLOVE

Edited by

ALLAN M. MASLOVE

Published by University of Toronto Press in cooperation with the
Fair Tax Commission of the Government of Ontario

UNIVERSITY OF TORONTO PRESS
Toronto Buffalo London

Printed in Canada
Reprinted in 2018
ISBN 978-0-8020-7195-8 (paper)

Printed on recycled paper

Canadian Cataloguing in Publication Data

Main entry under title:

Taxes as instruments of public policy

(Research studies of the Fair Tax Commission of Ontario)
Co-published by the Fair Tax Commission of the Government of Ontario.
Includes bibliographical references and index.
ISBN 978-0-8020-7195-8 (paper)

1. Taxation – Ontario.   2. Politicial planning – Ontario.   I. Sproule-Jones, Mark, 1941–
II. Maslove, Allan M., 1946–   III. Ontario. Fair Tax Commission.   IV. Series.

HJ2460.05T38 1994   339.5'25'09713   C94-931013-1

Contents

Foreword

The Ontario Fair Tax Commission was established to examine the province's tax system as an integrated whole and, in conjunction with its working groups, to analyse individual components of the system in detail.

It has been many years since the Ontario tax system was subjected to a comprehensive examination. However, a great deal of research on taxation has been undertaken over the past two decades. This work, based in several disciplines, has been both theoretical and applied, and in this context the research program of the Fair Tax Commission was formulated.

The research program has two broad purposes. The first is, of course, to support the deliberations of the commissioners. The second, more novel objective is to inform public discussions of tax matters so that the commission's formal and informal public consultations can be of maximum value. For this reason we have opted to publish volumes in the series of studies as they are ready, rather than holding them all until the commission has completed its work. While our approach is more difficult from a technical and administrative perspective, we believe that the benefits will justify our decision.

The research program seeks to synthesize the existing published work on taxation; to investigate the implications for Ontario of the general research work; and, where required, to conduct original research on the context and principles for tax reform and on specific tax questions. We thus hope to add to the existing body of knowledge without duplicating it. The studies included in these publications are those that we believe make a contribution to the literature on taxation.

I would like to extend my thanks to my fellow commissioners and to the members of the FTC secretariat. I also thank the many members of the working groups and the advisory groups who have contributed to the research program and to the overall work of the commission.

Monica Townson, Chair

Introduction

Taxation is primarily about raising revenues for provision of public services. Certainly, that is the popular view. The existence of tax structures, however, creates opportunities to fashion tax instruments for the pursuit of other policy objectives as well. In recent years, increasing attention has been directed to how tax instruments can be employed to redistribute income and to create incentives to generate more efficient outcomes in private markets. Tax measures are thus means to "get prices right" and, as such, are substitutes for other instruments of government – primarily direct spending and regulation – that are more commonly recognized as ways of achieving allocation goals.

The appropriateness of the policy objectives being pursued is not a tax matter to be investigated here. Rather, the tax issues addressed revolve around the merits and drawbacks of tax instruments, as compared with other possible routes to achieving policy objectives. For example, how effective are tax measures as a means to accomplish economic efficiency, as compared with direct spending or regulation? When should alternative instruments be used singly or in combination to reach an objective? What are the comparative administrative advantages of alternative instruments? Which instruments are more consistent with democratic accountability of governments?

The four papers in this volume deal with several facets of these issues. User fees, the subject of the first paper, are a category of taxes linked directly to consumption or use of specific goods and services; they are the counterparts of prices in private markets. The second and third papers discuss potential use of tax measures in two major areas of current public concern – investment in human capital, and conservation of the natural environment (specifically, combating the threat of global warming). The final paper provides an accounting record of existing tax expenditures in Ontario – tax measures that are used, in pursuit of economic or social policy objectives, to distribute financial benefits to firms and individuals.

User fees do not account for a large proportion of provincial revenues, but they are significant and, in recent years, have been growing at the municipal level. Sproule-Jones, in his paper, explores rationales and scope for reliance on user fees, along with limits of their applicability. To illustrate these principles, he examines the potential for user fees in four distinct policy areas. His paper shows the trade-offs among competing criteria involved in use of tax instruments.

Gunderson and Thirsk investigate whether and how the tax system impedes or promotes creation of human capital in Ontario. They begin by analysing rationales for government intervention in creation of human capital on either of two grounds – equity or efficiency. They develop models to analyse the effect of tax measures on decisions about investment in human capital. One of their conclusions is that the income tax system is not obviously biased against this form of investment. If inadequate investment exists anywhere, it is probably in worker training, and, accordingly, there may be an argument made for more use of tax incentives in this area.

Reducing carbon dioxide emissions has been identified as the key to combating global warming caused by greenhouse gases. Proposals for "carbon taxes" have been advanced for this purpose, and, indeed, some OECD countries have begun to implement them. These taxes are referred to as "market-based instruments" because they create incentives for users of energy to change their energy-consumption patterns, and they do so in ways that are more flexible than direct regulation. Lazar and Donner investigate the feasibility and potential effects of such a tax in Ontario. They find that the impact of the tax would fall disproportionately on a few industries, which might threaten their competitiveness vis-à-vis firms in jurisdictions not imposing such a tax. Lazar and Donner conclude that this would probably be a serious problem if Ontario were to introduce a carbon tax on its own; it would be preferable to do so along with other governments, following the terms of international accords.

Tax expenditures are preferential measures in the tax system that provide benefits to individuals and firms undertaking desired activities (for example, investment in research and development) or meeting specified conditions (for example, people with disabilities). These measures are expenditures – they represent revenues forgone, and direct spending measures could substitute for them. In the final paper, Block and Maslove introduce and explain the concept of tax expenditures, describe issues involved in identifying and measuring them, and, in general terms, discuss factors that influence the choice between direct taxes and tax expenditures. The paper concludes with estimates of the costs of Ontario's tax expenditures in the province's major tax systems, including those on personal and corporate income and on retail sales.

The intention of this volume – realized, we hope – is to develop a sense of the possibilities of and limits to pursuit of public policy objectives through tax instruments.

Allan M. Maslove

Taxes as Instruments of Public Policy

1 User Fees

MARK SPROULE-JONES

Introduction

"User fees," or "user charges," are the amounts of money levied on individuals for the use of goods and services from which they receive "special benefits." The fee payer engages in a transaction with a government or private organization and pays a fee in return for a measurable amount of a good or service (the special benefit). So, for example, a golfer pays green fees to a public or private club to play a round of golf; a student pays tuition fees to a public or private college or university for a course of study; or a homeowner pays water rates to a municipality or utility commission for litres of water consumed. This paper focuses on user fees paid to government rather than to private organizations, because user fees can often be substituted for taxes.

User fees are a form of benefit taxation in the sense that the feepayer receives benefits in return for the payment of fees. The feepayer may engage in a direct transaction with the service provider or may pay a levy earmarked for the service in question. I include both types of user fees in this study. User fees may be distinguished from other types of benefit taxation by the special nature of their benefits and the identifiable nature of (at least part) of their financing. The services from which the feepayer receives special benefits are "packageable" and deliverable to any individual or group of individuals. Their financing is based, at least in part, on the contributions of the identifiable individuals or groups of individuals that receive these services. Some further elaboration of these characteristics is provided in the section dealing with technical limits on applications of user fees.

User fees often do not have the compulsory character of income taxes. Feepayers often have a choice as to whether or not to buy a government good or service. So, for example, campers may choose to leave a provincial park at dusk rather than purchase a permit for overnight camping. Or a truck driver may choose to pay a bridge toll rather than take a more time-consuming alternative route. However, not all user fees have this voluntary character. Special assessments levied on property owners to pay for street lights or sidewalks are usually not subject to individual choice and are determined instead by a majority vote of property owners within an assessment area. Some authors (for example, Bird 1976, 3, 17) prefer to reserve the term "user fees" for compulsory levies and apply the term "user charges" in a generic way, to cover both voluntary and compulsory levies. I use both terms interchangeably in this paper to cover both compulsory and voluntary levies.

The paper has five sections. In "The Scope for User Fees," I review the magnitude of user fees and their relative importance as a revenue source for governments in Canada, especially for the government and municipalities of Ontario. "Why User Fees?" examines the philosophical, political, and economic reasons for adopting such levies to finance different government programs. Much of current public debate over user fees is couched in exclusively economic terms, considering them as a trade-off between the equity of charging the same fee to individuals of different income levels and the efficiencies of correctly pricing goods in the public sector. I present arguments to show that there are additional political and philosophical criteria that must be taken into account in assessing their value.

The next section summarizes "Technical Limits on User-Fee Applications." User fees are not always appropriate or feasible for many government programs, because of the ways in which the services must be consumed or produced. I note, in particular, that most government goods (functions) are composed of different activities, some of which may be easily measured and have user fees applied, and others where such fees cannot easily be imposed.

I illustrate these conclusions in "Four Cases" of government goods and services – domestic water-supply, management of water quality, health care, and university education – representing a range of activities for different kinds of government goods. I find scope for improvements in the application of user fees in all four examples.

Water-supply is a case in which user fees are the dominant form of revenue, but the method of application leads to inefficiencies as well as philosophical and political inequities. It is an excellent example of how user charges can be misapplied, despite the technical simplicity of assessing charges in this instance. In contrast, management of water quality is a complex, multi-activity good, in which Ontario could supplement its regulations by adopting user fees for the treatment of some pollutants. It offers an example of how user charges can be extended, with care, despite many technical complexities. Health care is the most costly provincial program, and one that enjoys significant public acceptance. However, here too there is scope for modest change by charging, for example, for "less essentials." This is a situation that amply demonstrates that there are valid philosophical and political reasons for limiting the scope of user fees. University tuition fees, as currently structured in Ontario, seem to merit more comprehensive reform. Tuition fees, as controlled by the province, possess limited economic advantages. They are politically unacceptable to many groups. They also transfer the (net) benefits of instruction to students of wealthier families and to students in professional programs such as medicine, pharmacy, or engineering.

The "Conclusion" reminds the reader of the potential scope for user fees and the precision with which they must be constructed if applied or extended.

The Scope of User Fees

User fees seem to be an endemic part of government machinery at all levels in Canada. Table 1 illustrates the types of fees that can be and are levied on goods and services used by the citizen. The list is not comprehensive; there is no single, complete set of data from which to compile such a list. The table does, however, give an indication of the wide range of items subject to a fee for use or purchase by citizens. There are, in addition, items available for use or purchase by other government agencies rather than by citizens; these are excluded from the table. Such items would include administrative services charged by a provincial or federal public works ministry to line ministries or support services such as laboratory services and training that may be charged to municipal organizations by provincial agencies.

One indicator of the magnitude and importance of user fees to governments in this country is provided by Statistics Canada. It summarizes all revenues paid into the consolidated revenue funds (or equivalents) of the federal, provincial, and local governments. This summary tends to understate the magnitude and significance of user

6   Mark Sproule-Jones

TABLE 1

Types of User Fees

Transportation
Subway and bus fares
Bridge and ferry tolls
Airport landing and departure fees
Hangar rentals
Dock and wharfage fees
Parking meter receipts

Policing
Special patrol service fees
Parking fees and charges
Fees for fingerprints and copies
Fees for extra service at stadiums and
   coliseums

Housing and Buildings
Street tree fees
Tract map filing fees
Development and utility connection
   charges
Lodging-house and nursing-home permits
Convention centre revenues
Building permits
Building inspectors fees

Recreation
Greens fees
Parking charges
Concession rentals
Admission and entrance fees
Club fees
Library charges
Camping permits

Utilities
Garbarge collection fees
Industrial waste charges
Sewer system fees
Water service charges
Electricity rates
Telephone booth rentals

Education
Tuition fees
Examination fees
Charges for books, libraries and
   equipment
Sports facilities charges
Concession rentals
Parking fees

Natural Resources
Land leases and rentals
Royalties and taxes on timber, minerals,
   water, and fish and wildlife
Veterinary services fees
Water storage leases
Grazing, pasture, and hay permits
Water transportation fees (e.g. logs)
Fishing and hunting licences

Tradesperson Licences
Auto wrecker
Barber
Electrician
Pawnbroker
Plumber
Street vendors
Taxi driver

Licences
Business licences
Marriage licences
Dog licences
Commercial motor vehicle licence and
   fees
Passenger vehicles' licence and fees
Operators' licence and fees
Theatre licences
Fire inspection fees
Taxi licences

Health and Hospitals
Ambulance charges
Concession rentals
Parking fees
Laboratory services
Health inspection fees
Inoculation fees
Pest eradicator fees

Sources: Bird (1976, 7–8); Mushkin and Vehorn (1977, 48).

fees, as the revenues of crown corporations and special boards tend not to be recorded in such totals. Nevertheless, some $47 billion is recorded as received from user fees – 17 per cent of all governmental revenues in 1990 (Table 2).

Queen's Park derives approximately 10 per cent of its revenue from user fees (Table 3) and the province's local governments, which include municipalities, school boards, and hospitals, receive 17 per cent of their revenues from user fees (Table 4).

The comparisons in Table 3 are interesting in two respects. First, Ontario decreased its employment of user fees by substituting payroll taxes for health insurance premiums in 1990. Thus, over 3 per cent of its revenue has been so replaced. Second, Ontario is less reliant on natural resources than other provinces, and, consequently, user fees on these sources make up less than 1 per cent of total revenues, compared with over 4 per cent for the other nine governments.

Table 4 reveals no similar major contrasts between local governments in Ontario and those elsewhere. However, previous work shows that if one disaggregates municipal from total local government revenues, principally by excluding school boards, one sees that municipalities, more than other general-purpose governments, raise sizeable sums through user fees (Sproule-Jones and White 1989). Table 5 shows that 25 per cent of municipal revenue comes from user fees, Canada-wide, with 5 per cent alone coming from the sale of water. Ontario municipalities rely on user fees to a lesser degree than the other provincial municipalities. Some 17 per cent of revenue comes from user fees.

User fees are growing and becoming more important to Ontario municipalities, rising from 12 to 17 per cent of revenues (Table 5). Even so, they still lag behind those of municipal governments in a number of other provinces. British Columbia's municipalities rely on user fees for 29 per cent of their total revenues; Alberta's, for 26 per cent; Saskatchewan's, for 19 per cent; and Prince Edward Island's, for 40 per cent (Sproule-Jones and White 1989).

In sum, while user fees are not the major source of revenue for any of the three levels of government in Canada, they raise, and have the potential to raise, significant sums of money for provision and production of government goods and services. Should we rely on them to a greater or a lesser degree? The next section develops criteria that can help us to answer that question.

TABLE 2
Consolidated Government Revenues, All Levels, from Fees and Similar Levies, 1990

	$ million, 1990	% of total consolidated revenue
Health and social insurance levies	22,003	8
Natural resource revenue	6,041	2
Privileges, licences, and permits	4,318	2
Sales of goods and services	10,372	4
Other own-source, non-tax revenue	3,755	1
Total consolidated revenue	272,566	100

Source: Statistics Canada (1992, Matrix 3159).

Why User Fees?

User fees and, indeed, the various tax methods that governments use to garner revenues are normally evaluated by economic criteria, such as efficiency, revenue-raising capacity, and administrative simplicity. All of these criteria are important and are discussed below. However, there are also important philosophical and political issues associated with the means by which communities finance governmental provision and production of goods and services.[1] The rationale for user fees is to be found in philosophical and political, as well as economic, analysis. Each of these types is addressed in the following sections.

Philosophical Rationale

Philosophical analyses of taxation and public finance are of two types. One type uses "end-state criteria" to evaluate fiscal issues. These focus on the outcomes of market, social, and political processes and on how various revenues and expenditures will affect these results. One such standard is that of a proper or just distribution of income, such as one that is largely egalitarian or (in contrast) reflects the natural and un-equal endowments of different individuals in society. User fees, which are paid by individuals regardless of income, may thus be judged as "unjust" by those analysts preferring an egalitarian distribution of income. They would, in contrast, be considered "just" by those prefer-ring that methods of raising revenue simply reflect and not distort people's endowments and capacity to pay for goods and services.

There are two fundamental problems with end-state criteria that remain insoluble in philosophical inquiry (Bish 1983). First, we have

TABLE 3
Provincial Government Revenues, All Provinces and Ontario, from Fees and Similar
Levies, 1990

	All provinces		Ontario	
	$ million	% of total gross revenue	$ million	% of total gross revenue
Health insurance premiums	4,775	4	1,394[a]	3
National reserve revenue	5,543	4	392	1
Privileges, licences, and permits	3,234	2	1,432	3
Sales of goods and services	2,169	2	700	2
Other own-source, non-tax revenue	844	1	306	1
Total gross revenue	132,837	100	45,844	100

Sources: Statistics Canada (1992, Matrices 2751, 2757).
[a] Estimated to fall to zero in 1992; replaced by payroll tax in 1990.

no way of measuring the value or utility of money (or its typical
derivation, that of work as opposed to leisure) to different people,
other than by observing how people behave. However, behaviour is
influenced by incentive structures, including the current pattern of
public finance. For example, a person who is already paying relatively
high municipal property taxes may be differently inclined to pay user
fees for municipal services than someone who pays relatively low
property taxes. End-state analyses fail to disentangle such problems.
A "just" distribution of income remains unmeasurable and of limited
practical value in governments' decision making.

Second, society has yet to devise an acceptable method of determining an appropriate end state and of ensuring conformity with this goal.
It is a truism to state that not everyone accepts egalitarianism or natural
endowments. We also seem unable to agree on how to deliberate and
decide upon any end-state criteria. Much of welfare economics is pred-
icated upon "benevolent despotism," in which a ruler can know and
aggregate individual preferences for collective solutions and then
implement such a collective solution without opposition (Sproule-
Jones 1972). Modern democratic forms of government are neither
omniscient in their decision-making capacities nor omnipotent in
effecting collective decisions, a point to which I return below in the
subsection on political rationale. Consequently, we have no practical

TABLE 4
Local Government Revenues, Canada and Ontario, from Fees and Similar Levies, 1990

	Canada-wide		Ontario-wide	
	$ million	% of total gross revenue	$ million	% of total gross revenue
Privileges, licences, and permits	428	1	196	1
Sales of goods and services	6,946	12	3,288	13
Other own-source, non-tax revenues	962	2	407	2
Total gross revenue	58,038	100	25,429	100

Sources: Statistics Canada (1992, Matrices 2764, 2770).

methods of establishing whether a user fee is appropriate or not in the light of such end-state criteria as justice and equality.

Because of such problems, philosophical discourse tends to reject end-state criteria and replace them with process criteria; it evaluates the rules or processes for making fiscal decisions, rather than the decisions themselves. Thus, if rules for establishing a user fee are considered fair, the user fee itself is fair. Institutional fairness or otherwise is used to evaluate fiscal decisions and their effects.

A particularly useful standard for evaluating user fees is that of "fiscal equivalence," a term coined by Mancur Olson (1969). Those who determine revenue and expenditures (or have representatives as agents acting on their behalf) are also those who benefit from and pay for the decisions, and so fiscal equivalence promotes self-correcting behaviour. Decision makers, who themselves know the nature and extent of the benefits of collective decisions, also pay for these decisions. If the benefits exceed the burdens, or vice-versa, self-correcting behaviour will bring them into balance. If there is no fiscal equivalence, self-correcting behaviour will not occur and society may well be destabilized as burdens are shifted away from the beneficiaries of public programs.

Fiscal equivalence suggests that user fees are the best way to finance those goods and services that can be "packaged" and "delivered" to identifiable individuals (concepts treated in the section below on technical limits on user-fee applications). Users get what they are prepared to pay for, and service levels can be adjusted to reflect the resulting

TABLE 5
Municipal Revenues, Canada and Ontario, from Fees and Similar Levies, 1981

	Canada-wide		Ontario-wide	
	$ million	% of total gross revenue	$ million	% of total gross revenue
Privileges, licences, and permits	190	1	58	1
Water	868	5	299	4
Rentals	199	1	67	1
Other sales of goods and services	1,968	11	705	10
Special assessments	329	2	36	1
Total gross revenue	17,968	100	6,951	100

Source: Sproule-Jones and White (1989, Tables 2 and 3).

revenues. Levels of service and of user fees emerge in a self-correcting process.

Fiscal equivalence can be applied spatially – to communities where goods and services are not produced for identifiable individuals but are used jointly by many citizens. In these cases, the geographic boundaries must be adjusted on a spatial basis to match the spread of beneficiaries and taxpayers. This is achieved typically through inter-governmental grants and contracts to pay for benefits and/or burdens that spill over political boundaries. Fiscal equivalence can, finally, be applied temporally, so that capital expenditures of governments are financed, over time, by designated capital budgets. Spatial and temporal fiscal equivalence is beyond the scope of this paper but parallels, in rationale, individual fiscal equivalence.

Political Rationale

Political factors are at the centre of governmental decisions about revenue policies and expenditure programs. They cannot be treated as constraints to achieving efficiency. Rather they are variables that express the priorities of any government, and, to the degree that taxes are concerned, they reflect the political power of government to coerce payments from citizens, corporations, and other groups.

User fees and various forms of taxation may be evaluated by two political criteria, both of which reflect the relationships between individual citizens and government decision makers. The first is that of representation; the second is that of accountability. Each is discussed in turn.

Representativeness is the degree to which the demands of individuals for revenue and expenditure programs are reflected in governmental decisions. Individuals would like their own preferences to match those of the government on all revenue and expenditure decisions. In any society, individuals will differ in their preferences, however, and it is highly unlikely that a perfect fit will occur in any one situation. Governments that represent diverse communities will be unable to represent fully all of their citizens' demands, and decisions will have to be made with less-than-unanimous consent. Perhaps the best that individuals can hope for is that, for a range of decisions over time, they are net beneficiaries of governmental decisions. Changes in the rules for voting, lobbying, and participation as well as in those for the conduct of parliaments, cabinets, and bureaucracies will not eliminate the problem of representation. Collective decision making implies a loss of control over individuals' decision making, notwithstanding democratic forms of representation.

By this criterion, user fees may thus represent the best form of revenue raising from the perspective of the individual citizen. To the degree that such fees are voluntary, the citizen can retain control over his or her selection of governmental programs. To the degree that the coercive types of taxation are used, the citizen loses control. This does not mean that taxation may not be attractive to those interests in society that can get their way. These interests may be coalitions put together by political parties or particularly powerful interest groups and bureaucracies. In such cases, there is no necessary match between the beneficiaries and the taxpayers of programs, a condition that I have identified as necessary for fiscal equivalence. Thus the implications of the political criterion of representation and the philosophical criterion of fiscal equivalence are consistent. Wherever it is technically possible to establish user fees (see the section below on technical limits on user-fee applications), they are preferable to alternative forms of taxation.

I turn now to the second political criterion – accountability. Governments in Canada have many rules designed to ensure that departments and managers producing goods and services remain accountable to politicians in cabinets and legislatures. These rules govern, among other things, the raising and spending of public monies.

Departments and managers, however, should also be accountable to the citizens who actually consume the goods and services that they produce. In the private marketplace, such accountability is called consumer sovereignty. In the governmental sector, there is no reason why citizen-consumers could not also be treated as consumer-sovereigns to the extent that this is technically feasible. Constitutionally, it is the governments of Canada and Ontario that share sovereign status in the province. However, there is no reason why in practice, rather than in constitutional theory, governments cannot treat citizen-consumers as if they were consumer-sovereigns.

If government departments and managers are to be accountable to the citizens who consume the goods and services that they produce, then user fees are the best way to raise revenues. There is one qualification to this criterion: the revenues would have to be earmarked for the government programs that are sold to citizen-consumers. User fees, when so earmarked, would enable service levels to be adjusted to meet the demands of citizen-consumers. Similarly, the citizen could better apportion his or her budget among goods and services that are not and need not be financed by taxes. Government programs should thus be made more responsive, and hence accountable, to citizens.

The political criteria of representation and accountability thus justify the role of user fees in public finance. They are consistent with, rather than in conflict with, the philosophical criterion of fiscal equivalence. They may or may not conflict, however, with economic criteria.

Economic Rationale

There is an economic rationale for the collection of user fees as a major source of government revenue. It consists of two major arguments. First, in the cases of goods and services that can be packaged and delivered to identifiable individuals, user fees can induce efficiency in government and also in the economy as a whole. Second, user fees can be a relatively simple way to recover the costs of government programs. I deal with the second argument first.

User fees are often a relatively painless way to recover the cost of government programs. Depending on the elasticity of demand for different goods and services, governments can raise substantial revenues by, in effect, selling some of their goods and services to citizens. Such governments must, however, choose between recovering costs and charging what the market may bear. The former route may involve simply setting user fees at a level representing the average cost of producing a given good or service. That way, total revenues from user fees will offset the total costs of the program, and no losses will occur to drain the treasury of tax revenues. If governments wish to raise revenue – that is, by generating profits – then the degree to which they can do so depends, in part, on the competitive nature of the markets for their goods and services. The classic case is the monopoly of the liquor stores in a province such as Ontario with regard to the sale of liquor and non-domestic wine. Profits amount to over $675 million per annum (Table 6). In contrast, wharfage fees collected by pleasure boating marinas that are owned by government tend to be set in the light of prices charged by public and private marinas in contiguous waterways (Sproule-Jones 1993, chap. 8).

A survey of 27 "upper-tier" (regional) and "lower-tier" (city) municipalities in southern Ontario, reported in Sproule-Jones and White (1989), revealed that none of them attempted to generate a profit when they applied user fees to their programs (the example of the Liquor Control Board of Ontario notwithstanding). Instead, all of them used the average cost-pricing model because it was simple to calculate. Only 13 of these municipalities, however, included both capital and overhead costs in their calculations. The others did not attempt even full recovery of costs. To my knowledge, there has been no other survey of the practice of setting user fees in Canada.

Economists nevertheless suggest that user fees should be based on marginal cost pricing rather than average cost pricing or revenue maximization (which is sometimes identical with marginal cost pricing). The reason is that of efficiency, which is the second of the two economic arguments for user fees.

The claims for efficiency parallel those previously mentioned for accountability. When user fees are set at a level that equates the marginal cost of government-produced goods with the marginal valuation or demand that citizen-consumers place on those goods, then efficiency will be the result. (It will also make services accountable to sovereign-consumers.) Efficiency is the result, because the user fees will directly reflect the opportunities that citizens forgo in the consumption of the good and, simultaneously, the opportunities that public managers forgo in the production of *that* particular good at *that* particular level. Neither consumers nor producers can be made better off by shifting their money into consuming or producing, respectively, alternative goods and services.

There is an extensive economic literature on the theory of marginal cost pricing and on when it may have to be modified or made more complex to meet particular market conditions. For example, in a decreasing-cost market for government goods, where marginal costs are below average costs, it may be appropriate for governments to

TABLE 6
Provincial Revenue ($ 000) from Administration of Liquor Control, 1989–90

	Net income from sales	Special liquor tax[a]	Licences and permits	Fines	Total revenue
Ontario	675,538	–	434,875	28	1,110,439
All provinces and territories	2,386,308	11,359	564,546	883	2,963,096

Source: Canadian Tax Foundation (1992, Table 11.8).
[a] Excludes provincial retail sales tax; includes special taxes in Prince Edward Island and Yukon, levied in addition to their provincial sales tax.

augment the revenues generated by user fees with tax revenues. The criterion of efficiency is not a simple one to apply in the real world of user fees. However, it may be even more difficult to apply the efficiency criterion in the cases of other revenue-raising instruments such as taxes.

Multiple Criteria

Analyses of the philosophical, political, and economic reasons for imposing user fees suggest that such levies may be an appropriate method of public finance on at least five grounds – fiscal equivalence, political representation, political accountability, revenue-raising capacity, and efficiency. These standards tend to be consistent with each other under most circumstances. However, the revenue-raising criterion can conflict with the others if the fees are not correctly designed. A charge merely to raise revenues may not be justifiable on philosophical, political, or efficiency grounds. In addition, there are technical limits to the scope of user fees. These limits are now discussed.

Technical Limits on User-Fee Applications

There are four major technical reasons why user fees cannot be adopted as the sole or major way that governments raise revenues. Two of these reasons have been either referred to or implied above.

First, many goods and services cannot be packaged and delivered to individual citizens. They are considered to be public or collective-consumption goods. Examples include national defence and clean air. Once one person has been provided with national defence or one person has breathed some clean air, lots of the two goods are available for others to consume or enjoy. This situation differs from that concerning many goods that are not consumed collectively. Goods such as an inoculation from a public health clinic or a bottle of wine from a liquor store are not available for others to consume once one person has acquired them. These latter are termed private goods, even though governments may supply many of them.

It is extremely difficult to put user fees on goods and services that are collectively consumed. Any one consumer may reason that he or she need not pay the user fee, because, if other people pay, the good will be available anyway. It will not be packaged and delivered only to those who pay the charge. Without everyone contributing in proportion to the benefits that they receive from consuming a public good, insufficient revenue will be raised and an insufficient supply of the good will be produced. A typical solution to the problem of providing and producing public goods is to resort to taxes that, by definition, force consumers to pay for the goods in question.

Consequently, there is a major class of goods to which user fees cannot be applied. However, there are often no technical reasons why some goods financed by taxes could not be paid for by user fees. Governments often provide private goods but finance them as if they were public goods, namely, through taxation. For example, only half of the municipal water-supply systems in Canada meter the water used by their customers, and some of these systems are financed by property taxes (Pearse, Bertrand, and MacLaren 1985, 103). We explore such cases in subsequent sections of this paper.

Second, it is frequently difficult to calculate the units with which to measure service levels, the costs to be included or excluded in calculating the average and marginal costs of any given level of service, and also the marginal costs as service levels may increase or decrease. These are all issues that must be addressed in the implementation of user fees, and as the survey of southern Ontario municipalities suggests, they can limit the scope of user-fee applications (Sproule-Jones and White 1989, 1483–84).

However, too much can be made of these difficulties in implementation. Since the development of program budgets and program evaluations in government in the 1970s, substantial experience exists within management or treasury board staffs in measuring service outputs and service costs. There is similar expertise in a number of local government agencies. It should not be too difficult for managers to agree on whether and how to include, for example, depreciation in their full-cost calculations. The major obstacle may well be one of incentives. Managers do not see the user-fee revenues for their programs returning to their agencies and have no incentive to alter costs and service levels in the light of these revenues. It is easier to stay with traditional budgetary systems. Moreover, "what are needed are not perfect prices, just better ones. Even bad prices have the virtue of making it clear that public services are not free" (Bird 1976, 238).

Third, and related to the previous two problems, there are some goods and services for which, for technical reasons, it is difficult to calculate appropriate user fees. Some of these are called toll (or club) goods, for which, once the good is produced, the marginal cost is close to zero. Examples include bridges and recreational facilities. Other kinds of goods difficult to price are those that generate externalities – that is, benefits or costs to people other than those directly benefiting from the goods. Both cases call for mixed financing. The operating costs of toll goods are probably financed best by general taxation, at least until congestion occurs, at which time a direct user charge may become desirable to ration demand. Externalities may also be funded by a separate kind of user fee, different from the actual fees used to finance the production of the good itself. For example, a pollution charge might be assessed against a hospital for the negative externalities from its incinerator, while at the same time hospital operations might be funded through taxes and user fees. The difficulty with externality charges is that the externality is often like a collective-consumption good for its recipients; it is available to other recipients for consumption after one person has experienced it. Consequently, it is difficult to calculate the exact dollar (negative or positive) value of the externality, when the externality is not traded on the market. I look into this case in more detail below. These kinds of difficulties in setting user charges are reviewed in detail in most public finance texts (for example, Musgrave, Musgrave, and Bird 1987, 679–95).

Fourth, many government goods and services involve more than one output. A relatively simple service such as that of solid waste (garbage) consists of two outputs or activities that make up the function – collection and disposal. Neither or both may be financed by a user fee. A more complex good such as university education consists of research activities, a variety of degree or teaching activities, and a number of activities for different communities and governments (such as cultural and sporting events, radio broadcasts, employment retraining, and job placement schemes). Again, one or more activities may be financed, at least in part, by user fees. The generic point is that some government activities or products in a multi-output service may not be technically amenable to financing by user charges. University research, because it is a public good, is normally thought of in these terms. In contrast, tuition fees can be and are levied by post-secondary educational institutions throughout the country and in most Western nations.

These technical difficulties all suggest that user fees must be adopted and applied with care. They may not be suitable for all goods and services, nor for all of the outputs that comprise any particular good or service. They also mean that any lessons that we can draw about the value of extending user fees to finance government programs in Ontario must rest on a careful, case-by-case scrutiny of different goods and services.

In the next section, I examine four cases to "elucidate" their lessons for public finance in Ontario.

Four Cases

I now examine four cases of governmentally produced goods and services in the province and apply the criteria set out in the section above dealing with user fees. The cases are selected to illustrate important features about the practicality of applying or extending user fees.

Case 1 is that of water-supply to domestic users. Water-supply is a private good. It can be "packaged" (that is, metered) and delivered to identifiable citizens. It is financed largely by user fees, but the practices of financing are criticized by economists for not approximating marginal cost-pricing standards.

In complete contrast, in case 2, water-quality management of lakes, rivers, and harbours is a public or collective-consumption good. Its benefits (or the converse, the costs of pollution) cannot be packaged and delivered to particular users. Users share in the benefits or costs. In these circumstances, it is very difficult to apply user fees, although for some activities they can and have been adopted. Moreover, environmental goods – exceptionally complex in their scientific and engineering aspects – illustrate the difficulty of "fine-tuning" user fees to particular cases.

Cases 3 and 4 concern health care and university education. Health care is Queen's Park's largest single expenditure (31.2 per cent of the budget in 1991) (Statistics Canada, CANSIM Matrices, 1991). It is also multi-functional and complex, making user-charge operations difficult to apply. In university education, a series of commissions recently appointed by the federal and provincial governments has recommended fee increases, and governments have never fully responded in a positive way. The Wright Commission (Ontario 1972) proposed that fees be increased by over one-third, the Bovey Commission (Ontario 1984) suggested that fees grow to reach 25 per cent of basic operating revenue, and the federal Macdonald Commission (Canada 1985) recommended higher fees and a voucher system.

These four cases are representative of many user-fee situations on several dimensions. I analyse and compare them using the criteria discussed in the section on user fees. The discussion emphasizes the economic yardsticks of revenue raising and efficiency, because most analyses of applications have been made by economists, and there are few data on the other political and philosophical criteria. These latter two standards will be addressed by two crude indicators. First, data will be reported that summarize public acceptance (or not) of user fees for a particular service or willingness to pay for better service. These data are indicators of demand for service, if not of representation directly. Second, some fragmentary data exist on the effects of changes in user fees on the number and type of users of services. The degree to which such changes would negatively affect users may indicate the level of fiscal equivalence in the current situation. One concern of the literature is the effect of fee changes on income classes; such changes should not reduce the accessibility of services to lower-income people. However, other groups in society may be harmed by user-fee changes, such as students by increases in tuition fees or people with large gardens by increases in water rates. There tend to be only anecdotal data on such groups. The discussion proceeds on the premises that the current revenue system creates winners and losers and that user fees, or increases in them, will change the breakdown of winners and losers. The information is, as noted, only a crude measure of fiscal equivalence.

Domestic Water-supply

Canadians use large amounts of water, at least in terms of international comparisons – approximately 360 litres/head/day (Tate and Lacelle 1987, cited in Pearse and Tate 1991). This figure ranks them second in the world, behind the United States, and roughly comparable with Australia and Switzerland (OECD 1989). Canadians get water mostly from departments of their municipalities, although public utilities, private utilities, and special boards also exist (Fortin 1985).

The prevailing method of financing water-supply is that of user fees. Eighty-six per cent of revenues from water distribution and 83 per cent of revenues from treatment come from user fees. Senior levels of government do contribute more to capital costs. Transfers from provincial governments average 35 per cent of total water system investments, with those in Ontario skewed towards smaller municipalities (Fortin 1985, 25–27). Fortin (p. 29) estimates that 95 per cent of water-supply costs are recovered in Ontario. The comparable figure for all Canada is 75 per cent.

Despite the dominance of user fees as a revenue source, economists criticize the prevailing system because of its inefficiencies. The inquiry on federal water policy states that "at present, pricing arrangements for water in Canada are rudimentary" (Pearse, Bertrand, and Mac-Laren 1985, 98). First, only half of the municipal suppliers, typically the larger systems, meter their water. As a result, municipalities do not know how much water they deliver to each household and how to charge on the basis of volume used. Second, the user-fee systems in operation do not permit marginal cost pricing as opposed to cost-recovery rates. Seventy-one per cent of Canadian municipalities, including those with the highest water use, set prices using a flat or declining block rate. A flat rate would be the $1.47 per 1,000 gallons that Ontario municipalities charge on average. A declining block rate would be the average Ontario charge of $1.69 for the first 1,000 gallons used and $1.08 for the last 1,000 gallons used (Fortin 1985, 41). Less than 2 per cent of communities use a volume-based schedule, in which the consumer pays more for each additional unit of water used. Even among those with a block rate, the first block is so great by volume that the effect is equivalent to a flat rate (Environment Canada 1990).

The result is that water is wasted by both consumers, who are not charged by volume used, and by producers, who do not see revenue accrue as they deliver more water. Further, the system is bigger than it need be to "deliver" the wasted water, and capital expenditures are necessarily larger. There are several indicators of wastage. First, installation of meters, without any general price increases, causes permanent reductions in water use from 10 to 50 per cent (McNeill 1991, 426). Table 7 shows the effects of metering on municipal water pumpage in three Ontario communities. Table 8 compares non-metered Metro Toronto and partly metered Hamilton-Wentworth with the totally metered large cities of Edmonton and Winnipeg. Per capita consumption falls with metering and volume-based charges. Consumption falls, especially in summer, after meters and volume-based charges are introduced. Ontarians use 70 per cent more water in summer dry weather conditions, mostly for watering residential lawns. Demand for water,

TABLE 7
Effects of Metering on Municipal Water Pumpage, 1984

Municipality	Pre-meter pumpage (litres) per capita-day	Post-meter pumpage (litres) per capita-day	Change (%)
Kingston	1,003	748	−25
Brockville	889	752	−15
Ottawa	597	433	−27

Source: Hamilton-Wentworth Regional Municipality (1989, 11).

especially in summer and for outdoor use, is price sensitive. One recent Canada-wide study finds that each dollar increase in the cost of 1,000 litres of water used would reduce water use by 45 per cent (21 per cent in Ontario).[2]

Second, leaks in the water distribution systems, because they appear costless, are permitted to continue, despite net benefits that might accrue from their reduction. Evidence is limited concerning extent of leakage, because in the absence of metering there is no good way to measure the difference between what is put into the system and what comes out. "Guesstimates" made by the Hamilton-Wentworth and Halton regional municipalities' departments of engineering – that 5 to 16 per cent leakage occurs – fall within commonly accepted North American values. A figure of 5 per cent is considered acceptable in western Europe (Environment Canada 1990). Hanke estimates that the net benefits of reducing leakage in Perth, Western Australia, from 15 to 5 per cent were over $2.5 million (Canadian) in 1977 (Hanke 1985, 71). Similar savings might result in Ontario.

Third, infrastructure costs are probably larger than necessary because more water is pumped through the municipal systems than would be needed under marginal cost pricing. Existing capital budgets in Canada averaged $99 per capita in 1983 (Fortin 1985, 30). No evidence exists on the capital budgets required to service lower volumes of supplied water, net of increased repairs to reduce leakages and net of meter-installation costs. We do know, however, that some 50 to 75 per cent of capital expenditures are designed to meet summertime peak loads, and costs of meter installation amount to only $150 each (Hamilton-Wentworth Regional Municipality 1989, 13, 15). Some savings in capital budgets would appear probable.

There would also be economic and other advantages from lower consumption of water in Ontario. First, there would be savings in treatment of waste water as water flows back from households

TABLE 8
Daily Consumption Demands (litres per capita excluding large industries)

Year	Non-metered		Totally metered		Partially metered
	Calgary	Metro Toronto	Edmonton	Winnipeg	Hamilton-Wentworth
1986	1,459	1,003	744	666	1,116
1987	1,433	1,157	734	718	1,343

Source: Hamilton-Wentworth Regional Municipality (1989, 12).

through sewage treatment plants. Evidence for the magnitude of these savings in Ontario is limited. Environment Canada estimates that a 21 per cent decrease in water-supply per annum should yield savings in the order of $1.5 million per year for the Hamilton Harbour watershed. Average costs of waste-water treatment are about 5 cents per cubic metre (Environment Canada 1990, 16). The major assumption behind such calculations is that efficient discharge standards can be met, because of the lower flows, without major modifications in treatment plants. There is some corroborating evidence from the United States that capital and operating savings can occur at treatment plants from lower water consumption. San Jose, California, calculates savings of $6.4 million per annum from a 10 per cent reduction in water-supply (Environment Canada 1990, 15).

Second, lower consumption rates might help those streams, lakes, and groundwater systems where uses are shared. Often, domestic water-supply is pumped from sources that must also provide water for fish, recreation, transportation, or storage. Insofar as such collective uses take place, marginal cost pricing can assist in assessing the appropriate trade-offs between uses. It would signal the value that households actually place on domestic water-supply and whether it is greater or less than the value accorded to alternative uses.

There are also philosophical and political factors that argue in favour of volume-based charges for domestic water-supply. First, the current system favours larger users of water, including industry and agriculture (to the extent that they hook up to community water systems), over smaller users. Bird (1976, 120) asserts that "what this means in practice is that lower-income consumers subsidize higher-income consumers who have dishwashers, bigger lawns to sprinkle, two cars to wash, and so on." This seems plausible even though supporting empirical evidence is lacking. There is apparently some lack of fiscal equivalence in the current system.

There also appears to be some public acceptance of user fees as a method to finance water-supply and water conservation. Loudon summarizes a number of recent studies and concludes that "the public accepts the 'user pay' philosophy, and would be willing to pay more if it can be related to a perceived need to provide good water quality" (Loudon 1990, 45). The caveat in his statement – the link between water-supply and water quality – is best illustrated in the 1990 survey of 1,523 Canadian households by Environics, which found that 66 per cent were prepared to pay more (43 per cent more than $50 per annum), over and above current annual household costs of $200, in order to improve water treatment (Environics 1990 in Loudon 1990, 44).

Again, some corroborating evidence exists in the United States. In a 1990 random sample of homeowners in Baltimore County, Maryland, for example, respondents were asked to rate the fairness of a number of finance measures, including user charges (such as water bills) and property taxes. Forty-five per cent rated user charges as very fair, while only 9 per cent rated property taxes as very fair. Conversely, 38 per cent believed that property taxes were very unfair, while only 11 per cent believed that user charges are very unfair (Lindsey 1990 in Apogee Research 1991, 33). These data, like the Canadian ones, indicate public acceptance of user fees as an instrument of public policy. They are silent on the issue of whether charges by volume are more acceptable than cost-recovery schemes.

In sum, water-supply is a private good produced largely by government, particularly at the municipal level. It is financed mostly by user fees, but on a cost-recovery, not a marginal-cost basis. Substantial evidence suggests the efficiency of moving towards volume-based pricing. However, these economic advantages must be considered along with philosophical and political criteria. The current system favours larger users of water and may well be regressive in its income effects. Some fiscal non-equivalence exists. Further, there is fragmentary evidence that user charges are a publicly acceptable method to finance water-supply systems, and that, consequently, user fees may possess political advantages over alternative methods of public finance.

Management of Water Quality

Water quality in a lake, river, or harbour is a complex collective-consumption good that cannot be packaged and delivered to any single user, such as a boater, fisher, swimmer, shipowner, or bird-watcher. Water-quality management consists of limiting the damage caused to such alternative users from discharges of various kinds of pollution. In the language of economics, abatement and management infrastructure should be undertaken to the point where their costs equal those of environmental damage. Here abatement costs cover pollution control and any losses resulting from production changes caused by pollution restriction; management infrastructure costs cover control and measuring; and damage costs are impairments of alternative uses. One method for ensuring efficient management of water quality is to charge polluters for their environmental damages. Despite a large theoretical economic literature on user fees for polluters, technical limitations preclude universal application of charges to pollution in different bodies of water. These are briefly discussed below. The current system of regulatory controls on the sources of pollution, on their collection, disposal, and reuse, and on the range of alternative uses permitted on each site is likely to remain the major instrument of water-quality management.

There are three major technical limitations to application of user-charge systems for managing water quality. First, pollutants differ in composition and effects, so that the good of water-quality management is in fact made up of different activities for different pollutants. Conventional sewage treatment plants are designed to reduce concentrations of pathogenic bacteria, suspended solids, and oxygen-consuming wastes found in effluent waste streams. The methods of reduction are, crudely put, disinfection, screening, and oxygenation, respectively. Another type of pollutant is that of nutrients such as phosphorus and nitrogen, which can be converted into chemical compounds by mixing with substances such as iron at treatment plants. Yet another type is that of toxic contaminants, such as persistent organic compounds and heavy metals. These are removed best (more cheaply) at source than by chemical precipitation in the pipe or other method on site. If governments are to impose user charges, they would have to differ charges for each type of pollutant.

Second, damages for each pollutant vary. Some pollutants, such as oxygen-consuming wastes, may, in certain concentrations, be continuously assimilated into ambient water. The same is the case for pathogens and suspended solids in marine environments. To the degree that assimilation is insufficient, damages from such pollutants are reasonably well-known (and continuous in response to loadings) and user charges could be applied at source. Although the full range of damages from nutrient loadings is less well-known, user charges could be applied there too. The damages from toxins can vary from lethal to sublethal and from organism to organism; the science is very imprecise. Queen's Park and Ottawa are therefore committed to "virtual elimination" of these pollutants from discharge into the water environment, and so user fees are inappropriate in this case.

Third, it is not always possible to identify the sources of pollution and who should pay any fees. The property rights of ownership are not clearly specified. Much pollution comes from non-point sources as run-off from agricultural and urban lands, and some is found in sediments built up over decades of waste disposal.

With these technical limitations in mind, it may be possible to bill those sources of conventional pollutants that cause measurable damage because of the limited assimilative capacities of particular lakes, rivers, and harbours. The fees could be on effluent loadings (amounts of contaminants discharged, rather than concentrations by volume) and set by Ontario's Ministry of Environment to reflect damage costs. Or the ministry could set a total permissible load of these pollutants for different sites and permit polluters to bid, in an auction, for part of this load. Either system could also be employed, incidentally, by a municipality in order to charge those industries and (perhaps) households that discharge wastes into the municipal sewer system.

A number of European countries utilize the former kind of user fee, including France, Germany, Hungary, and the Netherlands (Brown 1977; Brown and Johnson 1984). The actual charges are intended, however, not to capture damages, partly because of measuring difficulties, but to pay for treatment and are typically constructed on the basis of an index of pollution made up of various pollutants and the aggregate costs of treating them. Regardless of the merits of such indices, the charges cover only a small proportion of sewer and treatment costs. The maximum levy in the Netherlands, which has the stiffest rates, is only about one-third of total costs.

In Ontario, only municipalities employ some kind of user fee for sewage transport and treatment. Queen's Park relies on regulations as a method of control. The municipal systems are based on volumes of water consumed by household and/or liquid concentrations of a conventional pollutant for industries discharging into municipal sewers. Resulting revenues offset some of the operating and maintenance costs of sewer systems. Capital costs are financed by special assessments, development charges, and provincial grants. As indicated above, special assessments (and development charges, too) are user fees in the sense that they are directly related to property ownership.

There is increasing environmental concern with treating and charging property owners for storm-water run-off in urban areas (where storm drains exist), because storm water contains significant loadings of conventional pollutants and toxins, at least in the "first flush" of a rainstorm. In the United States, a number of communities levy user charges on property owners based mostly on volumes of storm water discharged, rather than contaminant loadings or concentrations in the water. Calculations are made of the square footage of impervious areas on a typical residential parcel, and charges calibrated to this figure (Apogee Research 1991, 22–23). No attempts are reported in the literature of charging property owners in rural areas for non-point source pollution.

It is difficult to assess the current system of water-quality management in Ontario in the light of the technical difficulties of controlling different pollutants and the current methods of public financing. In terms of the economic criteria of revenue raising and efficiency, the fact that about 75 per cent of capital expenditures on sewers and treatment plants are financed through special assessments and development charges, and that many municipalities assess a sewer surcharge on liquid wastes, indicates that the largest proportion of abatement costs are financed by users rather than by general taxpayers. There seems to be no economic reason why such costs could not be paid for completely by users. The full costs of pollution – of damages, especially – are unlikely to be so offset because of technical reasons. Full marginal cost pricing, and hence efficiency, must await the development of scientific and engineering data on damages and methods of control for different pollutants.

The philosophical criterion of fiscal equivalence can also be applied only partly to this good. A number of U.S. studies report that sewer charge systems benefit residential property owners and that a tax system benefits non-residential owners (Apogee Research 1991). This finding corroborates older Canadian evidence (Bird 1976). Given that some industries already incur most of their own abatement costs as direct discharges into a body of water rather than as discharges through a municipal sewer system, this conclusion must not be overemphasized. Fiscal equivalence is difficult to estimate when damages from pollution cannot be allocated to individual dischargers.

There is, of course, a great deal of public acceptance of increased environmental protection in Canada. Gallup reports that 68 per cent of Canadians would be willing to pay $25 more in income tax to protect the environment and that 54 per cent would pay $100 more.[3] Willingness to pay, in this context, is related increasingly to education, and hence to income. A shift to full recovery of abatement costs, which seems technically feasible, would probably not encounter major political opposition.

There are limits to the practical application of user fees in water-quality management in Ontario. Most of those limits are technical, and regulation is likely to remain the major instrument of management and pollution control. Nevertheless, there is more scope for full recovery of the abatement costs incurred by municipal sewage and treatment systems. Total recovery would be a step towards fiscal equivalence in public finance and would also be politically acceptable. Little more can be expected for the provision of a collective-consumption good.

Health Care

Health care is a complex, multi-activity good, in which the two most expensive sets of activities – hospital care and physician (medical) care – are financed by the general taxpayer rather than by the user. Most health-care activities can be packaged and delivered to identifiable individuals. Thus the good is made up largely of activities that are not collectively consumed (communicable disease control is a notable exception).

However, the complexities of health care make the good different in kind from the production and consumption of private goods such as apples, cars, and umbrellas. First, physicians and other health professionals are not simply producers of medical and hospital care. They are, after the first of a series of contacts with the patient, the primary "purchasers" of extra care through referrals, diagnostic tests, and recall visits. They act as agents for the patients who are the principals; the exact balance between the roles depends on the relative amounts of information that patient and physician possess and articulate. Proposals that recommend user fees levied solely on patients are often, as I note below, an ineffective way to produce greater efficiencies in treatments beyond primary care, precisely because they charge the wrong partner in this principal-agent relationship.

Second, there are significant elements of monopoly and monopsony in the system. Prices of health-care activities would differ significantly from those of a purely competitive system were supply and demand to be coordinated solely through market mechanisms. Major aspects of monopoly accrue to licensed professionals, and of monopsony to government health insurance plans that purchase medically necessary services.

Despite impressions to the contrary, substantial amounts of health-care expenditure in Canada are currently financed privately. There are some medical services that are not financed in whole or in part by the taxpayer in Ontario, including some optometric services and eye glasses, dentistry, prescription and non-prescription drugs (other than most of those for old age pensioners and those on welfare), prosthetics, and some chiropractic, osteopathic, and podiatry services. Costs of such medical services are equivalent in dollars to one-third of government-financed health care (calculated from Cuyler 1988, 9–12). Further, most preventive health care is produced, consumed, and financed by the individual citizen through decisions about diet, exercise, tobacco and alcohol consumption, and environmental conditions at home. Government health-care activities are targeted largely at the sick, not the well. The comments in this subsection pertain largely to those health-care services that are publicly financed.

In 1991, Queen's Park collected some $24 million of revenue from user fees exclusive of premiums paid to the Ontario Hospital Insurance Plan (OHIP) (Ontario 1991, 4–225). Fees range in type from sales of meals to ambulance users' co-payments. While $24 million is not an insignificant sum, it represents less than 2 per cent of the province's total outlay on its three major health-care expenditures – hospitals, medical care and drugs, and public health. The balance comes from the Ontario taxpayer and grants from Ottawa.

The grants from the government of Canada are authorized by the federal-provincial fiscal arrangements and the Established Programs Financing Act (EPF) of 1977, under a complex formula of transfer of income tax points and cash payments ($20 million in 1991). These payments are frozen at 1990 levels until 1994–95. Concurrently, under the Canada Health Act of 1984, Ottawa will deduct $1 in grants for every $1 that the province allows physicians and health-care professionals to "extra bill" and hospitals to levy user fees on in- and out-patient services. This arrangement makes it financially difficult for Queen's Park to extend the range of user fees currently in operation. However, given the freeze on grants, Ontario may soon consider replacing federal grants with own-source user fees.

User-fee options are evaluated, in the literature on health care, by economists largely by the criterion of efficiency. Economists have also emphasized the effects on access for lower-income groups of per-service and co-insurance fees levied by hospitals and physicians. Evidence is based on Canada's experience before and since public insurance was introduced, Saskatchewan's use (1968–71) of daily hospital charges and physicians' fees for office visits, and a major, $U.S. 80-million natural "experiment" (1982–84) conducted by Rand for the U.S. government in providing free outpatient medical treatment, including prescription drugs. (Overseas experience is also occasionally examined.) The fees considered are set by the health-care provider, not the consumer, and have been uniform across provinces. Table 9 presents a taxonomy from Barer, Evans, and Stoddard (1979) that presents some of the kinds of charges that could be levied.

The studies mentioned indicate that a $2.50-per-day user fee did not deter acute care hospitalization in Saskatchewan, perhaps because the real "purchaser" of hospital services is the physician, acting as agent for the patient. Larger fees, such as existed in Ontario before the public hospital plan of 1958, were financed by private co-insurance, although one-third of the population was uninsured. User fees appear to reduce office visits and other physician services for lower-income and elderly patients, but an increase in services to higher-income groups in Saskatchewan offset any losses in physician fees. The Rand studies suggest that the price elasticity of demand is -0.2, with the effects being felt by low-income patients, especially children. (This paragraph summarizes the findings in Manning et al. 1987; Warburton 1987; and Rachlis 1991).

In sum, the user-fee systems of per-service charges and co-insurance seem little to affect efficiency or levels of use but do appear to be regressive in their income effects (Barer, Evans, and Stoddart 1979, 112).

The potential for cost recovery of many medical services appears remote, given the large sums that would have to be raised through increased user fees. Barer, Evans, and Stoddard (1979) suggest that selective de-insurance of specific medical procedures, and their replacement by user fees, might offer the best single method of increasing the recovery of health-care costs. Direct billing of doctors, rather than patients, for secondary-care services such as diagnostic tests and drug prescriptions might also recover some costs and promote appropriate care (some level of compensation might have to be made through negotiation of medical fee schedules). In general, there seems to be limited scope for cost recovery unless the province is prepared to reinstitute OHIP fees and earmark them for health-care expenditures. (Such a measure would not serve to create incentives to conserve on health care unless it were related to use; it would be for cost recovery only.)

The defence of the present system rests, then, not on economic but

TABLE 9
Taxonomy of Fee Options

Charges determined by	
Non-provider	Provider
Uniform charges across provinces	
Co-insurance	
Deductibles	
Per-service charges	Co-insurance
Income– and income tax–linked proposals	Per-service charges
Differential charges across provinces	
Selective de-insurance (e.g. cosmetic surgery)	Major-risk medical (e.g. maximum limits on out-of-pocket expenses)
	Extra-billing
Parallel systems (e.g. private wards)	Service repackaging (e.g. health maintenance organization fees rather than a single physician's fees)

Source: Barer, Evans, and Stoddart (1979, 99).

on political criteria – especially substantial public acceptance. Gallup found in June 1992 that 87 per cent of Canadians and 90 per cent of Ontarians were very or somewhat satisfied with services.[4] More persuasive still were the responses to an August 1991 question: "Considering the quality and efficiency of services delivered, in general, do you think the amounts Canadians pay for health care and prescription drugs through direct fees, insurance premiums, and taxes is very high, high, about right, low, or very low?" About 34 per cent of Canadians and 37 per cent of Ontarians responded "about right." But only 19 per cent of Canadians (and 17 per cent of Ontarians) said "very high," compared with 57 per cent of Americans asked the same question.

It also appears obvious that the sick and their families are the major group that benefits from the system. Since lower-income people and the elderly tend to have higher rates of illness, these groups benefit disproportionately and seem to have the political power to redistribute resources in their direction.

It is possible to conclude as well that these groups benefit from the absence of fiscal non-equivalence in the system, and it is now unclear whether this situation can continue in its present form. For example, on 14 September 1992, TV Ontario broadcast a debate entitled "Can Canada Afford Universal Medicare?" This program publicized the ongoing concern among some heath-care professionals and analysts that increasing expenditures could no longer be sustained. This is the latest indicator of a series of so-called crises in the system, especially in its financing. Some modest experimentation with selective de-insurance (such as occurred with out-of-country expenditures above Ontario rates) and fees on physicians may be tried. No radical changes appear to be feasible, at least politically, on the revenue side.

University Education

University education may not be as complex a good as health care. It is, in Canada, produced almost entirely by government, and the public does not spend large sums in the private marketplace as it does with preventive health care. Nevertheless, it is a multi-activity good – programs in arts and science are different from those in medicine, engineering, law, and commerce – and its activities are produced jointly with the research function of a university.

The good of university education is consumed by the general public as well as by the student. The student gets private benefits that are packaged and delivered to him or her – higher earnings, compared with high school or community college graduates, and non-economic rewards from education "for its own sake." There are, however, social benefits as well – contributions to national income growth from a more educated work-force and the values and attitudes displayed by a more literate and numerate population. In short, the good is not a perfect private good, but one that has some, often vague, positive externalities.

Despite the good's private character, students have never paid the full cost of tuition. Prior to the First World War, tuition fees contributed, at best, 40 per cent of university revenue in Ontario; the balance came from private benefactors and Queen's Park. Prior to 1960, fees varied between 40 and 65 per cent of university revenue, and contributions from Ottawa began only in 1951 (other than grants to veterans). Fees fell gradually as a proportion of university funding throughout the 1960s, reached a low of 14 per cent in 1976, and rose gradually to 19 per cent in 1989–90. The balance of operating revenues comes from provincial grants (76 per cent) and a variety of small sources. Tuition fees included payments for a number of items charged by universities to students on a cost-recovery basis, until Queen's Park prohibited such billing in 1985. An example would be rental fees for musical instruments. Universities can still levy some auxiliary fees, such as for transcripts, athletics, or parking, but these generate only 1 per cent of operating revenue (Stager 1989, 5–33; Council of Ontario Universities 1991, 41).

The provincial grant to universities includes transfers from Ottawa under the EPF arrangements of 1977 – a cash grant and a so-called transfer of tax points, frozen at 1989–90 levels until 1994–95. The federal transfers amount to 112 per cent of the Ontario grant to universities, indicating that the province considers the tax-point transfers "other than a grant" and usable for other purposes. This kind of bookkeeping by Ontario and some other provinces "appears to be leading to assertions that the provinces are not pulling their weight in post-secondary education" (Leslie 1981, 196). Provinces maintain, on the contrary, that the expenditures of both levels of government were decoupled in 1977 and that their expenditures are now responsive to program design features intrinsic to post-secondary education. Ottawa's concerns are considered to focus on revenue-sharing rather than educational issues.

Ontario's government has not only controlled fee levels (by reducing its grants by one dollar for each tuition dollar raised) since 1971–72, but it has permitted some small variations in tuition fees for different university programs. Stager (1989, 32) calculates these tuition fees as a proportion of program cost, as indicated in Table 10.

We may now evaluate university financing in Ontario using the criteria advanced above. The information presented indicates that students pay only a small portion of university operating costs. Even if the social benefits from university education are high, they are not worth four times as much as the private benefits, as the proportion of taxpayer versus user revenues would imply. Consequently, there is some, but only a limited amount of, cost recovery in the present system.

Efficiency is also lacking, because of provincial laws and policies, not university administrations. Queen's Park prevents universities from practising marginal cost pricing either by enrolments per university or by enrolments per program. It prevents universities from "simulating" marginal cost pricing by allowing them to fix fees at a proportion, such as 20 per cent, of the marginal cost of student education. There is, consequently, no incentive for universities to economize in their use of factor inputs, and every incentive for them to compete with each other for reputational rankings in publications such as *Maclean's* (21 October 1991) rather than for instructional and research reasons.

The ostensible reason for the tuition fee policy is to preserve access for students from low-income families and, in recent years, for students who are female, have disabilities, are from a visible minority, or are aboriginal or francophone. Enrolment of these target groups seems to be largely unrelated to tuition fees, which represent only a small pro-

TABLE 10
Tuition Fees of Programs as % of Cost

Program of study	Actual fee as % of program cost[a]
General arts and science, journalism	26.7
Honours arts, rehabilitation medicine, library science, physical education, fine arts, commerce, law	19.6
Honours science, forestry, music, pharmacy, agriculture, education, nursing	15.4
Engineering, architecture, optometry	16.5
Medicine, dentistry	8.5

Source: Stager (1989, 32.2).
[a] Government grant (basic income units times formula weight) plus tuition fee.

portion of the total costs faced by any student at university; the total would have to include forgone earnings as a major item. It is estimated that tuition fees in Ontario represent only between 13 and 17 per cent of a student's total cost of enrolment per annum (Stager 1989, 38–39). Consequently, enrolment is inelastic with respect to fees. Leslie and Brinkman (1987)[5] estimate elasticity to be − 0.62 in their review of 25 studies. Other economic and non-economic factors affect enrolment by these groups much more than tuition fees.

The structure of public finance for university education redistributes income in favour of students at the expense of the general taxpayer. Students tend to come from families of higher income, and, consequently, the redistribution is regressive. Further, the general taxpayer is paying, out of current income, for capital investment in student skills, and there is some redistribution in favour of future generations. Both of these conditions violate the philosophical criterion of fiscal equivalence.

Policy on tuition fees redistributes resources towards students in particular programs. Table 10 illustrates how some students cover a much smaller portion of program costs than do others. Further, the rate of return in future earnings also varies by program. It seems, for example, unfair to charge a medical student 8.5 per cent of program costs in fees when his or her private rates of return (of benefits to costs) exceed 17 per cent, and then to charge an arts student 26.7 per cent when his or her rates of return are 3.8 per cent (Stager 1989, 74). This policy again violates fiscal equivalence.

Current policy seems defensible only on political grounds. Gallup polls in the early 1980s found that 25 per cent of respondents favoured an increase in fees, and 30 per cent, no change. In 1988, 57 per cent favoured an increase in government spending; 33 per cent an inflation-based increase; and only 6 per cent, a decrease (Livingston and Hart 1988 in Stager 1989, 85–86). The public appears to support higher university revenues, regardless of source.

There are, of course, groups that will be worse off if tuition fees are changed. Both student (Canadian Union of Students – CUS) and faculty (Ontario Council of University Faculty Associations – OCUFA) opposed the permitted 1992 fee increases of 7 per cent. No government seems to want to contemplate comprehensive reform of the system, such as has occurred recently in Australia, New Zealand, and the United Kingdom.

As with health care, reforms could come in two ways – the province could allow universities to set their own fees, or it could alter the level and type of fees that it stipulates for all institutions. The former policy lends itself better to the efficiency criterion. It allows universities to compete and adopt marginal cost pricing and to keep the rewards themselves. In either case, there are grounds for basing program fees on program costs, as a better measure for cost recovery and a better way to approach fiscal equivalence. Such an approach would have some political appeal on grounds of equitable treatment. The accessibility or affordability of university education would be better addressed through comprehensive reform of student assistance plans than through the "failed" policy of low tuition fees (COU 1992).

In sum, there is scope for reform of tuition fee policy in Ontario universities. Reform rests, however, with the province rather than with each institution. As the cases above also illustrated, the reforms should be selective and well-designed in order to meet economic and philosophical, as well as political, criteria.

Conclusion

User fees are a significant source of revenues for governments in this country. They bring in 17 per cent of all government revenues. They are used increasingly by municipal governments in all provinces, but especially in British Columbia and Alberta. There is thus potential for extending their growth in Ontario's local governments and also at the provincial level, where they represent only a small portion of revenues (7 per cent).

This study has two major lessons. First user fees must be constructed, applied, and calibrated to the precise nature of government programs. Not all government goods lend themselves to user fees, for technical reasons; only parts (activities) of government goods that are measurable and can be packaged and delivered to individual citizens. Thus a user fee could be put on the use of sewers and treatment plants to pay for the abatements of conventional pollutants, but it could not be put on toxic wastes, or fine-tuned to pay for damages, or assessed against non-point sources of pollutants. Each government activity must be assessed to see whether user fees are appropriate. I expect taxation revenue to remain a larger source of government revenue in Ontario for at least these technical reasons.

Second, there are legitimate philosophical, political, and economic reasons for levying user fees. Most of the writings on user fees are produced by economists who want more efficient government. I argue and show above that equally legitimate reasons – philosophical (fiscal equivalence), political (representation and accountability), and economic (cost recovery) – merit consideration in assessing the wisdom of user fees. Similarly, there is a very crude philosophical notion of equity – that lower-income people are disproportionately disadvantaged by user fees – that is wrong in both theory and practice and is used to stifle public debate and reconsideration of user fees. Redistribution, or "fiscal non-equivalence," seems to take place between all income classes, including from poor to rich, under our current system of taxes and fees. This fact is defensible on political grounds, of (say) ensuring accountability of programs to citizens' demands, as well as on economic grounds of (say) revenue raising. In assessing the merits of user fees, one ought to use economic, political, and philosophical criteria, rather than the standard economic criteria of efficiency and equity. Further, it may be legitimate to emphasize philosophical, political, and efficiency criteria when these conflict with the cost recovery popular in some governments.

Sometimes there are legal obstacles to applying or extending user fees. The Canada Health Act of 1984 prevents the province from permitting extra billing by doctors or user charges on basic medical and hospital care. Similarly, the conditions of provincial grants to universities prevent those institutions from raising or extending tuition charges. This adds an extra dimension to the politically acceptable ways of changing methods of public finance, as user fees must now meet the test of intergovernmental agreement for implementation, as well as generate agreement within the province.

In sum, no sweeping generalization about the value, or lack thereof, of user fees can be made. Appropriate reform can come only through scrutiny and examination of each government program.

Notes

I wish to acknowledge the help of Megan Sproule-Jones in preparing this study. I am grateful to Allan M. Maslove, research director, and an anonymous reviewer for helpful comments on an earlier draft.

1 These concerns are implied by the very title of the Fair Tax Commission.
2 See Environment Canada (1988) in Environment Canada (1990, 9). See also Fortin (1985, 12) for summaries of Canadian price-elasticity studies, and OECD (1989, 72) for overseas evidence.
3 See the Gallup Report (31 May 1990).
4 See ibid. (12 June 1992).
5 See Leslie and Brinkman (1987) in Stager (1989, 52).

Bibliography

Apogee Research 1991. *The User Pay Approach to Stormwater Management.* Toronto: Apogee Research International Ltd.

Barer, M.L., R.G. Evans, and G.L. Stoddart 1979. *Controlling Health Care Costs by Direct Charges to Patients: Snare or Delusion?* Toronto: Ontario Economic Council

Bird, Richard M. 1976. *Charging for Public Services: A New Look at an Old Idea.* Toronto: Canadian Tax Foundation

Bish, Robert L. 1983. *Basic Principles of Political Decentralization to Local Authorities.* Pretoria, South Africa: Bureau for Economic Policy Analysis

Brown, Gardner. 1977. "Charge and Subsidy Programmes of Several European Countries." In *The Practical Application of Economic Incentives to the Control of Pollution,* ed. James B. Stephenson, 409–22. Vancouver: University of British Columbia Press

Brown, Gardner, and Ralph W. Johnson. 1984. "Pollution Control by Effluent Charges." *Natural Resources Journal,* 24: 929–66

Canada. 1985. Macdonald Commission. *Report of the Royal Commission on the Economic Union and Development Prospects for Canada.* 3 vols. Ottawa: Supply and Services Canada

Canadian Tax Foundation (CTF). 1992. *Provincial and Municipal Finances 1991.* Toronto: CTF

Council of Ontario Universities (COU). 1989. *A Decade of Financial Information.* Toronto: COU
- 1991. *Financial Report of Ontario Universities: 1989–90.* Toronto: COU
- 1992. *Contingent Repayment Student Assistance Plans.* Toronto: COU
Cuyler, A.J. 1988. *Health Care Expenditures in Canada: Myth and Reality, Past and Future,* No. 82. Toronto: Canadian Tax Foundation
Environment Canada. 1990. *Water Demand Management.* Toronto: Inland Waters Directorate, Ontario Region
Fortin, M. 1985. "The User-Pay Principle and the Canadian Municipal Water Industry." In *The Economics of Municipal Water Supply: Applying the User-Pay Principle,* by Steve Hanke and M. Fortin, A1–AA60. Ottawa: Inquiry on Federal Water Policy
Gallup. Various dates. *The Gallup Report.* Toronto: Gallup Canada Inc.
Hamilton-Wentworth Regional Municipality. 1989. *Water Demand Strategy.* Hamilton: Department of Finance
Hanke, Steve H. 1985. "The User-Pay Principle and Market Socialism." In *The Economics of Municipal Water Supply: Applying the User-Pay Principle,* by Steve Hanke and M. Fortin, B1–BB90. Ottawa: Inquiry on Federal Water Policy
Leslie, Larry L., and P.T. Brickman. 1984. "Student Price Response in Higher Education." *Journal of Higher Education,* 58(2): 181–204.
Leslie, Peter M. 1981. "New Directions in Financing Canadian Universities." In *Financing Canadian Universities,* ed. David Nowland and Richard Bellaire. Toronto: OISE Press
Livingston, D.W., and D.J. Hart. 1988. *Public Attitudes towards Education in Ontario.* Toronto: Ontario Institute for Studies in Education
Loudon, Michael. 1990. "Public Acceptability of Municipal User-Polluter Pay." In *Towards "User Pay" for Municipal Water and Wastewater Services,* ed. Donna M. Leith, 37–46. Ottawa: Rawson Academy of Aquatic Science
Maclean's. 1991. "A Measure of Excellence." Toronto, October 21
McNeill, Roger C. 1991. "Water Pricing and Sustainable Development in the Fraser River Basin." In *Perspectives on Sustainable Development in Water Management: Towards Agreement in the Fraser River Basin,* ed. A.H.J. Dorcey, 417–29. Vancouver: Westwater Research Centre
Manning, Willard G., Joseph P. Newhouse, Naihua Duan, Emmett B. Keeler, Arleen Leibowitz, and M. Susan Marquis. 1987. "Health Insurance and the Demand for Medical Care." *American Economic Review,* 87:251–77
Musgrave, Richard A., Peggy B. Musgrave, and Richard M. Bird. 1987. *Public Finance in Theory and Practice.* Toronto: McGraw-Hill Ryerson Limited
Mushkim, Selma J., and Vehom, Charles L. 1977. "User Fees and Changes," *Government Finance,* November, 48, cited in Harry P. Hatry, *A Review of*

Private Approaches for Delivery of Public Services, 88–89. Washington, DC: Urban Institute Press, 1983.

Olson, Mancur. 1969. "The Principle of 'Fiscal Equivalence.' " *American Economic Review,* 69: 479–87

Ontario. 1972. Wright Commission. *Commission on Post-Secondary Education in Ontario: The Learning Society.* Toronto: Queen's Printer

Ontario. 1984. Bovey Commission. *Commission on the Future Development of Universities in Ontario, Ontario Universities: Options and Futures.* Toronto: Commission

Ontario. 1991. *Public Accounts of Ontario, 1990–91.* Vol. 1. Toronto: Queen's Printer

Organization of Economic Cooperation and Development (OECD). 1989. *Water Resource Management.* Paris: OECD

Pearse, Peter H., and Donald M. Tate. 1991. "Economic Instruments for Sustainable Development of Water Resources." In *Perspectives on Sustainable Development in Water Management: Towards Agreement in the Fraser River Basin,* ed. A.H.J. Dorcey, 431–51. Vancouver: Westwater Research Centre

Pearse, Peter H., F. Bertrand, and J.W. MacLaren. 1985. *Currents of Change: Final Report of Inquiry on Federal Water Policy.* Ottawa: Environment Canada

Rachlis, Michael M. 1991. "Summary of Presentation to the Committee on Government Operations of the U.S. House of Representatives." Toronto: Rachlis

Sproule-Jones, Mark. 1972. "Strategic Tensions in the Scale of Political Analysis." *British Journal of Political Science,* 2: 173–92

– 1993. *Governments at Work.* Toronto: University of Toronto Press

Sproule-Jones, Mark, and John White. 1989. "The Scope and Application of User Charges in Municipal Governments." *Canadian Tax Journal,* 37(6): 1476–85

Stager, David A.A. 1989. *Focus on Fees: Alternative Policies for University Tuition Fees.* Toronto: Council of Ontario Universities

Statistics Canada. 1992. CANSIM Matrices, 2751, 2757, 2764, 2770, 3159. Ottawa

Warburton, Rebecca. 1987. "User Fees for Acute Hospital Care, Physician Services and Drugs." Victoria, BC: Ministry of Health

2 Tax Treatment of Human Capital

MORLEY GUNDERSON and WAYNE R. THIRSK

Introduction

Consensus, even near-consensus, on policy issues is rare. In North America, however, there is general agreement that investing in education and training is absolutely crucial to meeting future competition and the resulting adjustments. This conclusion has been reached by almost every study, commission, or task force on competitiveness and adjustment in both Canada[1] and the United States.[2]

While there is general consensus on the importance of investing in human resources, there is no agreement on how such investment should best occur, and even less on who should pay. Disagreement over who should pay is fostered by the wide variety of "stakeholders" – albeit their vested interest does not appear to be matched by their willingness to invest. Individuals obviously have an interest in human resource development, both as consumers and as workers. Employers want a trained and educated work-force, and governments have a role (for reasons discussed below), though one complicated in Canada by divided federal-provincial responsibilities, especially in training. Unfortunately, divided and ill-defined responsibility often means none at all, with each party trying to shift the burden to others.

While there is little meeting of minds over who should pay for human resource development or the extent to which it should be subsidized, many people believe that human capital investments should not be penalized or unfairly treated through the tax system. This is especially the case given recent emphasis on the competitiveness of nations (and the individuals and organizations that constitute them), which depends increasingly on human capital and less on physical capital. Investment in human capital should not be penalized relative to that in physical capital, and perhaps – as discussed below – it should be treated more favourably.

This paper analyses the tax treatment of human capital, to determine whether it is encouraged or discouraged by tax treatment and whether the tax system is likely to cause inappropriate levels of such investment. While the focus here is normally on how it *is* treated, we also consider how it *ought* to be treated.

The first of the paper's six sections discusses the growing "Importance of Human Capital Investment" and the resulting need for reassessment of its tax treatment. The second section deals with the rationale for – and pitfalls of – "Government Involvement in Private Decision Making" in this area and offers alternative perspectives on the appropriate role for governments. "The Effect of Taxes on Human Capital Formation" outlines existing tax instruments that currently affect decisions on human capital investment in Ontario. In the light of these observations, we next see "Taxes on Financial and Physical Capital Reconsidered." Some "Empirical Evidence" suggests that there may be overinvestment in higher education and underinvestment in worker training. The "Conclusion" summarizes the paper and offers final observations on some of the main policy options, as well as on the information still needed for choosing among these options.

The focus throughout is on human capital investments through education and training. Earlier discussions of human capital in the 1960s also included investments in mobility, information, and health. Both types of investment involved costs in early periods (often forgone income) that would yield benefits later, often in increased earnings – hence the concept of human capital, analogous to investment in physical capital.

Obviously, there are also broader concepts of human capital investment, non-monetary as well as monetary. Having children is often categorized as investing in human capital, especially in agrarian societies, where there may be few other mechanisms of being provided for in one's old age. Prenatal medical care, and even basic nutrition, are often described as investments, in that they save on subsequent costs. Early child development, whether within the family or in child-care arrangements, can affect subsequent development and hence have an investment component. Even full employment can be social investment, to the extent that crime, stress, and social problems increase in periods of high unemployment.

While all of these areas are part of the broader concept of human capital investment, the focus here is on education and training. Occasionally, however, we mention some of these more general areas, especially when they relate to the more conventional education and training concepts.

Importance of Human Capital Investment

As indicated by Davies and St-Hilaire (1987, 75), investment in human capital in countries such as Canada is at least as large and likely to be substantially larger than investment in physical capital. They cite estimates of human capital stock in the United States ranging from 48 per cent of the total capital stock (Schultz, 1960), to 69 per cent (Kendrick, 1976), to 96 per cent (Jorgenson and Pachon, 1983); the last-named study also took into account the value of human capital in non-market activities. Freeman (1977) estimates human capital at 50 per cent of the total capital stock, and Kroch and Sjoblom (1986) estimate 73 per cent. It is thus surprising that so little research exists on how taxes affect human capital formation. Much of the available research concentrates on how taxation of human capital tends to affect the efficiency costs of choosing between consumption and income taxes.[3]

While issues surrounding human capital have always been very important, the significance of human capital investment has been expanding in recent years because of growing international competitiveness and the development of a more liberal trading system; changing workplace practices and human resource requirements; increased emphasis on the implications of "endogenous growth" and "efficiency wages"; and equity issues pertaining to the working poor and wage polarization. This paper deals with each of these issues in turn, with emphasis in each case on human capital investment.

International Competitiveness and High Value-Added Production

The 1970s and 1980s were characterized by intense global competition, especially from Japan and such newly industrialized Asian economies as Hong Kong, Singapore, South Korea, and Taiwan. This trend is likely to continue, given the recent Canada–United States Free Trade Agreement, a North American free trade agreement that includes also Mexico, and possible further extensions throughout Latin America. Competitive pressures from the European Union are also likely to increase, as are those from former Eastern Bloc countries, as they make the transition to market-based economies.

The pressure of competition is leading to dramatic industrial restructuring, especially when compounded by technological change, privatization, deregulation, and the shift from manufacturing to services. Adjustments have a "down side" (such as plant closings and mass layoffs) and an "up side" (such as new skill needs). Human capital investment is necessary for both types of adjustment – for example, for retraining, relocation, and training and education to meet the new skill requirements).

As well, the supply side of the labour market has changed, with an ageing work-force, the dominance of the two-earner family, and an increasingly diverse labour force in terms of such factors as ethnicity and gender. We see declining reliance on new young entrants or immigration to fill skill shortages and emphasis on developing indigenous training. Such changes have required rethinking of labour market policies; we should also rethink tax policies, especially vis-à-vis investment in human capital.

The competition from low-wage countries is particularly acute because labour costs in nations such as Brazil, Mexico, and the newly industrialized Asian economies are about 10 to 20 per cent of those in Canada. As well, labour standards and other elements of the "social wage" are either non-existent or not enforced. The increasing international mobility of capital, especially through multinationals, makes it easy for corporations to shift operations to take advantage of these low labour costs and to export products back into the higher-wage countries, given the reduction of tariff and non-tariff barriers to trade.

There is general recognition, however, that Canadians cannot – and ought not to – compete with those countries on the basis of low labour costs. Rather, we should develop "market niches" on the basis of customer service, quality, and a high-productivity, high value-added strategy. This, of course, entails human capital formation to ensure an educated and trained work-force, capable of providing the high value-added production and of adapting to the ever-changing pressures.

This observation is part and parcel of the more general proposition that the competitiveness of developed nations depends less on traditional sources of comparative advantage, such as access to land, resources, markets, and capital, and more on human resources. The shrinking of the global economy and improved transportation and communication make markets more open, physical capital more mobile, existing stocks of land highly productive, and new resource frontiers available. Countries such as Canada find comparative advantage shifting towards human resources, with obvious implications for investing in human capital.

This view has been forcefully presented by Robert Reich (1991) in *The Work of Nations*. Firms combine globally mobile capital, technology, raw materials, and management skills with immobile skilled and unskilled labour to produce output sold in a global market. Only countries that offer a large pool of skilled workers will be chosen for high-valued production.

While much of the difference in labour costs between Canada and low-wage countries is offset by our higher productivity, this is not the case with respect to our major trading partner – the United States. From the mid-1970s to the mid-1980s, labour compensation costs (including fringe benefits and adjustments for the exchange rate) in Canada were 80 to 90 per cent of those of the United States. However, over the 1980s, our competitive position deteriorated rapidly, largely because of an appreciating Canadian dollar (since 1986) and because productivity since the 1982–84 recession has been stagnant in Canada, while it has improved substantially in the United States. These developments are of considerable concern because they are occurring as Canada engages in more free trade with that country. Obviously, productivity is key to future competitiveness vis-à-vis low-wage countries and nations such as the United States that are "repositioning" themselves for the changing conditions. It is therefore crucial that the tax system encourage – or at least not discourage – optimal investment in human capital to meet the productivity challenge.

As becomes clearer below, optimal investment in human capital can have two operational definitions. Sometimes it refers to the absence of any opportunities to invest in education or training and receive a return in excess of the rate at which savers are willing to make funds available for investment. This criterion refers to the realization of an efficient volume of saving and investment. An alternative criterion is whether the gross (or before-tax) rate of return on human capital is the same as the gross rate of return on physical investment. Here the concern is with achieving an efficient composition of investment. Both criteria provide a useful benchmark or reference point in analysing the effect of taxation on investment decisions. The latter standard is invoked below, where we examine the returns to university education.

Changing Workplace Practices and New Human Resource Developments

The changing competitive pressures that have affected the labour market in general have also affected the workplace, as evidenced by new practices and human resource developments. While these changes may not have been as prominent in Canada as they have been in the United States (Long 1989), they nevertheless have been important in this country, and they will influence human capital development, both for firms and for employees.

For example, broader job classifications mean that employees need more general, generic skills to facilitate "multi-skilling." Only generic skills can provide the foundation on which to add subsequent retraining in the "lifelong learning" necessitated by constantly changing skill requirements. Learning how to learn – and relearn – will be more useful than acquiring a specific skill.

Similar implications for skill development follow from employees' increased participation and involvement in the workplace. As well, team production and quality circles require interpersonal "people skills," as does interaction with "downstream" suppliers and "upstream" customers. Emphasis on quality and on the role in assuring it of individual workers (rather than a quality control department) places a premium on self-responsibility and decision-making skills.

Compensation schemes that are contingent on performance can increase both the firm's and the individual's incentive to invest in education and training. As well, the greater individual risks associated with such contingent compensation may encourage investment in general skills to diversify against that risk. To the extent that flexible compensation reduces the need for layoffs as an adjustment mechanism, such workers may be available within the firm for retraining during slack periods and the return to the firm's investment in training will be greater.

Greater use of contingent compensation and contingent labour forces (for example, part-time, limited contracts, and subcontracting) can substantially shift risks from employers to employees. This can discourage employees from investing in human capital if they feel that they have little control over that risk; however, they may invest in more general skills to diversify against that risk.

In North America, labour adjustment usually occurs through the external labour market, often through layoffs, unemployment, and job searches. Adjustment can be particularly difficult for older workers who have moved up within the internal labour market of their organization and now find themselves displaced into the external labour market, where any hiring is only at the "entry level" in such organizations or in the low-wage service sector. This situation contrasts with many European countries and especially Japan, where "lifetime" employment provides a degree of job security and the associated low turnover gives employers an incentive to invest in training and retraining. As well, slack periods provide a "window" for such training. North America lacks proper incentives to train rather than a "training culture."

The ageing work-force also requires lifelong learning and adult retraining. As promotion opportunities become blocked by the large number of middle-aged "baby boomers," pressures exist for retraining for lateral transfers and possibly even "downtraining." Shortages in the labour pool resulting from the shrinking number of younger people entering the work-force may create more attractive short-run job opportunities for youths, which could induce them to leave school.

Employment-equity target groups such as women, visible minorities, Aboriginal people, and disabled persons have special training needs. Training may be necessary if they are recruited from outside the firm to meet targets, or if they are promoted from within. Women who leave the labour force to raise children also may later need retraining to facilitate their re-entry into the labour force. Injured workers require vocational rehabilitation, and employers may need special training to facilitate their duty to "reasonably accommodate" disabled workers.

Workplace practices and human resource requirements are changing rapidly. This shift, in turn, changes the optimal human capital requirements, though not always in one direction. In general, however, human capital investment becomes more important, especially basic general training and eduction that can facilitate constant retraining and lifelong learning. As well, interpersonal "people skills" are becoming more important, as are the special needs of groups targeted for equity.

Implications of Endogenous Economic Growth

Recent developments in growth theory may change policy, including that for human capital investment. In this subsection, the emphasis is on providing a "layperson's translation" of that literature and on extracting the implications for human capital investment.

In the literature on endogenous growth,[4] diminishing returns to growth do not appear to set in; rather, high income seems to sustain further growth. Poor countries, in contrast, can remain trapped in low growth because they do not have the resources to invest in physical or human capital or in public infrastructures; as a result, they remain poor. Parallels with poor regions or poor families are obvious. In contrast, wealthier countries seem able to sustain high growth and not reach diminishing returns because the combination of new developments and opportunities seems endless. This possibility that "growth begets further growth" may occur because of complementarities among investments in physical capital or human capital or even between physical and human capital. For example, when individuals invest in human capital, others often receive benefits – "when you learn, I learn." It is difficult, if not impossible, for individual agents always to appropriate fully all of the benefits that may spill over onto others in the process. Patents certainly do exist in the market for ideas, but it is not always possible to patent all ideas. In such circumstances, positive externalities are generated by decisions about human capital investment. This same phenomenon may occur in physical capital, when new products and innovations are developed, patents notwithstanding.

While such arguments provide a potential rationale for subsidies to the human capital formation that generates the positive externalities, caution should be used before embracing that policy conclusion. Certainly, markets can operate in subtle fashions to "internalize the externalities." Industrial development parks can arise, with the agglomeration externalities being internalized into land prices or other types of quid pro quo. Communities can try, through tax or other concessions, to attract or retain business that allegedly generates these positive "spillovers." Individuals may pay for education not only for its intrinsic value but for what could be considered network externalities or "spillover" benefits from others. If there are externalities, they probably differ across human capital investments, in which case targeting the support becomes difficult. Investments in physical capital can also generate externalities, and so those in human capital need not be unfairly treated relative to physical capital. Most important, once subsidies are forthcoming, rent-seeking will set in as agents try to appropriate subsidies for activities that they would have carried out anyway. For these reasons, an imperfect market solution must be compared to a probably imperfect public-sector solution.

Implications of Efficiency Wages

Efficiency wages are those paid above the competitive norm in order to induce effort and productivity from workers. Employers may pay such wages because of factors such as increased commitment and morale, or reductions in turnover and shirking, or savings in monitoring costs. Efficiency wages lead to queues for such prized jobs, and yet the employer will not lower wages or alter other working conditions in response to the queues because the wage premium serves the profit-maximizing function of inducing effort. In essence, the wage premiums pay for themselves.

Empirical evidence tends to confirm the existence of such efficiency wages, as shown, for example, by pure inter-industry wage differences that seem to prevail even after one controls for the effect of other wage-determining factors.[5] Such jobs correspond to our common-sense notion of "good jobs" – the wage premium is not simply compensation for non-pecuniary aspects of the job or for costly human capital acquisition. These jobs are valued, and in fact the prize elicits the positive behaviour.

The existence of efficiency wages can be used to rationalize industrial policies or even protectionist measures to encourage or preserve such positions. Other things being equal, countries with such jobs are better off than those without, since the premium benefits workers without penalizing employers. As indicated, the premium is not simply compensation for other elements of disutility associated with the job, nor does it simply redistribute monopoly profits. Policies that encourage creation of such "good jobs" can easily end up protecting positions that are not viable in the long run or that pay wage rents (wages in excess of one's next best alternative) out of monopoly profits and not for reasons of efficiency.

Efficiency wages are not tied directly to human capital investment. They may be more likely in jobs with a high human capital component because employers want to reduce turnover or elicit more effort. However, the relationship may not be sufficiently strong to merit considering use of the tax system to encourage such jobs. Before such a policy is considered, more information is needed on whether efficiency wages exist in the labour market; whether they are associated with human capital; whether such jobs merit being encouraged by public policy; and whether the tax system is an effective means of targeting such jobs.

Equity Issues

Most of the discussion above pertained to efficiency – the importance of human capital formation to meeting competitive challenges, to ensuring high value-added production, to meeting changing workplace practices and new human resource requirements, to encouraging continuous growth, and to ensuring "good jobs." Human capital formation can also address issues of equity and fairness, a dimension often overlooked.

This neglect stems in part from the perception that the disadvantaged are less able to benefit from additional education and training – although that is in fact often why they are disadvantaged in the first place. In such circumstances, it is more tempting to support the "winners," forgetting that they probably would be winners with or without assistance. However, the relevant measure of efficiency is added value and not final output, and we simply do not know how much more an additional dollar of human capital investment would increase earnings for an already well-educated and -trained employee than it would for a disadvantaged person. We know that the final earnings would be higher for the already prepared person, but, again, we do not know the extent of the increase in earnings that would result from the additional investment. Earnings may increase because the well-educated employee's ability to absorb the investment has already been revealed. In contrast, the disadvantaged employee may be in the increasing-returns portion of his/her "learning curve" and hence be able to benefit the most.

Even if human capital formation were inefficient for the disadvantaged, reasons of equity and fairness necessitate such investment. We may simply prefer a smaller pie that is more equitably divided to one that is unequally divided. Competitive changes affecting our labour market are increasing wage polarization and producing a "declining middle," and there is concern with the social ramifications of such growing inequality. This is particularly noticeable for the "working poor," whose earnings cannot take them out of poverty. Supporting the human capital formation of such disadvantaged workers may be a viable anti-poverty tool, or at least a mechanism to reduce inequality of wages.

Human capital policies enable the disadvantaged to "earn their income" rather than to receive it as a transfer payment. This is important for both taxpayers and recipients alike. Support for human capital formation for the disadvantaged is also consistent with the new emphasis on replacing passive income maintenance with more active programs that facilitate adjustment away from declining sectors and towards expanding ones. The trampoline may be just as important as, if not more so than, the safety net.

Support for human capital formation for workers hurt by technological change, free trade, or industrial restructuring may also reduce their resistance to such changes. Equity and efficiency issues need not always conflict. Workers in Japan, for example, tend to have a more cooperative attitude to such change in part because job security ensures that they will not be displaced and, in fact, will be retrained for the new job requirements. This situation contrasts with that in North America, where employees are likely to be displaced into the external labour market.

Clearly, human capital investment can encourage equity and fairness. Such objectives need not always conflict with, and may in fact enhance, efficiency. In the event of a conflict, a legitimate social trade-off can sacrifice some efficiency to achieve the distributional goals. Of course, these goals should be achieved as efficiently as possible. Facilitating the human capital formation of the disadvantaged may also be consistent with such efficient redistribution.

Government Involvement in Private Decision Making

Analysis of the increasing importance of investment in human resources suggests a number of rationales for government involvement. In this section, we expand more systematically on those rationales, relating them explicitly to where markets may fail to ensure adequate investment in human resources. Before doing so, we provide a brief, non-technical exposition of private actors' (employers' and individuals') decision making concerning human capital investment. We illustrate it with respect to training, although the general principles apply to any human capital decision.

Private Decisions on Human Capital Investment

Private parties will put money into human capital until the benefits from additional input are just equal to the cost of additional investment. At some point, the extra benefits per dollar are likely to diminish – for example, the additional value of the fifth university degree is likely to be smaller than that of the first, and it may even send a negative signal. As well, the benefits of additional human capital will shrink as more is acquired, simply because the acquisition takes time and therefore reduces the remaining period over which the benefits can accrue. The costs of obtaining additional human capital may also increase as more is acquired because one's time cost (and hence income forgone) grows as more human capital is acquired. These declining marginal benefits and increasing marginal costs ensure that at some point the latter will exceed the former, and it will no longer make economic sense to invest further.

For individuals, the costs of training and higher education are largely in the form of forgone earnings – often referred to as indirect, time, or opportunity costs of training. The benefits or returns from training usually occur later, in the form of increased earnings. This is the case, however, only for training that is generally usable in a number of firms, since only then will firms pay higher wages for such training. Even where the training is company specific, the firm may offer a higher wage to deter turnover and protect its investment. If the training is industry specific, then other firms will bid for such workers, but if the industry itself is declining then there may be little premium to such skills. Workers who are permanently displaced from such industries often experience large wage losses.

The distinction between general training and company-specific training affects the issue of who should pay for such training. Individuals should be willing to pay for the former (often in the form of a lower wage during the training period), since they will appropriate the returns later in the form of a higher wage. Employers will not be willing to provide such training (unless compensated, for example, by a lower wage during the training period), since they would still have to compete afterwards by paying a higher wage.

When the training is company specific, the employer will obtain a more productive worker and therefore should be willing to provide such training. Since the productivity is enhanced only in the sponsoring firm, then the firm will pay a higher wage to keep the trainee from moving elsewhere. The wage increase is less than the productivity increase, because the latter occurs only for the sponsor. However, since the trainee receives a higher wage, there is some monetary incentive for him or her to pay for a portion of the specific training.

While employers should thus clearly pay for most of the specific training, and employees for the general (and perhaps a small portion of the specific), the distinction is not always clear in practice. It is not always possible to delineate clearly company-specific from generally usable training – even the company-specific type reveals an ability to absorb such training. In addition, firms that provide company-specific training may still pay a higher wage so as not to lose the training embodied in their employee. In such circumstances, training becomes more of a shared investment, with both parties having an interest in the training but with neither having clear responsibility for paying.

This analysis of private decision making suggests areas – market imperfections, market failures, and equity rationales – where the private-sector participants may have insufficient incentives to invest in training, and hence where governments may in fact have a potential role.

Market Imperfections

Market imperfections arise where markets exist but where they may operate imperfectly. In the human capital area, for example, such investments can be fraught with risk and uncertainty over which the parties themselves feel they have little control. Employers may reluctantly agree to pay for training, only to have their trainees leave. Employees may reluctantly pay for training, only to have their firm close, or for the training to become obsolete, or for it to not to command a premium because a flood of other individuals undertook the same training. Training is often a joint product or even a by-product of the normal production process, in which case it is difficult to determine how much of it actually takes place. It may be difficult for trainees to diversify against the risk associated with human capital investments, since the investment is embodied in themselves as workers. Workers who lose their job may lose their basic wage, their human capital investment, and, if their job loss is because of a major plant closing, any investment that they have in the company as well as any reduction in the value of their home. Tying one's investment in human capital, one's home, and one's financial assets to the fortunes of one's employer – who also pays one's basic wage – is not a diversified investment portfolio. In physical capital investment, limited-liability companies are formed to sell shares to investors who can diversify by holding the shares of many firms.

Uncertainties also arise because it may be difficult to disentangle the extent to which training is general as opposed to specific, and hence to determine who should pay. Even if the training is purely company specific, employees may threaten to leave and take their training, even if it does not command a wage premium elsewhere.

Such problems in the market for human capital are often associated with any investment decision – risk and uncertainty are the essence of investment. The returns to human capital investments should take into account the associated risks and uncertainties, and institutional and contractual arrangements should emerge to deal with many of these issues. For example, employers who are concerned about losing their training investment may use deferred wages, whereby such workers are paid more later in their career if they remain with their employer. Seniority-based wages and pension benefit accruals may be forms of such deferred compensation.

Despite the similarity of most capital investment decisions, there are a number of areas where human capital investments may be different. Unlike physical capital, human capital (expected future earnings) cannot be used as collateral for a loan to finance the investment. As well, financial institutions may be reluctant to provide a loan to finance human capital formation because the recipient can influence subsequent returns through the extent to which he or she works afterwards. An individual who does not work later earns no return, and the creditor cannot "repossess" the investment. This moral hazard also exists vis-à-vis physical capital; however, there the lender can repossess the investment. Inability to finance human capital formation can be a problem, especially for low-income individuals, who cannot credibly signal their willingness and ability to repay any loans or who cannot afford to "self-finance" by taking a lower wage during training. Accepting a lower wage during a training period may also be hampered by wage-fixing legislation or by collective agreements, although training periods can be, and often are, exempt.

Women who engage in household work or who interrupt their labour-market career to raise a family can be thought of as engaging in household-specific human capital formation, even though there are typically no future monetary returns to such unpaid labour. The costs include forgone earnings as well as depreciation of labour-market skills. The benefits are non-monetary, including any physical returns associated with unpaid household work, such as raising a family. The benefits are shared with other family members, but the costs are borne largely by the women. In the event of a breakup of the household, women are seldom compensated for the permanent loss of their earnings associated with the abandonment or even interruption of their labour-market work, although in recent years the courts have begun to take women's household activities into account when dividing assets on separation or divorce. When plants close, workers also lose their investment in company-specific training. When "families close," women tend to lose their family-specific investment because they disproportionately bore the cost in the form of lost earnings potential.

Externalities, Poaching, and Insufficient Incentives

As indicated in the discussion of endogenous growth, training and education may generate externalities as others receive overspill benefits in the process. A suboptimal amount of training results, because the private parties do not take these additional positive benefits into account in their investment decision.

Firms that pay for general training also may not be able to appropriate the full benefits of their training because other firms may simply bid away the trained worker. The firm providing the training therefore has to "double-pay" – cover the training and then offer a higher wage so as not to lose the trainee. This classic "poaching problem" discourages firms' investment in general training in North America. In countries such as Japan, low turnover and lifetime employment encourage the large employers to invest in their staff. In North America, however, employers have little incentive to provide training if they run the risk of losing their trainees to other firms that "poach" rather than provide training. Of course, trainees should then be willing to pay for the training, because they receive the benefits in the form of a higher wage later. As we saw above, barriers or market imperfections may make it difficult, if not impossible, for individuals to pay for such human capital formation.

There may also be insufficient incentives for the private parties to innovate in the area of human capital formation. Parties that do so bear the full cost of their innovation, but they cannot appropriate the full benefits of any success, since it will quickly be emulated by others. Patents ensure that private individuals or firms can appropriate much of their returns to their innovations in physical capital, but not in human capital. An organization can patent new production technology that it develops, and this fact encourages innovation in that area. In contrast, one that sets up a new type of training program will have it emulated by competitors if it is successful. It bears the full cost if the program fails, but it shares the returns if it succeeds, and so there is little monetary incentive in this important area.

As well, if educational institutions implement changes to compete for new students, greater revenues do not offset the cost of expanding. Competitive pressures are blunted considerably by the way in which education is organized and financed.

Individual workers may also not have sufficient incentive to train co-workers, in spite of the potential value of such informal on-the-job training. If they train colleagues too well, they may train their replacement – a risky strategy without a reasonable degree of job security. The lifetime employment common in Japan, for example, encourages such efforts.

Externalities to investments in education and training may also exist in the form of tax revenues (or perhaps savings in transfer payments).

A private decision will increase an individual's income, which in turn will generate higher tax revenues, especially if the person moves into a higher marginal tax bracket. The increased education or training may reduce government expenditures in other areas, such as unemployment insurance or even welfare. If such programs have disincentives to work, they reduce the benefit period and hence private incentives to invest in human capital formation. Clearly, individuals' acquisition of more education and training can increase tax returns and/or lower government expenditures. Governments willing to subsidize some of the costs may appropriate the returns through higher taxes and/or reduced expenditures. The paper looks below at estimated rates of return to higher education.

Equity Issues

Public support for human capital formation may also be justified on grounds of equity or fairness. As we saw above, such support may be particularly appealing because it enables recipients to earn their income. As well, it helps the move from passive income maintenance (which can discourage adjustment from declining sectors) towards a more active strategy to encourage adjustment to expanding sectors. Such assistance may also reduce resistance to efficient change and even encourage cooperative efforts.

Making training or education a condition of eligibility for income support (workfare) for the employable may be a viable way of allocating scarce funds for income support. It may also reduce long-run dependence on income maintenance and encourage skill development.

More Interventionist Strategies

We have seen the rationale for government intervention in human capital formation, largely when markets fail to ensure optimal investment or to meet certain equity objectives. A more interventionist strategy would not require markets to fail before governments enter. Rather, governments could be regarded as being a leader, or at least forge partnerships with the private parties. Investment in human resources is regarded as a social investment, with particular emphasis on free education as a mechanism to provide equality of opportunity.

Deterioration of human capital stock may become irreversible beyond some point. Institutional structures for education and training take time to be established; teachers themselves have to be trained before they can impart their training. As well, individuals who miss basic education cannot simply enter the education system later in their career (or non-career). Their lack of education may have started them down a path that is very difficult to reverse. The phrase "lost generation" is not usually taken to refer to a *temporary* loss of opportunities. The appropriate analogy can be with elements of the environment or natural resources. It is not always feasible to replace the ozone layer or forests or lakes if they are allowed to "depreciate," especially if the process becomes self-perpetuating. Similar elements of irreversibility may apply to human capital.

The relevant model of the more interventionist strategy would be public education, where general instruction is publicly provided at least from kindergarten to grade 13. While there is serious discussion about expanded private initiatives in that sector, few people talk about having government provide support only when there are well-defined market failures or equity problems.

According to that perspective, public provision should be extended to other areas of human capital formation. At a bare minimum, public provision of education should be extended to childcare years prior to kindergarten, when the foundation for subsequent human capital formation is laid down. Tuition fees should be no more required in higher education than in kindergarten through grade 13. Training should be supported in the same fashion as public education.

Certainly, arguments can be brought against this perspective. It may simply reflect the view of people who have a strong preference for public education and training. The reasons may implicitly be efficiency and equity. This is not the forum, however, to deal with that debate. We intend this analysis to show the broad spectrum of views on government involvement in formation of human capital, including implications for the role of government.

Range of Options for Government Intervention

Assuming that governments have a role in human capital formation, what is the appropriate nature and degree of that involvement? The range of options can be categorized roughly according to the extent to which governments will intervene in the operation of market mechanisms in investment decisions.

At the least interventionist end, governments would do little except enforce private contractual arrangements, just as it does with other investment decisions. Non-interventionist governments would remove any artificial or regulatory barriers to human capital formation. They might, for example, exempt workers in training programs from minimum wage legislation. (Of course, such legislation itself would probably be eliminated by a complete non-interventionist strategy!)

A minimalist role would have governments facilitating private decision making by providing information on changing occupational demands, job opportunities, and availability of education and training programs and other human capital investments. While private markets for such information do exist (in fact, acquisition of labour market information is an investment decision vis-à-vis human capital, and want ads convey occupational demands), the rationale for government intervention rests largely on information as "public goods." Use of the information by one party does not detract from its use by another, and it is difficult to exclude non-payers once the information is provided.

A slightly expanded public-sector role would involve intervention only in response to well-defined market failures. Markets would be judged innocent until proven guilty. Possible market failures include individuals' inability to use their human capital as collateral to finance their investment, possible "poaching," and markets' failure to deal with equity and fairness.

The interventionist end of the spectrum would see governments as leaders, with human capital being regarded as a social investment in the public infrastructure of society. The focus would be not so much on who should pay and how public decision making should mesh with private decision making, but rather on how to ensure the optimal provision of each type of human capital as well as the total amount of human capital relative to other expenditures, such as health, roads, and social services.

To whatever degree governments intervene, they will have to decide on the use of tax instruments versus other instruments for achieving their goals. In extreme non-intervention, for example, they will want to make sure that the tax system does not penalize investments in human capital relative to other investments. With strong intervention, they may want to use tax incentives to subsidize human capital investments.

We next consider the impact of taxes on human capital formation.

The Effect of Taxes on Human Capital Formation

The theoretically expected impact of taxes on human capital formation can best be illustrated by a sequence of cases that illustrate the various effects of the tax system and reveal the behavioural mechanisms through which taxes affect investment decisions. We build on the simple model outlined above, in which private investors (firms and individuals) invest in human capital until the extra benefits from such investment just equal the additional cost, and this return will in turn just equal the private returns from other investments, such as those in financial assets or physical capital. We can analyse the effect of taxes on human capital in terms of how taxes affect the costs and benefits of human capital investments relative to other investments. The returns here are after-tax figures, which drive private investment decisions.

Proportional Income Tax on Human Capital

Consider first the simplest case – a proportional income tax on human capital, a fixed labour supply, riskless investment returns, and no out-of-pocket education costs. Under a proportional income tax, the marginal tax rate is constant, so that extra income is reduced by the same proportion, irrespective of the level of income. This arrangement reduces the benefits to human capital formation because resulting higher earnings are taxed.

However, the proportional tax also reduces the (opportunity) cost of human capital formation because the main cost – earnings forgone while creating human capital – is also reduced in the same proportion. The costs are reduced because the person acquiring the human capital is now forgoing what would have been after-tax earnings.

If the costs of human capital formation are all in the form of forgone income, then these two effects offset each other, and a proportional income tax has no net effect on such investment decisions.[6] If a person's post-training wage is effectively reduced by 50 per cent because of a tax, and the cost during the training period is also reduced by 50 per cent because the trainee is forgoing after-tax wages, then the return is unaffected by taxation. This argument applies equally to any tax system with a constant marginal tax rate.

This result can be demonstrated simply. For example, in Figure 1 the benefits and costs of human capital investment are shown on the vertical axis, and the amount of investment on the horizontal axis. Benefits, B, are a downward-sloping function of the amount of investment because of diminishing returns and represent the present value of the additional wages arising from human capital formation. Costs, C, slope upwards as larger investments entail the sacrifice of more forgone earnings. With no taxes of any kind, investment would proceed until

FIGURE 1
Human Capital Investment under a Proportional Income Tax

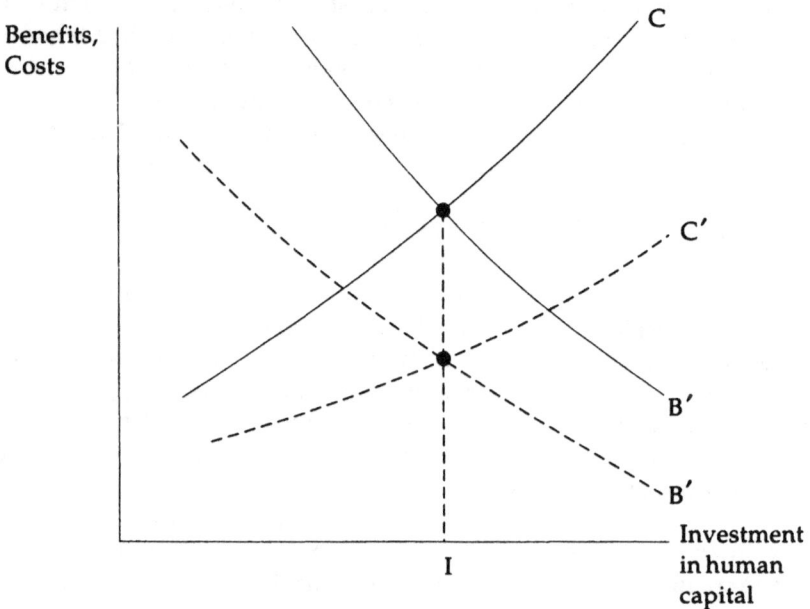

costs and benefits were equated (B = C). With a proportional income tax, at rate t, the investor will equate after-tax costs, $(1 - t)C$, with after-tax benefits, $(1 - t)B$ or:

$$(1 - t)C = (1 - t)B \tag{1}$$

In Figure 1, the proportional tax will shift both B and C downwards by the same proportional amount, as shown by the dotted lines C' and B'. As is easily seen, these downward-shifted curves will intersect at the same level of human capital investment as was chosen in the absence of this income tax.

Thus the proportional income tax is neutral with respect to human capital formation, because it does not alter the after-tax rate of return to such investments as both costs and benefits are affected proportionately. Human capital investments are unusual in that the main expense (forgone income) is implicitly given a full and immediate write-off or tax deduction – the trainee does not pay tax on the income during the training period if no income is earned. There often is a mistaken impression that taxes reduce human capital formation by taxing subsequent earnings. This assumption ignores the favourable tax treatment given to the costs of human capital formation.

The same neutrality of a proportional corporate tax applies to firms that invest in training, since their wage costs for trainees are immediately and fully deductible as part of normal labour costs. Of course, these deductions are explicit in that the wages paid during the training period are a business expense, as are any costs of materials used in training. The returns to investment in the form of higher productivity and hence corporate earnings are taxed at the same rate as the savings experienced from the deduction. Benefits are reduced in the same proportion as costs.

Progressive Tax on Human Capital

Under a progressive income tax, the tax rate increases with the level of income so that a larger portion of income is taxed as income rises. This situation alters the calculations based on a proportional tax, in that the benefits of human capital formation are taxed at a higher rate. The benefits accrue at a future time, when the trainee's income is likely to be higher, especially because the human capital formation is likely to increase income. As well, people are likely to make such investment decisions at a stage in their life when their earnings (and hence forgone income or opportunity cost) are low. The forgone income, in contrast, is an (implicit) tax deduction that occurs during the investment period, when earnings are otherwise low. As Davies (1986, 204) points out, forgone earnings may even push the investor into a lower tax bracket. A progressive income tax thus reduces the after-tax rate of return to human capital formation and hence discourages such activity.

Students who give up four years of earnings when their marginal tax rate would have been only 25 per cent (because of their low earnings at that stage in their life) implicitly "save" only 25 per cent of their earnings by not paying taxes. Their cost of human capital formation is reduced by 25 per cent because they are paying in after-tax (forgone) income, which is reduced by the tax. However, if their marginal tax rate is 50 per cent on their later earnings, then their benefits from creating human capital drop by half. Their marginal tax rate may be 50 per cent when they are receiving the benefits simply because they are in a stage of life when earnings are usually higher and hence they are in a higher tax bracket. As well, additional earnings from higher education may "bump" them into the higher tax bracket. Clearly, the reduction in benefits from the 50 per cent tax rate is greater than the cost saving that occurred when the marginal tax rate was 25 per cent. Relative to the proportional tax, which was neutral vis-à-vis human capital formation, a progressive tax discourages such efforts.

This result is, of course, a natural by-product of the fact that a progressive income tax is designed to tax disproportionately those with greater ability to pay, even if that ability comes from greater human capital formation. As well, it is a by-product of the unusual nature of the main cost of human capital formation – forgone income (and hence saved taxes) in a period when marginal tax rates are likely to be low.

In Figure 2, forgone earnings, C, are taxed at the rate t_1, while benefits are taxed at the higher rate t_2. Once again, the investor will seek to equate after-tax costs and benefits or

$$(1 - t_1)C = (1 - t_2)B \tag{2}$$

These after-tax functions are depicted as dotted lines, and, because t_2 exceeds t_1, the benefit curve is shifted downwards more than the cost curve. Compared with a no-tax equilibrium, the progressive income tax induces a decline in human capital investment from I_0 to I_1.

A progressive tax reduces human capital formation because costs are usually incurred when marginal tax rates are low and benefits are received when they are high. This pattern need not always hold. For example, adult education may occur during a period when marginal tax rates are high, with the returns being expected later, when income and hence marginal tax rates could be lower. However, even in that case the marginal tax rate may not be high if the retraining resulted from a layoff. As well, if earnings (and hence marginal taxes) were high, it is unlikely that individuals would interrupt their peak earnings for retraining. Even if they are "paying" in after-tax dollars, the cost would be very high.

The progressive tax case does not apply to employers because the corporate income tax is proportional and hence neutral; it has no net effect on decisions about human capital investment (as we saw in the previous subsection). If the progressive income tax discourages human capital formation for individuals who engage in general education and training, and the proportional corporate income tax has no effect on the decision of firms to provide company-specific training, then the combination of the two systems may impart some bias towards company-specific training, which is not discouraged by the tax system.

FIGURE 2
A Progressive Income Tax on Human Capital Investment

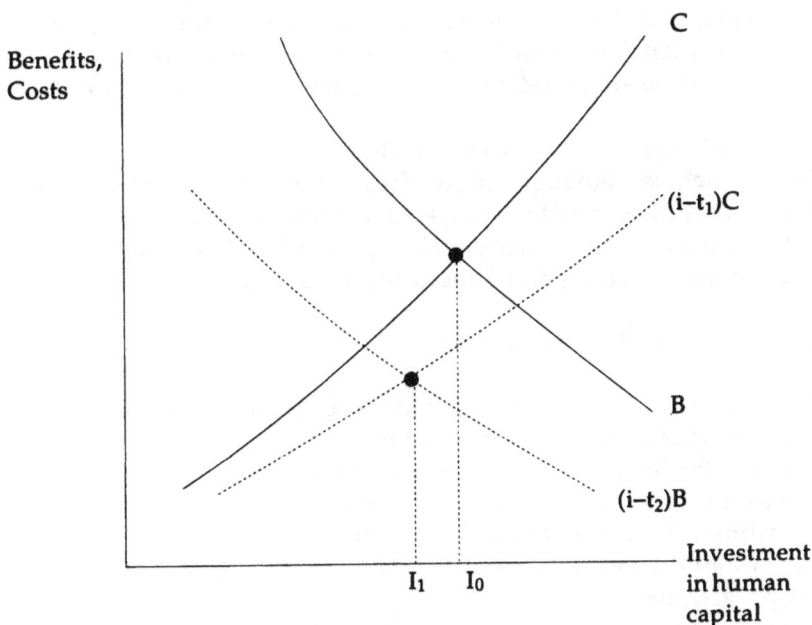

Costs Other than Forgone Income

We based discussion of both the proportional and the progressive tax on the assumption that all costs of human capital formation were in the form of forgone income – the "time cost" invested. While this is likely to be the largest, but underemphasized, cost, other expenses can obviously be involved. Such "goods costs," or purchased inputs (including tuition), are direct costs.

Obviously, the relative proportion of time cost and goods cost can vary. For grade school, the costs are exclusively direct and involve the inputs of teachers, buildings, and supplies. Universities necessitate such direct costs (a portion of which may be paid for from tuition), but the bulk of the cost is the student's forgone income.

The effect of adding goods costs to the above analysis depends on whether these costs are tax deductible. If they are, then they get the same tax treatment as forgone income. For example, if the tax rate is 25 per cent, then a dollar's worth of goods used as an input into human capital formation "costs" only 75 cents, just as a dollar's worth of time given up costs only 75 cents because one implicitly saves 25 cents by not having to pay income tax on the forgone earnings. If goods and time costs are both fully deductible and therefore get the same tax treatment, then the conclusion above about the impact of taxes on human capital formation holds. That is, a proportional income tax would have no effect and a progressive income tax would discourage it.

In most tax systems, however, including Canada's, goods costs are not deductible, although tuition fees are partially deductible. If α denotes the fraction of total costs that are non-deductible goods costs, the optimal investment decision in a proportional income tax system equates after-tax costs and returns and appears as:

$$\alpha C + (1 - \alpha)C (1 - t) = (1 - t)B. \tag{3}$$

Diagrammatically, the non-deductibility of goods costs means that, in the context of Figure 1, the cost curve will not shift downwards by as much as the benefit curve in the post-tax equilibrium. Compared to a no-tax situation, the lack of deductibility of goods costs will deter investment in human capital. In a progressive income tax system, that absence of deductibility would compound the negative effect of the tax progressively.

Even if goods costs are not tax deductible, they may be extensively subsidized, which encourages formation of human capital. Becker (1975) and Hansen (1963), for example, both indicate that over two-thirds of the direct cost of higher education is subsidized. In essence, the favourable tax treatment of forgone income may be crucial: it is the largest component of most human capital investments; the goods component may also receive some favourable tax treatment and is often subsidized, putting it on the same footing as the forgone income.

Also, while goods costs are usually not tax deductible (and this may discourage human capital formation), some of the benefits of creating human capital accrue in (untaxed) household production – a form of "implicit subsidy."

A Proportional Income Tax on Human and Physical Capital

Investments in physical capital are also subject to income taxation, and both physical capital and human capital are substitutes in investors' wealth portfolios. Income from investment in the former is taxed in many instances at both the personal and company levels; some assets, such as owner-occupied housing, are tax preferred and do not have their (imputed) income streams taxed at any level.[7] Ignoring these exceptions, taxation of physical capital biases a proportional income tax in favour of human capital.

The tendency towards excessive investment in human capital can be illustrated with the aid of Figure 3. There, the benefits and the costs of such investment in the absence of any taxes are shown as B and C, respectively. Without taxes, investment in the amount I_0 would occur. With a proportional income tax and no investment alternative to human capital, after-tax cost and benefit schedules shift downwards by the same proportion as in Figure 1. When physical capital exists as an investment option, the after-tax cost curve for human capital will shift downwards in the presence of the income tax, but the evaluation of after-tax benefits will not shift the benefit curve.

The benefit curve is stable because of the tax-induced decline in the discount rate that is appropriate for measuring the present value of the future benefits from human capital investment. In the no-tax situation, future benefits, B_j, are discounted at the market interest rate i. When interest income earned on investment in physical capital is taxed at the rate t, the investor's opportunity cost for investing in human capital is transformed from i to $i(1 - t)$, or the after-tax interest rate. When the after-tax benefits of investing in human capital, $B_j (1 - t)$ are discounted at the after-tax interest rate $i(1 - t)$, the result is the same as when the before-tax benefit, B_j, is discounted at the market interest rate i. Taxation of both wage and interest income reduces the benefits from human capital investment and the discount rate in the same proportion.

From the investors' perspective, proportional taxation of the income from both physical and human capital lowers the costs of human capital investment – from C to C^1 in Figure 3, while leaving unchanged the present value of the benefits from that investment. In Figure 3, this tax system will encourage expansion in human capital investment from I_0 to I_1.

This post-tax equilibrium signals misallocation of the economy's investment resources. In this simple tax world, the before-tax yield on physical capital, r^p, will exceed the before-tax yield on human capital investment, r^n, by the proportion $1/(1 - t)$. This is implicitly shown in Figure 3, where, in the new equilibrium, the rate of return on human capital investment, r^n, is equated to the after-tax rate of return on

FIGURE 3
A Proportional Income Tax on Physical and Human Capital

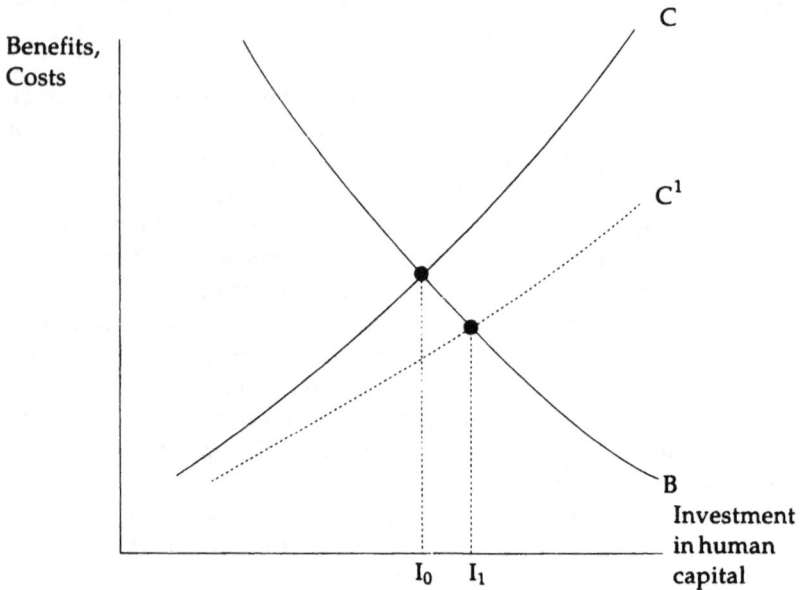

physical capital, $r^p(1 - t)$. In other words, this tax system causes too much of the economy's investment resources to be devoted to human capital. More efficient use would require less human, and more physical, investment.

This conclusion rests on a partial-equilibrium view of the investment process. As we mention below, in a general-equilibrium approach, the investment distortion may be much smaller. Davies and Whalley (1991), for example, find that adopting a neutral wage or expenditure tax to replace the personal income tax would provoke little change in the amount of investment in human capital. Tax substitution would stimulate such greater savings that, in a new long-run equilibrium, the before-tax rate of return on physical capital would be driven down to almost its initial net-of-tax value.

Our inefficiency result also rests on the particular tax treatment accorded to physical capital. If, for example, the normal rate of return on marginal physical investments were exempt from income tax, the rate of return on human capital investment would be equated at the margin to the before-tax rate of return on physical investment and there would be no distortion. A capital tax regime that allowed full "expensing," or immediate write-off, of all the costs of investment in physical capital would achieve this outcome.

Canada's corporate tax system does not permit full expensing, but its rather complex features must be carefully considered in calculating effective tax rates on different marginal investments in physical investment. Boadway, Bruce, and Mintz (1987) patiently outline the method of determining marginal effective tax rates and estimate these rates for different types of physical investment contemplated by Canadian corporations.

Finally, the income tax subsidy to human capital investment shown in Figure 3 may be economically justifiable if externalities abound or, more precisely, if the externalities attached to human capital investment exceed those emanating from physical investment. In that case, the social benefit schedule would lie above the private benefit schedule shown in Figure 3, making investment in human capital in excess of I_0 socially worthwhile.

Debt-Financed Human Capital Investment

The analysis to this point has assumed that an investor in human capital sacrifices alternative investment in physical capital to pay for education or training. Some investors, however, may borrow to finance their human capital formation. In this case, a proportional income tax will not encourage excessive investment in human capital, as long as interest expense is not deductible from taxable income. Debt-financed investments in human capital would receive neutral tax treatment.

The explanation for this outcome lies in the choice of the discount rate that is appropriate for a borrower. If interest costs are non-deductible, the investor faces a cost of finance, and a discount rate, that are equal to the market interest rate i rather than the after-tax interest rate $i(1 - t)$. When the benefits of human capital investment are discounted at the market interest rate, the situation portrayed in Figure 1 is relevant, not the one shown in Figure 3. If, however, interest expense on educational loans were deductible, Figure 3 would apply.

Incorporating the Work-Incentive Effects of Taxes (Relaxing the Assumption of Fixed Labour Supply)

The analysis above assumed that the tax had no effect on work incentives and, hence, no effect on the period over which the benefits of the human capital investments subsequently accrue. However, human capital is an unusual investment: it is embodied in the individual, and therefore economic returns depend on the subsequent period over which the individual engages in paid employment. The influence of taxes on human capital formation thus depends on their effect not only on the cost of the goods and time inputs but also on work incentives.[8]

In theory, income taxes have opposing effects on the incentive to engage in paid employment. On the one hand, they lessen the incentive by reducing after-tax returns to labour-market work. This situation can induce substitution of non-taxed forms of work, such as household production or pure leisure, for paid employment and/or reduction of labour market work by reduced hours or occasional non-participation (for example, through delayed entry or early retirement).

On the other hand, higher income taxes also lessen the worker's wealth, inducing him or her to work more to offset this loss. People may put in more hours or enter or stay in the labour force for longer periods. This income or wealth effect depends in part on the extent to which the taxpayer values public expenditures financed from taxes. If their positive value is exactly equal to the negative value of the tax increase, then, of course, there is no change in the person's net wealth. However, if the public expenditures are valued less than the tax increase, then net wealth drops.

Since these "substitution" and "income" effects, respectively, have opposing influences on the incentive to take paid employment, economic theory by itself does not tell us the net effect of income taxes on such incentives. This is akin to the notion that labour supply schedules may slope upwards or bend backwards. They will slope upwards if a wage increase (akin to a tax decrease) induces more labour-market work because the greater economic returns to paid employment induce substitution into such work, which offsets any tendency for the higher income to enable the individual to afford not to work as much. They will slope backwards if the opposite is true – that is, if the income effect outweighs the substitution effect. Since income tax increases are analogous to a reduction in the net wage, then income taxes (i.e., a movement down the labour supply schedule) will reduce labour-market work incentives if the labour supply schedule slopes forward, and they will increase it if the schedule bends backwards.

Since economic theory does not tell us unambiguously whether income taxes will increase or decrease incentives for labour-market work, we must appeal to the empirical evidence. Summaries[9] suggest that increases in wages lead to a rise in labour-market work (i.e., the substitution effect outweighs the income effect, although both are present, acting in opposite directions). For women, this positive net effect of wage increases on labour supply is especially strong. For men, the net effect is generally negative, as they reduce their labour supply in response to a wage increase. The stronger positive effect for women outweighs the weaker negative effect for men, producing an overall positive net effect for both sexes. In recent years, however, the labour-supply response of women has been becoming more like that of men, suggesting that the aggregate labour-supply response is becoming less positive.

This finding implies that income tax increases, which are the equivalent to a reduction in the net wage, would decrease overall labour supply. They would strongly decrease labour supply for women, and weakly increase it for men, with the combined effect being negative. As indicated, the response for women is becoming more like that for men, suggesting that the aggregate response to a tax increase may be becoming "less negative," even approaching zero. There is considerable variation in the magnitude of the expected overall reduction, although the evidence suggests that an income tax increase that would reduce net wages by 1 per cent would reduce hours supplied to the labour market by about one-quarter of 1 per cent. The magnitude could range anywhere, however, from no response to a reduction in labour supply of almost one-half of 1 per cent.

To the extent that income taxes reduce the incentive to work in the labour market, then this reduces the subsequent benefit period from which to recoup the cost of human capital formation. This reduction in benefits lowers the economic returns to such investment. The negative effect of income taxes on work incentives lowers the use of human capital.[10] As indicated, this effect is stronger for women than it is for men.

Taxes on Financial and Physical Capital Reconsidered

As we have seen, income taxes discourage human capital formation in a variety of ways. The progressive nature of the tax system discouraged such investments, since the benefits would be taxed at a rate higher than would apply when the costs were incurred. The direct expenses may not be tax deductible even though the benefits are taxed. And income taxes may reduce labour-market work and hence the period over which benefits accrue. All these forces discourage formation of human capital.

However, the income tax on the return from physical capital works in the opposite direction. It is therefore conceptually impossible to determine the net impact of income taxes on the decision to invest in human capital. Davies and St-Hilaire (1987) argue on balance that the income tax system alone probably discourages human capital investment when compared to either a lump-sum tax or an expenditure tax. They believe that the interest-rate effect on the incentive for accumulation of physical capital is likely to be weak, except for older workers. They also point out, however, that significant subsidies apply to many kinds of human capital investment and counteract any net discouragement caused by the income tax system.

Clearly it requires a general-equilibrium analysis to sort out the relative strengths of the different effects that we have identified. Unfortunately, none of the modelling efforts to date has addressed this issue but instead focused on the effect of different tax reforms. Before we assess this literature, we briefly examine how income taxes affect the investor's assessment of the relative riskiness of investments in physical and in human capital.

Taxation of Risk Returns

Investing in human capital is often regarded as riskier than investing in physical capital, although refugees have often lost the latter while retaining much of the former. Compared to physical capital, human capital provides fewer opportunities for risk diversification. Capital markets provide an array of risk-pooling and -spreading services. By comparison, an investor in human capital is forced to put more of his or her eggs in a single basket and faces a more variable (or risky) flow of returns for the same expected rate of return. These differences could result in systematic underinvestment in human capital. A higher effective tax rate on the income from physical capital investment would reduce this bias.

Eaton and Rosen (1980) confirm this conclusion in a riskless setting. But they also show that in a risky world, with constant relative risk aversion (i.e., when willingness to accept risk increases with higher income levels), the interest-income component of the personal income tax reduces income and makes investment in the riskier asset (human capital) less attractive.

The earnings component of the personal income tax also reduces the risk or variability of the return from human capital. This, in turn, would induce risk-averse individuals to invest more in human capital relative to other investments that would have the same expected return but greater variability or uncertainty.

Income taxes reduce uncertainty about return because, as we have seen, the main cost of investment in human capital is forgone income. Income taxes on the higher earnings reduce the benefits and the costs, because one is forgoing after-tax dollars. This parallel reduction in benefits and costs can leave the expected return the same (under a proportional tax and with all expenses in the form of forgone income), or it can reduce the expected return (under a progressive tax, or if non-deductible direct expenses are involved). In either case, however, the tax will reduce the variability about that expected return because the tax takes a fixed and certain amount out of both the cost and benefit side of the equation. It is somewhat like sharing the risk with a partner, who gets a share of the benefits in return for sharing some of the cost.

It is difficult to judge the practical importance of this risk factor in decisions about human capital investment. It is unlikely, however, that it would be of great significance, certainly relative to the other factors associated with the tax treatment of human capital.

If human capital is inherently a more risky venue than other loci of investment, institutional change and new policies could offset this bias by redistributing risks. One such possibility is the development of income-contingent repayment schemes for student loans. As in the current Canada Student Loan Plan, the government would guarantee the loan to the lender but would make the amount to be repaid, and the length of the repayment period, contingent on the student's future economic success. Society would share in the risk of the student's investment.

The Clinton administration in the United States has introduced a scheme of this type, but using the Internal Revenue Service to collect outstanding debts. If loans are easy to obtain and defaulters pay no penalty, these schemes could shift too much risk to society from the investor and could encourage excessive amounts of human capital investment.

General Equilibrium Effects through Changes in Saving

We have seen adjustments in human capital investment as taxes affect its costs and benefits and relative to other investment decisions. These are partial equilibrium effects in that they focus on the direct effects of taxes on the decision to invest. They do not deal with general equilibrium effects, whereby taxes affect other markets, which in turn influence the market for human capital. The following discussion is based on Trostel (1991) and Davies and Whalley (1991).

Taxation of physical capital induces excessive substitution towards human capital in the short run but reduces aggregate savings and hence the aggregate capital stock in the long run. According to neoclassical growth theory, this, in turn, will raise the interest rate and lower the wage rate because reduced capital stock lowers the productivity of labour.

The rise in the interest rate will lead to a substitution away from human capital and into physical capital to get the higher return from the latter. The reduction in the wage rate should shrink labour supply (assuming that the aggregate labour-supply schedule slopes upwards, as the evidence suggests). This contraction, in turn, discourages formation of human capital by reducing the period over which it is used in the labour market. These induced general-equilibrium changes in factor prices therefore discourage excessive human capital formation.

General Equilibrium Effects through Changes in Output

Taxes can reduce future output and income, leaving fewer goods available for investing in human capital. Trostel (1991) labels this an income effect (because less income is available for investing in human capital) or a crowding-out effect (because the tax bite on income or output crowds out such investment). This general equilibrium effect of taxes through changes in output or income thereby discourages formation of human capital.

This reasoning, however, shows the tenuous nature of general equilibrium analyses, at least for this issue. As we saw above, taxes need not reduce real income or output. Rather, they are used for public expenditures, which presumably have some value to taxpayers. This value may be less than the displaced private-sector consumption, but it could also be greater, because only government spending could purchase the public goods. Rather than crowding out private-sector consumption or investment, government spending may simply displace it with public equivalents.

For example, taxes are used for public education. The taxes do reduce the resources available for private education, and the investment in public education does crowd out investment in private education. But surely this substitutes public for private investment rather than reducing overall human capital formation. Whether overall wealth is increased or reduced by the tax-expenditure package depends on the value of the public versus private investment.

Even if income or wealth is decreased by the tax-expenditure package, it is not obvious that this situation should affect decisions on investment, including that in human capital. Such decisions are based on expected benefits versus expected costs (including forgone income and possibly borrowing costs). Unless these real factors are affected by changes in wealth, then the investment decision should not be altered. If borrowing is not feasible (for reasons discussed above) and the reduced wealth from taxes (to the extent that it does occur) makes self-financing of human capital investment more difficult, then this mechanism should be explicitly stated. The same applies if reduced income or wealth expands labour supply, which in turn increases the benefits of human capital formation.

General Equilibrium Effects through Deficit Financing

Trostel (1991) also discusses general equilibrium effects created when public investments in human capital are paid for through deficit financing. Such financing involves delayed or deferred taxation. Delayed taxes are greater than taxes paid earlier and compound any negative effects of taxes on human capital formation. This reasoning seems to assume, however, that taxes reduce human capital formation, while we have seen that they have both positive and negative effects.

Delayed taxes reduce not current wages but future after-tax wages. Any negative effect on work incentives is delayed into the future, which is when the human capital formation is to be used as part of the subsequent labour-market work. The effect is to reduce human capital formation.

As with the other general equilibrium effects, it seems difficult to evaluate this impact through deficit financing. If the investments in human capital are economically worthwhile and generate growth in incomes, then the debt is easily repaid out of the higher income. Even if delayed taxes are higher, they may be repaid more easily if growth is higher. Net wages in the future may be reduced by delayed taxes, but the higher gross wages generated by human capital formation may still leave them higher. Clearly, possible general equilibrium effects from deficit financing are difficult to evaluate.

Summary of Tax Effects on Human Capital Formation

Table 1 summarizes the channels through which taxes affect human capital formation. A proportional income tax, by itself, would have no net effect because the tax reduces marginal benefits and marginal cost (forgone income) by the same proportion (assuming that all costs are in the form of forgone income and that the tax has no effect on work incentives). There is often a mistaken impression that such a tax would reduce human capital formation by taxing subsequent earnings. However, the costs in income forgone are (implicitly) given a full and immediate write-off.

A progressive tax, however, discourages formation of human capital, because the tax write-off happens when the investment is being made and, hence, when taxable earnings are low, while the higher tax rate applies later, when earnings rise. Non-deductibility of direct expenses discourages such investment. Any negative effect of taxes on work incentives would also reduce the benefit period during which the human capital is used. This, too, discourages human capital formation.

In the opposite direction, an income tax would reduce the after-tax rate of return on physical capital more than on human capital, given the (implicit) expense deduction of forgone income. This would cause substitution from physical to human capital. As well, taxes may reduce the variability of the returns to human capital formation and encourage such investment.

Clearly, these partial equilibrium effects have opposing influences. Some possible general equilibrium effects, however, discourage human capital investments. Taxes may reduce savings and hence the capital stock and thus increase interest rates and reduce wages (and hence work incentives) in the long run. Taxes may also reduce income and output and therefore the goods available for investing in human capital. As well, if the tax increases are deferred, they will be larger in the future (hence amplifying any negative effects of taxes) and will accordingly lead to subsequent reductions in work incentives, which will lessen use of human capital.

As we have seen, the plausibility of these general equilibrium effects is difficult to assess. In a sense, in general equilibrium "anything goes." After all, a tax increase led to the Boston Tea Party, which led to a revolution with profound effects on human capital formation! The effects specified here discourage formation of human capital, and,

TABLE 1
Summary of Effect of Taxes on Human Capital Formation

Tax aspect	Mechanism for affecting human capital formation	Effect
Proportional tax	Reduction in cost from immediate and full (implicit) write-off of forgone income expense exactly offsetting reduced benefits from tax on higher earnings	Neutral
Progressive tax	Benefits from higher earnings taxed at high marginal tax rate, while lower rate applies to forgone income write-off	Decrease
Expenses other than forgone income	If other expenses not deductible, then cost of human capital formation higher	Decrease
Work incentives	Taxes reducing labour supply and therefore use of human capital	Decrease
Tax on physical and financial capital	Reduces after-tax return more than for human capital, since expenses for physical capital not fully deductible, thereby inducing a substitution from physical to human capital	Increase
Reduced uncertainty after taxes	Taxes reducing variation in returns from human capital because they reduce both benefits and forgone income costs	Increase
General equilibrium (GE) effects on savings (factor price effects)	Tax on capital income reducing savings and capital stock and therefore increasing the interest rate and reducing wages (and labour supply), both of which reduce human capital formation	Decrease
GE crowding effects on income and output	Taxes reducing income and output and therefore goods available for investment in human capital	Decrease
Deficit financing (deferred taxes)	Implies higher taxes, which compound their negative effect; also reduces after-tax wage (and work incentive) in later period when use of human capital most likely	Decrease

because of this outcome, their cumulative effect merits serious consideration.

Empirical Evidence

As is so often the case, the economic forces at work have opposing influences on behaviour. In this case, taxes have an ambiguous effect on human capital formation; hence our appeal to the empirical evidence. Unfortunately, in this area there is remarkably little conclusive evidence. On partial equilibrium effects, there have been no studies that have estimated the different results. Studies outlining the mechanisms whereby taxes affect human capital formation emphasize their bi-directionality and their tendency to offset each other, possibly even encouraging human capital formation.[11]

Rosen (1982) does estimate how the decision to undertake on-the-job training (OJT) is affected by a number of variables, reflecting the expected return on training, as well as the individual's marginal tax rate. His data are from the U.S. Panel Study of Income Dynamics for the year 1976. He finds that higher marginal tax rates encourage investment in OJT somewhat. Specifically, an increase of one-third would expand (OJT) by only 2.4 per cent. He concludes: "The positive value suggests that individuals are induced by the income tax to engage in OJT. Apparently the effect that dominates is the one which gives an individual an incentive to substitute human capital for physical capital as a means for carrying consumption into the future" (447).

The one general equilibrium study that focuses on the effect of taxes on human capital formation – Trostel (1991) – does provide simulation results indicating that income taxes discourage human capital formation, mainly through the general equilibrium effects discussed above. Specifically, a 1 per cent increase in taxes (for example, increasing the tax rate from 40 to 40.4 per cent) is associated with a 0.39 per cent reduction in human capital formation.

Although analysis does not permit quantification of the separate effect of each mechanism, simulations indicate the relative importance of some factors. Most discouraging appears to be lack of deductibility for direct expenses (other than forgone income). If all the costs of acquiring more human capital were deductible, the negative effect of income taxation would be halved. Next in importance, taxes reduce income and output available for investing in human capital formation and weaken work incentives and reduce use of human capital. The short-term reduction in the after-tax interest rate that results from taxing capital income is offset by the long-term increase in the before-tax interest rate produced by the smaller savings and capital stock.

Trostel's model did not incorporate progressive taxes (which should further inhibit human capital formation) or reduction in the uncertainty resulting from possible tax charges (which should facilitate such formation). However, Trostel suggested that because these two effects work in opposite directions, and because the progressive tax effect is likely to be larger, their omission would reaffirm that taxes reduce formation of human capital.

The empirical literature suggests that taxes may slow human capital formation. However, in our single U.S. study, some of the mechanisms are perhaps tenuous, and the conclusions contrast sharply with the earlier "informed opinion" that any net effect of taxes would be small or slightly positive. Given the uncertainty of the evidence, more study is needed.

Federal Personal Income Taxation and Formal Education

Because the Canadian provinces generally conform to Ottawa's definition of taxable personal income under the Tax Collection Agreement, it is federal tax legislation that influences human capital formation. Current laws tilt modestly in support of its acquisition through formal education. Income used to support a student does not receive preferential tax treatment, but a number of direct education costs are effectively deductible through two tax credits. Other measures relating to formation of human capital include:

- Scholarships, fellowships, and bursaries are fully taxable.
- Research grants are fully taxable if they exceed research-related expenses.
- Any reimbursement or accountable advance used to defray educational costs is also fully taxable.
- Interest expense on student loans is not deductible, although repayment is not required under the Canada Student Loan Plan until the student finds a job and earns income.
- A student loan obtained from a corporation is taxable, while later repayments are deductible. If the student has no taxable income, this treatment could result in a net tax saving.

As a partial offset against direct education costs, two tax credits are currently available. The post-secondary tuition credit allows students (or their parents or grandparents, if it is of no value to the student) to claim a tax credit equal to 17 per cent of their tuition fees. It is not claimable if tuition is paid by an employer (and is excluded from a student's taxable income) or if tuition costs are reimbursed to the student's parent and are excluded from the parent's taxable income. An education credit, equal to 17 per cent of $60 for each month of full-time attendance at a post-secondary institution, is available to help pay for non-tuition expenses. Use of a credit for these expenses confers a benefit independent of income level. Unused credits up to $600 can be transferred to a spouse, parent, or grandparent who would normally claim the student as a dependant.

While the education credit provides a modest training incentive, its impact is selective. It is of no use to people enrolled in part-time studies who cannot afford to give up their job for full-time study. And it is available only for publicly provided training courses. Private training is ineligible, presumably because of difficulty in monitoring the quality and content of an employer's training program. Effective monitoring could facilitate generalization of the credit. In the conclusion of our paper, we outline a new Quebec tax credit designed to stimulate business investment in human capital.

Registered education savings plans (RESPs) are another tax device intended to stimulate investment in human capital. Contributions to RESPs are non-deductible, but the interest income accrued within the plan is non-taxable while payouts (no later than 21 years after the plan is established) are taxable in the hands of the beneficiary. Schmidt (1991) gives an example of the tax savings associated with an RESP. Assuming that a contribution of $1500 (the maximum limit, beginning in 1991) earns 10 per cent and is paid out in 21 years, a beneficiary taxed at the rate of 35 per cent would receive $48,168. If the same initial investment were made outside an RESP and interest income were taxed at 50 per cent, the balance would be only $24,758.

As seen above, taxation of the income from physical capital will indirectly encourage greater investment in human capital. Canadian taxation of savings, however, goes a long way towards removing this stimulus. To the extent that savings contributions to registered pension and savings plans are not inframarginal, the marginal effective tax rate on these savings is zero and investment in both physical and human capital receives the same expenditure tax treatment.

Wealth transfer taxes on estates and bequests might also induce taxpayers to leave a larger bequest in the form of a human capital legacy, but this stimulus is also absent in Canada. However, during periods of high inflation, deemed realization of capital gains at death introduces a substantial element of taxation on wealth, rather than on income.

Corporate Income Taxes and Worker Training

Company-sponsored training schemes receive cash flow or expenditure tax treatment under both federal and provincial law. Training expenses are immediately deductible, and any income benefits reaped by the company are taxable only upon realization.

The absence of perfect loss offsets, however, may erode the value of the training cost deduction for loss-making firms. Currently, incorporated firms under federal law may carry losses backward for three years and forward for seven. Unless an unprofitable firm is able to deduct training costs against earlier profits and receive a tax refund, the value of a dollar's worth of current training expense will be diminished if it is carried forward and may be ultimately worthless if there are no future profits to set the deduction against. Since losses are more widespread during an economic recession, the incentive for firm-provided training may be dampened at exactly the time when more training would be seen as desirable by both the firm and its employees. Additionally, since early losses occur in many new small firms, imperfect loss offsets may especially discourage their training efforts.

As indicated above, the willingness of companies to offer formal on-the-job training (OJT) depends on the division of costs and benefits between the company and trainees. If much of this training is of a general nature, the firm would be willing to provide it only if the worker were to pay for it by accepting a lower training wage or, if not, labour's turnover rate is sufficiently low that any investment by the firm in training is "protected." It is well documented, for example, that large Japanese firms, because of their commitment to long-term employment, provide more worker training than large firms in other countries.

This suggests that certain non-tax elements of the fiscal system that influence workers' attachment to the labour force and turnover rates may determine supply and demand for training more than do the relevant features of the tax system. For instance, if welfare programs discourage participation in the work-force because of their effectively high marginal tax rates, they also inhibit acquisition of job-related human capital. Similarly, if unemployment insurance encourages voluntary worker terminations and firm layoffs, it too erodes the incentive to provide OJT.

It is well beyond the scope of this paper to examine how various non-tax factors affect the opportunities for workers to receive OJT. Instead, we present some empirical evidence on Canada's investment in human capital – results of a recent study on returns to university education in Canada and international comparisons of investment in OJT. The evidence suggests strongly that there is currently no under-investment in formal university education, but that job-related training may be inadequate. Accordingly, tax measures to stimulate greater investment in university education do not appear to be warranted, and tax measures to encourage more worker training by firms may be desirable, although the evidence is surprisingly weak.

Investment Returns from University Education

Table 2 presents the results of one of the most recent efforts to measure the rate of return from university education for Canadian men with either three or four years of university studies. The rate of return is calculated as the discount rate that equates the present value of the earnings differential between university and high-school graduates with the present value of the costs of obtaining a university education. Data are drawn from the 1981 census.

There are two alternative ways of assessing the benefits and costs of holding a university degree. First, we can consider only the private or after-tax benefits enjoyed by the university graduate (ignoring any benefits to others), and only the private costs actually borne by the graduate (omitting any covered by others). With this approach, we can calculate the private rate of return, measuring the incentive for the individual to attend university. Second, we can consider all monetary pre-tax benefits (no matter to whom they accrue) and all costs (regard-less of who pays them). This approach yields a social rate of return, which provides a benchmark for assessing the merit of devoting more public resources to universities rather than to other types of public investment.

Ontario's social and private rates of return are mid-range for the five regions. Private rates of return have been calculated by considering as costs only forgone earnings and out-of-pocket expenses and as benefits only income differentials (between university and high-school grad-uates) net of taxes. Forgone earnings are assumed to be two-thirds (not 100 per cent) of the incomes earned by high-school graduates between the ages of 18 to 20 in order to take into account the earning opportun-ities that university students have through part-time and summer work. The social rates of return are calculated by considering as part of costs the government grants made to universities and by measuring benefits as before-tax earning differentials.

TABLE 2
Social and Private Rates of Return to University Education in Canada

Region	Years of study	Private rate of return (percentage)	Social rate of return (percentage)
Atlantic	3	14	9
	4	12	8
Quebec	3	14	10
	4	13	9
Ontario	3	11	8
	4	9	7
Prairies	3	9	7
	4	7	6
British Columbia	3	10	7
	4	8	6

Source: Vaillancourt and Henriques (1986)

With what should these rates of return be compared? For the individual, an alternative investment in long-term government bonds would yield, on a historical basis, a real after-tax return of between 1 and 3 per cent. Depending on the province, men can obtain a return varying between 7 and 14 per cent after taxes by investing the same sum in a university education. Not surprising, university enrolments continued to climb in the 1980s, particularly in the Atlantic region and Quebec, where private rates of return are highest.

Canada's Treasury Board uses a 10 per cent real rate of return as the criterion for determining the desirability of public-sector investment projects. In other words, the board assumes that the funds are drawn from a variety of alternative uses, including private-sector investment, whose real opportunity costs to the economy amount to 10 per cent.[12] If we use a social opportunity cost of 10 per cent as a standard for comparison, we find university education at best marginally attractive. According to Table 2, the social rate of return across the country varies between 6 and 10 per cent. Even a lower benchmark rate of 7.5 per cent, as favoured by Burgess (1981), would leave Quebec and the Atlantic region as the only parts of Canada where there was clear economic justification for more investment in higher education.

Generally, social returns are less than private returns because the higher social costs (government grants to universities) outweigh the higher social benefits (the difference in the present value of taxes paid between university and high-school graduates). In all provinces, tuition fees pay for only about 15 to 20 per cent of university operating costs. Therefore, social costs include most of the remaining operating costs, which are covered by government grants. The size of this subsidy casts doubt on the view that too little has been invested in universities.

This conclusion contrasts with much earlier efforts to measure social and private rates of return on investment in higher education. For Ontario males in 1961, for example, Stager (1972) calculated the private rate of return as 15.4 per cent and the estimated social rate of return as 12.5 per cent. Declining payoff to investment in higher education over the period 1961–81 is common for a number of developed countries. During the 1980s in the United States, but much less so in Canada, a trend towards wage polarization helped to restore both social and private rates of return to their earlier, and higher, levels.

How accurate are these estimated rates of return? Unfortunately, they cannot capture all of the relevant effects. Allowing for future productivity growth by university-trained workers would raise the rates of return, both private and social, by perhaps as much as one percentage point. At the same time, the social rates of return may be somewhat overstated if credentials rather than skills acquired are also valued in the labour market. A further omitted factor is the value of any external benefits enjoyed by society if, for example, university graduates contribute to successful investment in research and development. Such external benefits are notoriously difficult to assess.

A recent study by Constantatos and West (1991) for all of Canada included in the calculus the "hidden" costs of taxation ignored by earlier studies. Drawing on 1981 census data for males, they determined the sensitivity of the social rate of return to alternative assumptions concerning the "true" cost of tax finance and the fraction of education-related income differentials that could be attributed to ability factors. Under the most favourable set of assumptions (zero hidden costs of taxation and no ability differentials), the social rate of return was 9.9 per cent. Under the least favourable (tax distortions amounting to 80 per cent of each dollar of tax revenue and a 35 per cent ability factor), it plummeted to 6.2 per cent.

On-the-Job Training in Canada

There is some evidence, albeit slender, that employer-based formal training yields relatively high returns and that income taxes influence workers' willingness to accept training. Unfortunately, the kind of information needed to substantiate these conclusions is "panel data" that are often either non-existent or of poor quality. In the United States,

Mincer (1989) relied on such data to obtain estimates of the rate of return to OJT that ranged between 15 and 34 per cent (with an assumed depreciation rate of 4 per cent annually) and between 8 and 26 per cent (with depreciation at 10 per cent).

As we saw above, Rosen (1982) had discovered from panel data that payments of income taxes induced workers' participation in OJT. He attributed this result to income taxes' encouragement of substitution of human for physical capital. Davies and St-Hilaire (1987) are sceptical about the strength of this substitution effect in Canada. If it exists, they argue, it would be relevant for prime-age workers between 25 and 40 who may face high marginal tax rates, but the effect would be relatively weak, given tax shelters (RRSPs), light taxation of capital gains, and the fairly low effective tax rate on corporate income.

Canada undertakes less OJT than other industrialized countries (see Tables 3 and 4). Japan provides formal OJT for over one-third of its labour force. In Canada, only 6.7 per cent of all workers receive OJT, nearly less than half the number in the United States. As a fraction of the total wage bill, Canadian expenditures on OJT may be less than half of those in the United States.

Why is Canada at the bottom of the international heap? The most plausible explanation is that either the costs of training are higher or the returns from training are lower in Canada than elsewhere. Since the technology of training is not country specific, however, it is not obvious that international cost differences are significant factor. More probably, the returns are lower than elsewhere. But why?

Four factors, or some combination of them, occur to us as possible sources of relatively low returns to training in Canada. First, real minimum wages are higher in Canada than in most U.S. jurisdictions, and they may inhibit employers' willingness to offer general training, although several Canadian provinces allow a somewhat lower training wage. Second, as the Economic Council of Canada (1992) has emphasized, the amount of training provided is closely related to the size of the firm. The council found that only 13.1 per cent of small firms had a training budget, compared to 58.6 per cent of large ones. The latter offer more opportunities for internal advancement and promotion "from within." Their turnover rates may therefore be lower, and their return from OJT correspondingly higher. Canadian firms may be on average smaller.

Labour turnover may be generally more rapid in Canada and act as a strong disincentive to offer training. Canada's relatively generous unemployment insurance system could make it less costly for employ-

TABLE 3
Enterprise-Related Training in Several OECD Countries, 1990

Country (with rank in brackets)	% of workers receiving training
Japan (1)	36.7 (within last two years)
Australia (2)	34.9 (in-house)
Sweden (3)	25.4 (all workers)
Great Britain (4)	14.4 (all workers)
West Germany (5)	12.7 (all workers)
	76.0 (15–19 year olds)
United States (6)	11.8 (all workers, formal training)
Canada (1985) (7)	6.7 (all workers, formal training)
France (8)	4.6 (all workers)
	43.0 (15–19 year olds)
	26.6 (employees in firms 10+ years)

Source: Lynch (1992)
Note: Except for Canada, the data are derived from OCED, *Employment Outlook*, July 1991. Canadian data were obtained from Statistics Canada, 1985 Adult Training Survey, 1986.

ers to lay off workers and employees to quit as well as preserving more jobs in seasonal activities with low training requirements.[13]

Finally, Canada's formal education system may, on average, be of higher quality than that in other countries. If so, and if OJT and formal education are close substitutes for each other, Canada may do a relatively better job in the latter and may require less effort than other countries on the former. The Economic Council (1992), however, questions the quality of Canada's primary and secondary education, pointing out, for example, that the drop-out rate for high-school students has been rising and is currently estimated to be 30 per cent.

All these factors involve non-tax rationales for Canada's relatively weak performance in worker training. If these factors lie at the heart of the problem, it is not clear that the tax system should be adjusted in order to try and correct the problem. It is likely to be more efficient to tackle economic problems directly rather than indirectly, through related markets. For example, if certain features of unemployment insurance inhibit OJT, it is preferable to modify the insurance system directly rather than tinker with the tax system to combat its unwanted effects. It is with this admonition in mind that we explore next a range of tax policy options that might be appropriate for further research.

TABLE 4
Average Percentage of Total Wage Bill Spent on Training in Several OECD Countries

Country	% spent on training
Japan[c]	0.4
Australia (private sector)	1.7
United Kingdom	1.3 (1984)
West Germany	1.8 (1984)
United States[a]	1.8 (larger firms)
Canada[b]	0.9 (1987)
France	1.6 (1984)

Source: Lynch (1992)
[a] Information obtained from OECD, *Employment Outlook*, July 1991, and *Training Magazine*, 1988.
[b] Data are from Canadian Labour Market and Productivity Centre, 1987 Household Survey. The CLMPC found that firms spent $1.4 billion on training and concluded that "the amount spent on training is no more than half that in the United States."
[c] Training expenditures as a percentage of monthly labour costs. Because monthly labour costs exceed the wage bill in every country, this figure for Japan is biased downwards and cannot be strictly compared with the data for other OECD countries.

Conclusion: Tax Reform and Human Capital Formation

We argue above that, in principle, income taxes have an ambiguous effect on efficient levels of human capital accumulation. Progressivity and an inability to deduct fully all the expenses of acquiring human capital could result in too little investment. However, taxes on income from physical capital create incentives for excessive investment in human capital.

The empirical record for estimated rates of return on human capital and investment levels in different kinds of such capital does not support the hypothesis that taxes distort investments in human capital. There is no empirical support for the notion that there is no shortage of university graduates or that investment in higher education has apparently been inadequate in the past.[14]

Tax treatment of income earned by university graduates does not conform entirely to the theoretically ideal structure for a tax either on personal expenditure or on personal income. Ideally, all the direct expenses of producing human capital, such as tuition and books, would be immediately deductible or depreciable if they were not subsidized and did not involve personal consumption. In fact, tuition costs are heavily subsidized, so that in all Canadian provinces the social rate of return from university education is less than the individual's private rate of return. This result, and the fact that a federal tuition and education tax credit already exists, make it difficult to argue persuasively for more liberalized tax treatment of education expenses. In short, there is no obvious need for altering tax treatment of human capital acquired from post-secondary education.

The same may not be said, however, for the human capital acquired through formal on-the-job training (OJT). A growing body of evidence indicates that employer-based training is weak by international standards. Relatively low investment in worker training appears to be rooted in such non-tax factors as rigid minimum wage laws and generous unemployment insurance. If this diagnosis is correct, the best policy response would be to attack the problem directly by reforming the regulatory and expenditure policies that inhibit OJT. For example, work-sharing programs and wage subsidies paid to employers by unemployment insurance might lengthen job tenures and raise the rate of return to OJT.

If, however, political or institutional rigidities prevent appropriate adjustments in expenditures, the tax system could be altered to counteract unwanted effects from expenditures. The argument should run along the lines that the social rate of return from more OJT exceeds the employer's private rate of return, and only tax instruments can address this discrepancy. A better-trained and more adaptable work-force may be less susceptible to prolonged bouts of unemployment in the face of economic shocks and may more easily attract both foreign and domestic investors. These effects of OJT serve to raise the social return to it beyond what a private employer can capture from investment in OJT and justify some sort of subsidy to reduce the costs of private-sector training.

Although we have not carefully considered the most desirable form for such a subsidy, we feel that there is some merit in considering introduction of a training tax credit for employers. The tax credit would be equivalent to an earmarked expenditure and would reward only the behaviour that is sought by the policy. The trick, however, would be to design the credit in such a way that it would not reward training that would have been given in any event. To maximize the marginal effectiveness of the credit, it might, for example, apply only to training expenditures in excess of some minimum, or base level.

An exhaustive search of current provincial and territorial legislation reveals that only Quebec, and then only recently, has used tax credits to encourage worker training.[15] While the Quebec scheme may not be ideal, it contains several noteworthy features. Introduced in the

1990–91 provincial budget, it is comprehensive and offers a credit for the cost of preparing a human resource development plan (HRDP), the cost of buying courses from a certified training centre, and the worker's wages that are paid during the training period, provided that the training occurs during normal working hours. Tax credits for these expenditures are refundable and therefore of equal value to both profitable and unprofitable firms.

The scheme avoids subsidizing inframarginal training by making all required training programs, conferences, and seminars ineligible. The tax credits are also reasonably well targeted with respect to type of worker and firm and timing of applications. They are available only to workers whose normal work week exceeds 15 hours, and higher rates of credit prevail for smaller businesses, which are less likely to offer training than larger firms, for expenses involved in developing an HRDP and for training courses completed before 1993. To limit abuse, an HRDP can be credited only once in each three-year period and must be purchased from a recognized educational institution or registered consultant. Moreover, only $10,000 worth of HRDP expenditure is creditable.

For small and medium-sized businesses, the rate of credit is 30 per cent for HRDP expenses and 20 per cent for training and wage costs – if completed before 1993, these rates rise to 50 and 40 per cent, respectively. For large businesses, the credit rates are 20 per cent for HRDP cost and 10 per cent for training and wage costs, augmented to 30 and 20 per cent, respectively, before 1993. By almost any standard, these are generous subsidy rates that should alter training behaviour. The value of the credit is not included in taxable income but is reduced in size by the amount of any subsidy given to training. If another credit can also be obtained – for example, the one for research and development – the company can claim only one of these credits.

When it was introduced, the scheme was anticipated to cost $67 million in 1990–91 and $100 million in 1991–92. Over 100,000 workers had benefited from this program, according to the 1992–93 budget. In view of its perceived success, the program was modified in the last budget to stretch eligibility for the enriched credit rates from 1993 to 1 January 1995.

To complement the business tax credit, the 1991–92 budget also introduced an individual training assistance program that, from 1992 to 1994, will be restricted to salaried workers. Eligible employees must have resided in the province for at least one year and have participated in the labour market for at least six years. Eligible training activities are limited to short-term (less than 12 months) vocational training courses offered by certified institutions. This program offers a loan guarantee; a training allowance based on the size of the loan, the worker's family situation, and employment income received during training; and an income tax deduction for all interest payments and repayment of principal. This deduction is available only if the loan is repaid within 10 years. For this program, $16 million has been set aside for 1992–93, and $59 million for 1993–94. Beyond the initial phase (to 1994), the anticipated cost is $100 million annually.

We are not endorsing the particular features of Quebec's program. However, we do feel that it addresses an urgent labour-market problem in Canada and that several of its elements would appear desirable for any future program in Ontario or elsewhere. It is too early to judge the program's effectiveness and to develop a finer appreciation of its strengths and weaknesses.

It does seem to us, however, that Quebec's program offers more, and is more attractive, than the alternative "play or pay" training widely discussed in the United States and adopted in several countries, including Papua–New Guinea. Under such an option, companies are assessed a fraction (1–2 per cent) of their payrolls to cover the costs of additional manpower training. Firms, however, can credit the costs of any in-house or externally supplied training that they provide against this assessment. No payroll tax is due if the company "plays" the training game to the limit of its creditable assessment. In contrast to the Quebec scheme, this approach relies on use of the fiscal stick instead of the fiscal carrot. In principle, either the carrot or the stick can yield acceptable results. In practice, however, the stick may be more difficult to administer because of the difficulty in distinguishing between legitimate "in-house" training outlays and those thinly disguised to gain tax credits.

Notes

1 See, for example, the Canadian Labour Market and Productivity Centre (1989, 1990); the Economic Council of Canada (1990, 1991) and its study, *Perspective 2000*, by Newton, Schweitzer, and Voyer (1990); A. de Grandpré's (1989) report, *Adjusting to Win*; the Macdonald Commission's (1985) report; the Ontario Council of Regents (1989) report, *Vision 2000*, on community colleges; the Ontario Premier's Council reports (1988, 1990); Porter (1991) for the Business Council on National Issues; Prosper-

ity Secretariat (1992) for the government of Canada; and Strand (1991) for the British Columbia Task Force on Employment and Training.

This same conclusion is reached in four earlier reports – all reviewed in Davies (1986) – the Dodge report, the Allmand report, the Economic Council's *In Short Supply*, and the CEIC Skill Development Leave Task Force report, *Learning a Living in Canada*.

2 See, for example, the American Assembly report from 65 leaders of business, labour, academe, and government (Starr 1988); the American Association of Community Colleges and Junior Colleges (1990) report, *Productive America*; the American Society for Training and Development's (1988) report, *Gaining the Competitive Edge*; the Business Higher Education Forum's (1985) report; the Conference Board report (Lusterman 1985); *The Cuomo Commission Report* (Kaden and Smith 1988); and the Hudson Institute's report, *Workforce 2000* (Johnston and Packer 1987).

3 Examples of such studies include Davies and St-Hilaire (1987); Davies and Whalley (1991); Driffill and Rosen (1983); Eaton and Rosen (1980); Hamilton (1987); Lord (1989); and Perroni (1992).

4 See, for example, Romer (1986) and Lucas (1988).

5 Gera and Grenier (1991) provide empirical evidence for Canada and review some of the more extensive evidence for the United States.

6 Formal proofs of this proposition are given in Boskin (1975); Davies and St-Hilaire (1987); Eaton and Rosen (1980); and Heckman (1976).

7 Because interest payments on mortgage-financed housing are not deductible in Canada, debt-financed housing enjoys expenditure tax treatment in much the same manner as human capital investment. We consider the case of debt-financed human capital in the next subsection.

8 Garfinkel (1973) and Kesselman (1976) emphasize these work-incentive effects of taxes and income maintenance programs and their subsequent effects on human capital formation.

9 Trostel (1991) refers to 50 studies reviewed by Hansson and Stuart (1985), who find an average wage elasticity of labour supply of 0.10 – an uncompensated figure that reflects the net effect of the opposing income and substitution effects. However, they find that the more recent studies tend to find higher elasticities, averaging about 0.44. These may be preferred estimates, given that they are based on more recent data and more sophisticated estimating techniques. Trostel (1991) also refers to the elasticity estimates used in other tax studies as typically ranging from 0 to 0.30. In view of the higher figures found in the more recent studies, a range of 0 to 0.50 would seem reasonable, with the mid-point of 0.25 perhaps being a good "guesstimate." The empirical evidence on the elasticity of labour supply is also summarized in Killingsworth and Heck-

man (1986) for females, and in Pencavel (1986) for males. Those reviews also confirm that the wage increases generally induce a small net reduction in the labour supply of men (i.e., their labour supply schedule bends backward, as the income effect dominates the substitution effect) and a larger positive increase for women (i.e., their schedule slopes upward, as substitution dominates income).

10 Eaton and Rosen (1980) and Driffill and Rosen (1983) provide a formal analysis of the impact of taxes on human capital formation when labour supply is endogenous. They conclude that taxes would increase such formation because they assume that taxes would expand labour supply and, therefore, use of human capital. This analysis implies that labour supply bends backward, which may be true for men but not for the economy as a whole, given the stronger forward slope of labour supply for women.

11 See, for example, Boskin (1975); Driffill and Rosen (1983); Eaton and Rosen (1980); and Heckman (1976).

12 There is notable lack of consensus concerning the 10 per cent rate. Burgess (1981), and more recently Constantatos and West (1991), have suggested a range of 7 to 7.75 per cent. Burgess (1988) has also indicated that the real costs of foreign borrowing may be significantly higher than most analyses have suggested. The range of uncertainty between 7.5 and 10 per cent probably reveals our ignorance on this matter.

13 See Green and Cousineau (1976) for a detailed discussion of these points in a Canadian context.

14 However, reduced levels of current funding for post-secondary institutions in many provinces could be a source of concern for the future.

15 We wish to acknowledge the skilful research assistance of Dagny Mofid in conducting this search.

Bibliography

American Association of Community Colleges and Junior Colleges. 1990. *Productive America: Two Year Colleges Unite to Improve Productivity in the Nation's Workforce.* Washington, DC: Council of Occupational Education

American Society for Training and Development. 1988. *Gaining the Competitive Edge.* Alexandria, Va.: Society

Becker, Gary. 1975. *Human Capital.* 2nd ed. New York: Columbia University Press

Boadway, R.W., N. Bruce, and J. Mintz. 1987. *Taxes on Capital Income in Canada: Analysis and Policy.* Canadian Tax Paper No. 80, Canadian Tax Foundation, Toronto

Boskin, M.J. 1975. "Notes on the Tax Treatment of Human Capital." In *Conference on Tax Research*, 185–95. Office of Tax Analysis, Department of the Treasury, Washington, DC

Burgess, D.F. 1981. "The Social Discount Rate in Canada: Theory and Evidence." *Canadian Public Policy*, 7: 383–94

– 1988. "On the Relevance of Export Demand Conditions for Capital Income Taxation in Open Economies." *Canadian Journal of Economics*, 21: 285–311

Business Higher Education Forum. 1985. *Toward a Competitiveness Agenda*. Proceedings of Special Joint Session with Members of Congress, Washington, DC

Canadian Labour Market and Productivity Centre (CLMPC). 1989. *Focus on Adjustment*. Ottawa: Centre

– 1990. *Report of the CLMPC Task Forces on the Labour Market Development Strategy*. Ottawa: Centre

Canadian Manufacturers' Association. 1989. *The Aggressive Economy: Daring to Compete*. Toronto: Association

Constantatos, C., and E.G. West. 1991. "Measuring Returns from Education: Some Neglected Factors." *Canadian Public Policy*, 12: 127–38

Davies, James. 1986. "Training and Skill Development." In *Adapting to Change: Labour Market Adjustment in Canada*, ed. W. Craig Riddell, 163–219. Toronto: University of Toronto Press

Davies, James, and France St-Hilaire. 1987. *Reforming Capital Income Taxation in Canada: Efficiency and Distributional Effects of Alternative Options*. Ottawa: Economic Council of Canada

Davies, James, and John Whalley. 1991. "Taxes and Human Capital Formation: How Important Is Human Capital?" In *National Savings and Economic Performance*, ed. Douglas Bernheim and John Shoven, 163–97. Chicago: University of Chicago Press

de Grandpré, A. 1989. *Adjusting to Win*. Report of the Advisory Council on Adjustment. Ottawa: Supply and Services

Driffill, John, and Harvey Rosen. 1983. "Taxation and Excess Burden: A Life-cycle Perspective." *International Economic Review*, 24: 671–83

Eaton, Jonathan, and Harvey Rosen. 1980. "Taxation, Human Capital and Uncertainty." *American Economic Review*, 70: 705–15

Economic Council of Canada. 1990. *Good Jobs, Bad Jobs: Employment in the Service Economy*. Ottawa: Supply and Services

– 1991. *Employment in the Service Economy*. Ottawa: Supply and Services

– 1992 *A Lot to Learn: Education and Training in Canada*. Ottawa: Supply and Services

Employment and Immigration Canada. 1989. *Success in the Works: A Labour Force Development Strategy*. Hull: CEIC

Freeman, Richard. 1977. "Investment in Human Capital and Knowledge." In *Capital for Productivity and Jobs*, 129–38. Englewood Cliffs, NJ: Prentice-Hall

Garfinkel, I. 1973. "A Skeptical Note on the Optimality of Wage Subsidy Programs." *American Economic Review*, 63: 447–53

Gera, S., and G. Grenier. 1991. "Interindustry Wage Differentials and Efficiency Wages: Some Canadian Evidence." In *Canadian Unemployment*, ed. S. Gera. Ottawa: Economic Council of Canada

Green, C., and J.M. Cousineau. 1976. *Unemployment in Canada: The Impact of Unemployment Insurance*. Ottawa: Economic Council of Canada

Hamilton, J. 1987. "Optimal Wage and Income Taxation with Wage Uncertainty." *International Economic Review*, 28: 373–88

Hansen, W. Lee. 1963. "Total and Private Rates of Return to Investment in Schooling." *Journal of Political Economy*, 71: 128–40

Hansson, Ingemar, and Charles Stuart. 1985. "Tax Revenue and the Marginal Cost of Public Funds in Sweden." *Journal of Public Economics*, 27: 331–53

Heckman, James, 1976. "A Life-Cycle Model of Earnings, Learning, and Consumption." *Journal of Political Economy*, 84: S11–S44

Johnston, W., and A. Packer. 1987. *Workforce 2000: Work and Workers for the Twenty-first Century*. Indianapolis, Ind.: Hudson Institute

Jorgenson, Dale, and A. Pachon. 1983. "The Accumulation of Human/Nonhuman Capital." In *The Determinants of National Savings and Wealth*, ed. F. Modigliani and R. Hemmings. New York: St Martins Press

Kaden, L., and L. Smith. 1988. *The Cuomo Commission Report: A New American Formula for a Strong Economy*. New York: Simon and Schuster

Kendrick, John. 1976. *The Formation and Stocks of Total Capital*. New York: Columbia University Press

Kesselman, Jonathan. 1976. "Tax Effects on Job Search, Training and Work Effort." *Journal of Public Economics*, 6: 255–72

Killingsworth, Mark, and James Heckman. 1986. "Female Labor Supply: A Survey." In *Handbook of Labor Economics*, ed. Orley Ashenfelter and Richard Layard, 103–204. New York: North Holland

Kotlikoff, Laurence, and Lawrence Summers. 1979. "Tax Incidence in a Life-Cycle Model with Variable Labor Supply." *Quarterly Journal of Economics*, 93: 705–18

Kroch, E., and K. Sjoblom. 1986. "Education and the National Wealth of the United States." *Review of Income and Wealth*, March: 87–106

Long, Richard. 1989. "Patterns of Workplace Innovation in Canada." *Relations industrielles/Industrial Relations*, 44: 805–26

Lord, William. 1989. "The Transition from Payroll to Consumption Receipts with Endogenous Human Capital." *Journal of Public Economics*, 38: 53–73

Lucas, Robert E., Jr. 1988. "On the Mechanics of Economic Development." *Journal of Monetary Economics*, 22: 3–42

Lusterman, S. 1985. "Trends in Corporate Education and Training." Conference Board Report. New York: Conference Board

Lynch, Lisa M. 1992. "International Comparisons of Private Sector Training." Paper prepared for the Canadian Employment Research Forum, Ottawa, March

Macdonald Commission. 1985. *Report of the Royal Commission on the Economic Union and Development Prospects for Canada*, Vol. 2. Ottawa: Supply and Services

Mincer, J. 1989. "Job Training: Costs, Returns and Wage Profiles." National Bureau of Economic Research, Paper No. 3208, Cambridge, Mass.

Newton, K., T. Schweitzer, and J.P. Voyer, eds. 1990. *Perspective 2000.* Ottawa: Economic Council of Canada

Ontario Council of Regents. 1989. *Vision 2000: A Review of the Mandate of Ontario's System of Applied Arts and Technology.* Toronto: Council

Ontario Premier's Council. 1988. *Competing in the New Global Economy.* Toronto: Queen's Printer

– 1990. *People and Skills in the New Global Economy.* Toronto: Queen's Printer

Pencavel, John. 1986. "Labor Supply of Men: A Survey." In *Handbook of Labor Economics*, ed. Orley Ashenfelter and Richard Layard, 3–102. New York: North Holland

Perroni, Carlo. 1992. "Assessing the Dynamic Efficiency Gains from Tax Reform When Human Capital Is Endogenous." Mimeo. University of Western Ontario, Department of Economics

Porter, Michael. 1991. *Canada at the Crossroads: The Reality of a New Competitive Environment.* Ottawa: Business Council on National Issues

Prosperity Secretariat. 1992. *Canada's Prosperity: Challenges and Prospects.* Ottawa: Government of Canada

Reich, Robert. 1991. *The Work of Nations: Preparing Ourselves for Twenty-first Century Capitalism.* New York: Knopf

Romer, Paul. 1986. "Increasing Returns and Long-Run Growth." *Journal of Political Economy*, 94: 1002–37

Rosen, Harvey. 1982. "Taxation and On-the-Job Training Decisions." *Review of Economics and Statistics*, 64: 442–49

Schultz, T.W. 1960. "Capital Formation by Education." *Journal of Political Economy*, 68: 571–83

Schmidt, R. 1991. "Students and Taxation." *Canadian Tax Journal*, 39: 673–89

Stager, D. 1972. "Allocation of Resources in Canadian Education." In *Canadian Higher Education in the Seventies*, ed. S. Ostry, 199–238. Ottawa: Information Canada

Starr, Martin, ed. 1988. *Global Competitiveness: Getting the U.S. Back on Track.*
New York: W.W. Norton
Strand, Kenneth. 1991. *Learning and Work.* Report of the British Columbia
Task Force on Employment and Training. Victoria, BC
Trostel, Philip. 1991. "The Effect of Taxation on Human Capital." Mimeo.
North Carolina State University, Department of Economics
Vaillancourt, F., and D. Henriques. 1986. "The Return to University School-
ing in Canada." *Canadian Public Policy*, 12(3): 449–58

3 The Economic Effects of an Environment Tax

ARTHUR DONNER and FRED LAZAR

Introduction

International and Domestic Focus on Greenhouse Gases

In June 1988, the government of Canada sponsored a conference in Toronto to address "The Changing Atmosphere and Implications for Global Security." The gathering was attended by more than 300 scientists and policy makers from 46 countries, UN organizations, and non-governmental organizations (NGUs). The delegates called on governments to ratify the Montreal Protocol (1987)[1] and to set energy policies to reduce carbon dioxide emissions to levels approximately 20 per cent below 1988 levels by the year 2005. Several countries and the European Community have adopted the recommended emission targets for carbon dioxide (see Table 1). However, the targets in the Toronto Protocol are not legally binding, and, with a few exceptions (Finland, the Netherlands, and Sweden), these nations have not yet set out, let alone implemented, concrete policy initiatives to achieve the targets.[2]

As can be seen in Table 1, Ottawa has committed itself to stabilizing the emission of carbon dioxide and other greenhouse gases at 1990 levels by 2000. It announced this commitment in its Green Plan of December 1990. But, thus far, it has done little more than set out policy alternatives. For example, the National Action Strategy on Global Warming, developed by the federal, provincial, and territorial governments and released in November 1990, proposed that governments in Canada begin studying potential longer-term measures to reduce emis-

TABLE 1
Commitments by OECD Countries to Reduce Emissions of Greenhouse Gases[a]

Country	Gases included	Action	Base year	Target year[a]
United States	All GHGs	Stabilization[b]	1990	2000
Japan	CO_2	Stabilization	1990	2000
Germany	CO_2	25% reduction	1987	2005
France	CO_2	Stabilization	1990	2000
Italy	CO_2	20% reduction	1988	2005
United Kingdom	CO_2	Stabilization	1990	2005
United Kingdom	All GHGs	20% reduction	1990	2005
Canada	CO_2, N_2O, CH_4	Stablization	1990	2000
Australia	CO_2	20% reduction	1988	2005
Australia	CO_2, N_2O, CH_4	Stabilization	1988	2000
Austria	CO_2	20% reduction	1988	2000
Belgium	CO_2	Stabilization	1990	2000
Denmark	CO_2	20% reduction	1988	2005
Finland	CO_2	Stabilization	1990	2000
Greece	CO_2	Stabilization	1990	2000
Ireland	CO_2	Stabilization	1990	2000
Netherlands	CO_2	Stabilization	1989–90	1995
New Zealand	CO_2	20% reduction	1988	2005
Norway	CO_2	Stabilization	1989	2000
Portugal	CO_2	Stabilization	1990	2000
Spain	CO_2	Stabilization	1990	2000
Sweden	CO_2	Stabilization	1990	2000
Switzerland	CO_2	Stabilization	1990	2000

Source: Hoeller and Wallin (1991)
[a] All countries have agreed to phase out most CFCs by the year 2000.
[b] No target for CO_2, N_2O, CH_4. Stabilization of GHCs is achieved primarily by reducing CFC emissions.

sions. Among the measures suggested were economic instruments, such as taxes and emission-trading programs, and "measures to make markets work more efficiently, such as regulatory/institutional changes affecting electric and gas utilities, and lifestyle changes, such as increased use of urban transit" (Environment Canada 1992, 36).

Ottawa is not alone in its concern about continued accumulation of greenhouse gases in the atmosphere. In March 1990, the Liberal government at Queen's Park (Ontario 1990) released *Global Warming: Towards a Strategy for Ontario*, which proposed that the province stabilize emissions of greenhouse gases, particularly carbon dioxide, at 1989 levels by the year 2000. The NDP has, as party policy, a planning target of a 20 per cent reduction in carbon dioxide emissions from 1988 levels by 2005 (Homung 1990, 34). Neither the Liberal nor the successor NDP government developed or introduced specific policies. Nevertheless, the Toronto Protocol of 1988, the March 1990 document, and NDP policy provide the rationale for studying the economic feasibility of Ontario's using some form of taxation to reduce carbon dioxide emission.[3]

Taxation as a Policy Instrument for Reducing Carbon Dioxide Emissions

The range of policy instruments available to government aimed at stabilizing greenhouse gas emission fall into three broad categories: command and control, market-based incentives, and information dissemination (Australia, Industry Commission, 1991, 45). Command and control involve regulatory or direct control of emissions – namely, specifying allowable levels and/or setting energy efficiency standards for machinery, equipment, appliances, automobiles, and the like. Market-based incentives include policies that affect production costs or output prices (as through taxation of emissions), outputs or inputs associated with emissions, subsidization of emission reductions, and "allocation of emission permits which would be tradeable among current and potential greenhouse gas emitters" (Australia, Industry Commission, 1991, 45).

The Australian body set out several criteria for assessing possible policy instruments: efficiency, dependability, information requirements, ease of monitoring and enforcement, flexibility, equity, and continuing incentive (1991, 47). More recently, the government of Canada set out a complementary list of criteria that included effectiveness in achieving environmental objectives; impact on international competitiveness; distributional effects; transition and adjustment costs; administrative, monitoring, and compliance costs; jurisdictional issues; and acceptability to industry and the public (Environment Canada 1992, 3).

Regardless of the standards that might be used, it appears that Ottawa favours market-based incentives. In its discussion paper (Environment Canada, 1992), Ottawa argued that market-based or economic incentives have many advantages over regulation. Economic instruments are more cost-effective in achieving an environmental objective. They provide a continuous and dynamic incentive for firms to search for and adopt new technologies to control pollution and accommodate entry into an industry and any resultant growth without adding to emission levels (3, 17). A carbon tax – an input tax on the carbon content of fossil fuels – would rank high on a list of economic instruments to stabilize carbon dioxide.

In general, an input tax does not create the incentive to develop and invest in "end-of-pipe" emission reduction technologies. Reducing the quantity of harmful outputs would not reduce input tax liabilities unless fewer of the taxed inputs were used to achieve these results. In the case of carbon dioxide emissions, the potential incentive from an output tax is rather limited, since there are no cost-efficient technologies available commercially. Moreover, because the ratio between carbon dioxide emissions from the combustion of fossil fuels and the carbon content of these fuels is roughly the same for all fossil fuels examined in this study (about 3.6 tonnes of carbon dioxide per tonne of carbon content), an output tax would not provide additional incentives for individuals and firms to substitute the fuels that generate less carbon dioxide. Therefore an input tax based on the carbon content of fossil fuels should be as effective as an output tax on carbon dioxide emissions in encouraging substitution from solid to liquid and then to gaseous fuels (see Tables 2 and 3).

Over time, the two might not be equally effective, since an output tax would provide a greater incentive to search for and commercialize cost-efficient technologies to reduce carbon dioxide emissions produced by the combustion of fossil fuels. But here we follow common practice among students of this subject and concentrate on an input tax. As well, a carbon or other form of input tax should have some administrative advantages over an output tax. Fewer firms and individuals would be subject to an input tax, which could be collected "upstream" from the producers, importers, or distributors of the fossil fuels, rather than from the "downstream" consumers. In addition, there would be no need to monitor emissions in order to calculate the tax payable.[4]

Furthermore, there are precedents for a carbon tax. All OECD countries tax oil products, and many tax natural gas. Hoeller and Wallin (1991) have estimated the existing implicit carbon taxes in the OECD (see Table 4). In 1988, the implicit carbon tax on oil products ranged from U.S.$65 per ton in the United States to U.S.$351 per ton in France. In Canada, the implicit tax of U.S.$108 per ton is relatively low, exceeding only the U.S. tax.

Finland, the Netherlands, and Sweden have recently implemented explicit carbon taxes. Finland introduced a carbon tax of approximately U.S.$1.50 per ton at the beginning of 1990 as part of tax reform (OECD 1991, 73). A tax of about U.S.$6.50 per ton was introduced in the Neth-

TABLE 2
Carbon Dioxide Emissions from Fossil Fuels (Various Units)

Fuels	T/TJ[a]	Relative to natural gas[b]	T/NU[c]	NU
Solid: Coal				
Canadian bituminous	91.6	184.4	2.52	
U.S. bituminous	83.8	168.6	2.48	tonnes
Lignite	93.8	188.8	1.49	
Gaseous				
Natural gas	49.7	100.0	1.88	megalitres
Liquid				
Motor gasoline	68.0	136.8	2.36	
Kerosene	67.6	136.2	2.55	
Aviation gasoline	69.4	139.6	2.33	
Aviation turbo	70.8	142.6	2.55	
Diesel oil	70.7	142.3	2.73	kilolitres
Light fuel oil	73.1	147.2	2.83	
Heavy fuel oil	74.0	148.9	3.09	
Petroleum coke	100.1	201.5	2.89	
Propane	60.3	121.4	1.54	

Source: Jacques (1992)

[a] T/TJ: tonnes of carbon dioxide per terajoule of energy.

[b] Natural gas index = 100.0.

[c] T/NU: tonnes of carbon dioxide per natural unit of fuel.

erlands in February 1990 and was intended to raise revenues (around U.S.\$80 million annually) earmarked for environmental protection (OECD 1991, 73). The government "has also announced its support for an international CO_2 tax, and, in cooperation with the other signatories to the Hague Declaration of 1989, an international climate fund which would be used to finance research into climate change, forest management projects, technology transfers to developing countries and the management of internationally important ecosystems" (OECD 1991, 73).

In January 1991, Sweden enacted a carbon tax of approximately U.S.\$50 per ton as part of a tax reform package that also included reducing existing energy taxes on fossil fuels by 50 per cent. Bergman (1991) has noted that the sum of the ordinary energy tax and the carbon tax cannot exceed 1.7 per cent of the total value of output for firms in Sweden. Consequently, "neither the energy-intensive industries nor future power production based on fossil fuels have to pay the carbon tax. In other words, the carbon tax is essentially a tax on gasoline and fossil fuels for residential and commercial heating purposes" (107).

TABLE 3
Carbon Content of Fossil Fuels (Various Units)

Fuels	T/TJ[a]	Relative to natural gas[b]	T/NU[c]	NU
Solid: Coal				
Canadian bituminous	22.7	167.4[c]	0.69	
U.S. bituminous	23.4	172.9	0.68	tonnes
Lignite	27.1	200.0	0.41	
Gaseous				
Natural gas	13.6	100.0	0.51	megalitres
Liquid				
Motor gasoline	18.5	136.7	0.64	
Kerosene	18.4	136.0	0.70	
Aviation gasoline	18.9	139.5	0.63	
Aviation turbo	19.3	142.6	0.69	
Diesel oil	19.3	142.1	0.75	kilolitres
Light fuel oil	19.9	147.0	0.77	
Heavy fuel oil	20.2	148.8	0.84	
Petroleum coke	18.6	136.9	0.79	
Propane	16.3	120.3	0.42	

Source: Jacques (1992)
[a] T/TJ: tonnes of carbon per terajoule of energy.
[b] Natural gas index = 100.0.
[c] T/NU: tonnes of carbon per natural unit of fuel.

The OECD (1991, 68) and the government of Canada (Environment Canada 1992, 18) have suggested that if a carbon tax lowers carbon dioxide emissions by encouraging energy conservation and fuel substitutions, emissions of other greenhouse gases would also decline. A carbon tax should decrease use of energy in general and substitute "cleaner" fuels, such as natural gas, for "dirty" fuels, such as coal. Bye, Bye, and Lorentsen (1989) show that a carbon tax designed to decrease Norway's emissions of carbon dioxide by 20 per cent would lead indirectly to reductions of 21 and 14 per cent for sulphur dioxide and nitrogen oxides, respectively.

Feasibility of an Input/Environment Tax for Ontario

Despite the precedents, it is important to ask whether a carbon or other type of input tax is a feasible option for a sub-national jurisdiction such as Ontario. (Unless we are discussing a specific variant of the tax, we use the term "environment tax" to refer to an input tax for which a

TABLE 4
Implicit Carbon Taxes (U.S. $ per Ton of Carbon), OECD Countries, 1988

Country	Oil	Gas	Coal[a]	Total[b]
United States	65	0	0	28
Japan	130	2	−2	79
Germany	212	23	−28	95
France	351	38	0	229
Italy	317	80	0	223
United Kingdom	297	0	−10	106
Canada	108	0	0	52
Austria	287	39	0	150
Belgium	162	35	−24	86
Denmark	297	110	0	147
Finland	189	0	0	107
Ireland	227	4	0	138
Netherlands	221	27	0	89
New Zealand	235	0	0	117
Norway	258	0	0	182
Portugal	205	131	0	150
Spain	176	19	−25	112
Sweden	268	13	6	214
Switzerland	224	2	18	198

Source: Hoeller and Wallin (1991)
[a] A negative value denotes a subsidy.
[b] We ignore subsidies in calculating the average implicit carbon tax.

reduction in carbon dioxide emissions could be one objective.) The answer depends, in part, on the objective for the tax; on whether Ontario unilaterally introduces the tax or acts in concert with other jurisdictions, both within and outside Canada; and on whether Ontario has the constitutional powers to impose such a levy.

Regardless of whether the tax is introduced for revenue or environmental purposes, there are two potentially negative effects that will have to be considered by policy makers. Many empirical studies have shown that energy and capital are complementary factors of production. Jorgenson and Wilcoxen (1991, 5) have pointed out that carbon taxes are likely to reduce the rate of return on capital and the rate of capital accumulation. This, in turn, can lower competitiveness and slow productivity growth.

Furthermore, international competitiveness and industrial and regional effects influence the design and implementation of a carbon tax (Environment Canada 1992, 9). An environment tax would fall most heavily on a few sectors of the economy, and if Ontario were to introduce the tax unilaterally, without exemptions or offsets, the competitive position of Ontario-based firms in these sectors could deteriorate. The adjustment costs could be highly concentrated and thus greater in duration than under more even distribution of the effects and subsequent adjustments across sectors and regions. This particular concern – the industrial effects of a carbon or energy tax in Ontario – provides the principal motivation for this study.

Most countries that have adopted the targets in the Toronto guidelines for carbon dioxide emissions have been reluctant to adopt a carbon tax unilaterally because of concerns about international competitiveness. Many have expressed an interest in participating in a global effort to reduce such emissions and would be willing to accept a "global" carbon tax as part of the package, as long as the competitive effects were neutral. Sweden ensured that its carbon tax would not hurt its industries. Therefore, the Ontario government (Queen's Park) should weigh costs in competitiveness against the revenue or environmental benefits of a tax, especially if Ontario is one of very few jurisdictions that intends to proceed with this type of tax.

As well, environmental benefits might be minimal. Carbon dioxide emissions in Ontario would decline, but imports of energy-intensive products would increase because of rising prices in domestic industries. Since "production of imported goods will presumably cause more emission than domestic production because the foreign competition will not have to pay the tax, the environmental consequence of the unilateral tax may therefore be quite small" (OECD 1991, 83). Revenues also might fall if Ontario-based firms relocate and/or replace domestic with external suppliers.

The effects might become critical if Ontario relies only on an environment tax to stabilize carbon dioxide emissions. The province's Ministry of Energy has estimated that such emissions will increase by 21 per cent between 1988 and 2005 without any fundamental change in current policies (see Ontario Global Warming Coalition 1991, 6, 7). To offset this expected growth, the tax might have to be quite large and substantially increase prices of fossil fuels for Ontario users.

Finally, the constitution might constrain Queen's Park. Gibbons and Valiante (1991, 22–24) observe:

An Ontario tax on consumption of carbon-based products would be constitutionally valid provided that it could be classified as a 'direct' tax, as a tax of any kind on the production of electricity or as a charge that is part of a valid regulatory program ... Provincial taxes on fuel consumption payable by the final consumer of the fuel have been upheld, but if the same fuel is used as a feedstock in manufacturing a product, the tax would be indirect and not within the provincial authority ... Provincial charges whose primary purpose is not revenue generation can be constitutional even if indirect if they are intended to operate for a valid provincial regulatory purpose. Valid provincial purposes must be those within the ambit of provincial powers under the Constitution ... The characterization of a regulatory scheme must relate to an area of provincial responsibility ... and not simply relate to 'the environment' ... Even if the purpose of a regulatory scheme is to protect an important provincial interest, provincial controls that have a detrimental effect on extraprovincial interests may be vulnerable. Overall, a carbon tax imposed by Ontario on the final sale of fossil fuels would likely be constitutionally valid as 'direct taxation' and may also be justified as a regulatory fee within the context of a valid environmental regulatory program.

Outline of Paper

This study has two key objectives: to assess the potential effects of an environment tax on the competitive position of Ontario-based manufacturing and resource industries and to suggest initiatives that Queen's Park could consider if it wants to stabilize carbon dioxide emissions while keeping domestic industries competitive. The next section sets out the data used to estimate tax rates, the sectoral effects of the taxes, the effects of the taxes on energy prices, and the potential effects on energy use and carbon dioxide emissions. Among the data we describe are carbon intensities of fossil fuels, energy use by sector, and carbon content and carbon dioxide emissions by sector. For most of our analysis, 1989 serves as the base year; economic activity in Ontario peaked then, and we wish to separate the influence of the recession on the use of energy from the resulting carbon dioxide emissions.

In "Environment Taxes and Their Incidence," we estimate carbon tax rates, energy tax rates, and ad valorem rates for energy inputs that would generate $1 billion (an arbitrary figure) in provincial revenue. It becomes a simple and straightforward exercise to scale tax rates up or down to yield any multiple of this figure. The incidence of this tax on the four major sectors – residential, commercial, industrial, and transportation – and on major subsectors within the last two is estimated and discussed.

Next, we estimate the potential short-term (one year) and long-term

(15 years) effects of the various taxes on energy use and carbon dioxide emissions by sector, and in aggregate, using energy demand elasticities for Ontario. These results are presented in the section "Tax Effects."

"Effects of an Environment Tax" considers how various taxes will affect cost structures of major manufacturing and resource industries. The analysis does not allow for inter-fuel substitutions, energy conservation, or replacement of Ontario suppliers with suppliers elsewhere.

"Survey" presents the results of our examination of manufacturing and resource companies. We asked firms to predict the possible effects of a carbon tax on their costs, prices, financial performance, competitiveness, and investment decisions. We asked them also to suggest how the tax should be structured and how the revenues might be used so as to minimize harm to competitiveness.

In the conclusion, we set out an action plan that could serve as a starting point for Queen's Park in its efforts to stabilize carbon dioxide emissions, while preserving as much as possible of Ontario's cost competitiveness and its attractiveness to investors.

Background Information

Fossil Fuels: Carbon Intensity and Sectoral Use

Fossil fuels can be categorized into solid, gaseous, and liquid fuels. Coal falls into the first category, natural gas into the second, and refined petroleum products into the third. Use of these various types of fossil fuels as energy inputs results in emission of carbon dioxide (see Table 3). The factors are expressed both on a common base, that is, tonnes (T) of carbon dioxide per terajoule (TJ) of energy, and in terms of the natural units of each fuel (litres, tonnes).[5]

Use of natural gas contributes the least to emission of carbon dioxide. Coal and petroleum coke are the most harmful, at least vis-à-vis accumulation of carbon dioxide. Refined petroleum products, in the middle ground, emit between 36 and 49 per cent more carbon dioxide per terajoule of energy generated than does natural gas.

Carbon dioxide emitted into the atmosphere by the combustion of fossil fuels is not identical to the carbon content in these fuels. Carbon content could provide a base for one version of an environment tax. (see Table 4). Natural gas has the lowest carbon content (13.6 tonnes per terajoule), while petroleum coke and coal exceed 20 tonnes per terajoule. The carbon contents for refined petroleum products are 18 to 19 tonnes.

Table 5 summarizes 1989 energy use in Ontario for the residential, commercial, industrial, and transportation sectors.[6] The residential and commercial sectors relied primarily on natural gas and electricity. Natural gas provided approximately 44 per cent of the total energy requirements of industry, followed by bituminous coal, at about 22 per cent. In transportation, motor gasoline and diesel fuel were, by far, the major categories of energy used.

Coal, used in the making of coke, which is then used to make iron, is treated as an energy input for the iron and steel industry by Statistics Canada. Most of the calculations and tables presented in this paper are based on this assumption. However, a recent Revenue Canada administrative decision determined that coal serves as a feedstock for the iron and steel industry. In calculating carbon, energy, and ad valorem taxes and estimating their incidence and effects, we considered use of fossil fuels and electricity only as direct energy inputs, not as feedstocks. For example, fossil fuels used as a feedstock for the petrochemicals, plastics, and asphalt industries are not included in Table 5. While we generally follow Statistics Canada's convention for the iron and steel industry, we do report some results based on the treatment of coal as a feedstock for both the iron and steel and the cement industries.[7] We highlight the cases where we adjust the taxes to reflect such treatment of coal.

Table 6 sets out the energy expenditures by sector in 1989. The four sectors spent $20.9 billion in total on their energy requirements; spending on electricity totalled $6.9 billion; on motor gasoline, $6.5 billion; and on natural gas, $3.2 billion.

Transportation led with expenditures of $8.2 billion, or approximately 39 per cent of the total expenditures reported in Table 6. The residential sector accounted for $4.7 billion in spending on natural gas, refined petroleum products, and electricity (22 per cent of total spending on energy), while industrial users spent $4.3 billion (20 per cent).[8]

Table 7 disaggregates the total expenditures of industry and transportation by major subsector. The industrial sector includes manufacturing, agriculture, construction, mining, and forestry. In this sector, the heaviest users of energy in 1989 were iron and steel ($763 million) and pulp and paper, agriculture, and chemicals, each at over $400 million. If the iron and steel figures are adjusted to remove the use of coal as a feedstock, its expenditures drop to $450 million. A similar adjustment reduces the figure for the cement industry by about $19 million, to $70 million.

In transportation, retail pump sales of $6.5 billion for motor gasoline

TABLE 5
Fuel/Energy Use (PJ), by Sector, Ontario, 1989

Fuels/energy	Residential	Commercial	Industrial[a]	Transportation	Total
Solid					
Canadian					
bituminous			25.9		25.9
U.S. bituminous			164.5		164.5
Lignite					
Gaseous					
Natural gas	269.5	163	380.1	0.5	813.3
Liquid					
Motor gasoline		17.1	9.8	424.1	451.0
Kerosene	3.7	1.3	0.6		5.6
Aviation gasoline		1.1		0.2	1.3
Aviation turbo		5.9		51.8	57.7
Diesel oil		25.8	32.5	114.9	173.2
Light fuel oil	56.6	15.3	4.7		76.6
Heavy fuel oil	0.1	3.1	42.1	13.9	59.2
Petroleum coke			13.3		
Propane	3.9	7.5	14.7	11.1	37.2
Electricity	161.9	145.2	178.9	1.3	487.3
Total	495.7	385.3	867.2	617.8	2,366.0

Source: Statistics Canada (1990) Tables 8B and 8D
[a] Included in the totals for liquid fuels and natural gas for this sector are quantities
used to generate electricity for own use.

and other petroleum products dominate. Spending, primarily on diesel
fuel, by trucks and urban transit exceeded $830 million. Domestic
airlines spent $350 million on aviation fuels, but foreign airlines spent
in Ontario less than one-quarter of this amount. Foreign airlines could
be in a better position to avoid the effect of any Ontario environment
tax and, consequently, might gain an additional cost advantage over
domestic carriers.

Carbon Content and Carbon Dioxide Emissions by Sector

Table 8 presents data on the carbon content of the energy inputs used
by each of the four sectors.[9] Industry used inputs with approximately
15,000 kilotonnes of carbon; transportation's energy requirements contained just over 11,500 kilotonnes. By far the largest total carbon con-

TABLE 6
Expenditures ($ million) on Fuels/Energy by Sector, 1989

Fuels/energy	Residential	Commercial	Industrial	Transportation	Total
Solid					
Canadian					
bituminous			27.1		27.1
U.S. bituminous			312.7		312.7
Lignite					
Gaseous					
Natural Gas	1,401.3	672.5	1,075.6	1.3	3,150.7
Liquid					
Motor gasoline		246.8	141.4	6,138.8	6,526.8
Kerosene	38.1	13.2	5.9		57.2
Aviation gasoline		9.3		2.1	11.4
Aviation turbo		49.0		427.6	476.6
Diesel oil		325.4	410.0	1,449.7	2,185.1
Light fuel oil	463.5	125.3	38.6		627.4
Heavy fuel oil	0.4	8.4	114.1	37.6	160.5
Petroleum coke			43.6		43.6
Propane	56.0	89.7	76.6	157.7	380.0
Electricity	2,711.3	2,173.2	2,008.0	20.2	6,912.7
Total	4,670.6	3,712.8	4,253.5	8,234.9	20,871.8

Sources: Tables B1 and 5

tent was contained in the motor gasoline used in automobiles (7863 kilotonnes).

Tables 9 and 10 provide estimates of carbon dioxide emissions.[10] Direct use of fossil fuels by the four sectors contributed 117,600 kilotonnes of carbon dioxide. Electricity generation by Ontario Hydro added another 32,200 kilotonnes. As a result of the procedure used to allocate Hydro's emissions (see notes 9 and 10), we find that the four sectors in aggregate emitted, directly and indirectly, approximately 150,000 kilotonnes of carbon dioxide in 1989. Industry and transportation accounted for almost two-thirds of the total.

Aggregate carbon dioxide emissions from the industrial sector drop by 15,500 kilotonnes (35 per cent of the total reported, and 10 per cent of the total for all sectors) when we remove use of coal as a feedstock from the analysis. Iron and steel generated almost 19,000 kilotonnes (10.6 per cent of the total). If coal is classified as a feedstock, then emissions attributed to iron and steel decline sharply.[11] For policy purposes, the treatment of coal in the iron and steel industry becomes

TABLE 7
Expenditures ($ million) on Fuel/Energy Inputs, Industry and Transportation, 1989

Sectors and subsectors	Expenditures	% of totals in Table 6
Industrial		
Agriculture	422.8	2.0
Construction	143.0	0.7
Mining	311.7	1.5
Forestry	21.0	0.1
Manufacturing	3,508.9	16.8
Chemicals	412.2	2.0
Iron and steel	762.6	3.6
Smelting and refining	76.8	0.4
Cement	88.6	0.4
Pulp, paper, and sawmills	496.4	2.4
Total	4,253.5	20.4
Transportation		
Rail	178.3	0.8
Domestic airlines	345.2	1.6
Foreign airlines	84.6	0.4
Domestic marine	67.2	0.3
Foreign marine	74.4	0.4
Truck and urban transit	834.2	4.0
Retail pump sales	6,478.0	31.0
Total	8,243.9	39.4

Sources: Table 6 and see Table 5.

very important in terms both of environmental objectives and of minimizing damage to the competitiveness of Ontario-based industries.

The single largest source of carbon dioxide emissions was the use of motor gasoline in automobiles. In 1989, emissions allocated to retail pump sales totalled 30,900 kilotonnes (23.6 per cent of total emissions in Ontario). Use of taxes and the price mechanism to achieve environmental objectives would add to the existing federal and provincial taxes on motor gasoline and might rekindle cross-border shopping.

The rather meagre 4.7 cents (U.S.) per gallon tax approved by Congress does little to help Canada with the cross-border problem. But if higher and broader energy taxes are approved in the future and/or the state governments in New York and Michigan impose their own carbon or other energy tax, this dilemma would be mitigated. In addition, the decline in the value of the Canadian dollar from a peak of 89 cents (U.S.) to the current level of between 74 and 76 cents (U.S.) has lessened

TABLE 8
Total Carbon Content (Kilotonnes) of Fuels/Energy Used, by Sector, 1989

Fuels/energy	Residential	Commercial	Industrial	Transportation
Solid				
Canadian bituminous			588.07	
U.S. bituminous			3,858.06	
Lignite				
Gaseous				
Natural gas	3,655.33	2,214.02	5,156.29	6.35
Liquid				
Motor gasoline		316.16	181.16	7,862.62
Kerosene	68.60	23.73	10.55	
Aviation gasoline		19.90		4.56
Aviation turbo		114.63		1,000.16
Diesel oil		497.23	626.48	2,215.43
Light fuel oil	1,127.73	304.88	93.82	
Heavy fuel oil	2.99	62.22	850.43	280.14
Petroleum coke			246.47	
Propane	64.45	121.67	240.20	181.63
Electricity	2,834.27	2,541.61	3,133.06	23.60
Total (excluding electricity)	4,919.10	3,674.44	11,851.53	11,550.89
Total (including electricity)	7,753.37	6,216.05	14,984.59	11,574.49

Sources: Tables 4 and 5

cross-border shopping. If the Canadian dollar remains at its present level or depreciates further, and if Queen's Park and Ottawa fully coordinate their efforts to collect sales taxes on goods purchased in the United States, shopping across the border need not be a major factor in deliberations on an environment tax.

Environment Taxes and Their Incidence

Magnitude of Carbon, Energy, and Ad Valorem Taxes

In order to compare meaningfully different types of taxes to reduce energy use and stimulate inter-fuel substitutions, we selected tax rates to generate $1 billion in revenues (in 1989), prior to any behavioural changes in the four sectors.[12] The figure simplifies estimation of tax rates and tax effects for other revenue targets. Three tax bases are

TABLE 9
Total Carbon Dioxide Emissions (Kilotonnes), by Sector, 1989

Fuels/energy	Residential	Commercial	Industrial	Transportation	Total
Solid					
Canadian					
bituminous			2,372		2,372
U.S. bituminous			13,780		13,780
Lignite					
Gaseous					
Natural gas	13,388	8,109	18,885	23	40,405
Liquid					
Motor gasoline		1,159	664	28,829	30,652
Kerosene	252	87	39		378
Aviation gasoline		73		17	90
Aviation turbo		420		3,667	4,087
Diesel oil		1,823	2,297	8,123	12,243
Light fuel oil	4,135	1,118	344	5,597	11,194
Heavy fuel oil	11	228	3,118	1,027	4,384
Petroleum coke			1,328		1,328
Propane	238	450	887	671	2,246
Electricity	10,348	9,280	11,439	86	31,153
Total (excluding					
electricity)	18,023	13,467	43,715	42,358	117,563
Total (including					
electricity)	28,371	22,747	55,154	42,444	148,715

Sources: Tables 3 and 5

examined – carbon content of fossil fuels; energy content of fossil fuels and electricity; and retail prices of fuels and electricity. How these tax systems might operate is discussed briefly in the final section.

The carbon tax required to generate $1 billion in revenue works out to $24.68 per tonne of carbon content.[13] The tax rises to $27.59 per tonne, an increase of 11.8 per cent, when the aggregate carbon content of all fossil fuels used in Ontario as an energy input excludes coal used as a feedstock in the iron and steel and the cement industries.

The energy tax necessary to produce $1 billion in revenues in 1989 is $422.65 per terajoule of energy content.[14] Except in the iron and steel and the cement industries, the energy tax is not levied when fossil fuels are used as feedstocks in the production process. The energy tax, when it is corrected to exclude use of coal as a feedstock, increases by 8.4 per cent to $458.15 per terajoule.

The ad valorem tax rate is 4.79 per cent. Applying this figure to total

TABLE 10
Total Carbon Dioxide Emissions (Kilotonnes), Industry and Transportation, 1989

Sectors and subsectors	Emissions	% of totals in Table 9
Industrial		
Agriculture	2,723	1.5
Construction	874	0.5
Mining	2,385	1.3
Forestry	123	0.1
Manufacturing	49,449	27.5
Chemicals	4,340	2.4
Iron and steel	18,988	10.6
Smelting and refining	896	0.5
Cement	2,829	1.6
Pulp, paper, and sawmills	4,727	2.6
Transportation		
Rail	1,969	1.1
Domestic airlines	2,959	1.6
Foreign airlines	725	0.4
Domestic marine	838	0.5
Foreign marine	772	0.4
Truck and urban transit	4,289	2.4
Retail pump sales	30,892	23.6

Sources: Table 3 and see Table 5.

expenditures on energy by all four sectors in 1989 (Table 6) yields $1 billion in tax revenues.[15] The ad valorem rate is marginally higher (at 4.87 per cent) after adjustments for iron and steel and for cement.

In absolute dollar terms, the "unadjusted" carbon tax affects coal most heavily, with the per-terajoule tax ranging from $560 to $670 (see Table 11). For petroleum products and electricity, it falls in the range of $400 to $500 per terajoule. This tax translates into $335 per terajoule for natural gas. The energy tax is uniform across all fuel types and electricity, as expected. The ad valorem tax favours coal and, to a lesser degree, natural gas, heavy fuel oil, petroleum coke, and propane for industrial use. This tax, when expressed in dollars per terajoule, is heaviest on electricity, diesel fuel oil, motor gasoline, and propane for uses other than industrial. (Appendix A estimates the effects of these taxes on a basic unit for each of the fossil fuels and electricity.)

The ad valorem tax offers no scope for encouraging inter-fuel substitutions, where technically possible, because it produces the same relative increases in the retail prices of all fuels and electricity – 4.8 per cent (see Table 12). The other two taxes can generate substitutions. The carbon tax is more likely to reduce aggregate emissions of carbon

TABLE 11
Taxes ($/TJ) to Generate $1 Billion in Revenues, 1989

Fuels/energy	Carbon	Energy	Ad valorem
Basic rate	$ 24.68/tonne	$422.65/TJ	4.79%
Solid: Coal			
Canadian bituminous	560.39	422.65	50.10
U.S. bituminous	578.70	422.65	91.03
Lignite	669.65	422.65	29.51
Gaseous			
Natural gas			
Residential	334.77	422.65	249.09
Commercial	334.77	422.65	197.34
Industrial/transportation	334.77	422.65	135.53
Liquid: refined petroleum products			
Motor gasoline	457.57	422.65	693.35
Kerosene	455.35	422.65	491.08
Aviation gasoline	466.95	422.65	424.13
Aviation turbo	476.82	422.65	395.68
Diesel oil	475.83	422.65	604.32
Light fuel oil	492.12	422.65	392.56
Heavy fuel oil	498.08	422.65	129.71
Petroleum coke	458.34	422.65	157.44
Propane			
Residential/transportation	402.78	422.65	678.63
Commercial	402.78	422.65	576.38
Industrial	402.78	422.65	249.16
Electricity			
Residential	432.15[a]	422.65	802.33
Commercial	432.15	422.65	717.17
Industrial	432.15	422.65	537.54

[a] Derived by prorating carbon content of fossil fuels used by Ontario Hydro over electricity used by the four sectors.

dioxide, since it translates into a smaller relative increase in the price of natural gas than does the energy tax. With either a carbon tax or an energy tax, the price of natural gas increases relative to that of electricity and light fuel oil. Consequently, the residential, commercial, and industrial sectors might substitute electricity for natural gas.[16]

Some readers may find it counterintuitive that the carbon tax produces a larger relative increase in the price of natural gas than in the prices of most other fuels and electricity, especially since Table 11

TABLE 12
Relative Effects (% Increase) on Fuel/Energy Prices of Taxes to Generate $1 Billion in Revenues, 1989

Fuels/energy	Carbon	Energy	Ad valorem
Solid: Coal			
Canadian bituminous	53.6	40.4	4.8
U.S. bituminous	30.4	22.2	4.8
Lignite	108.7	68.6	4.8
Gaseous			
Natural gas			
Residential	6.4	8.1	4.8
Commercial	8.1	10.3	4.8
Industrial/transportation	11.8	14.9	4.8
Liquid			
Motor gasoline	3.2	2.9	4.8
Kerosene	4.4	4.1	4.8
Aviation gasoline	5.3	4.8	4.8
Aviation turbo	5.8	5.1	4.8
Diesel oil	3.8	3.4	4.8
Light fuel oil	6.0	5.2	4.8
Heavy fuel oil	18.4	15.6	4.8
Petroleum coke	14.0	12.9	4.8
Propane			
Residential/transportation	2.8	3.0	4.8
Commercial	3.4	3.5	4.8
Industrial	7.7	8.1	4.8
Electricity			
Residential	2.6	2.5	4.8
Commercial	2.9	2.8	4.8
Industrial	3.8	3.8	4.8

Sources: Taxes in $/TJ (Table 11) as proportion of fuel/energy prices expressed in $/TJ (Table B1)

shows, when these taxes are expressed in dollars per terajoule, that they generally tend to be lowest for natural gas. These results, however, reflect the much higher retail prices per unit for these other energy sources. The higher prices, in turn, stem from significantly larger explicit (implicit, in the case of electricity) provincial and federal taxes.[17] Consequently, the carbon or energy tax might not induce inter-fuel substitutions to reinforce either levy's conservation effects on emission of carbon dioxide.

Sectoral Effects of a Carbon Tax

We combine carbon taxes for each fuel and for electricity (Table 11) with sectoral energy use by fuel/electricity (Table 5) to produce the impact of the carbon tax by sector in Table 13.[18] Of the $1 billion in revenues that a tax of $24.68 per tonne of carbon content would generate, industry would bear the greatest burden, paying about 36 per cent ($359.6 million) of the total tax.

Given the assumptions underlying Table 13, the transportation sector would pay roughly 29 per cent ($285.7 million) of the total tax; the residential, 19 per cent ($191.4 million); and the commercial, 15 per cent ($153.4 million). The largest single source of tax revenues would be motor gasoline used in transportation ($194 million). Other major consumers would be the industrial sector, for the use of natural gas ($127.3 million) and coal ($109.7 million); the residential sector, for natural gas ($90.2 million); and the industrial sector, for electricity ($77.3 million).

Sectoral effects would change moderately if we use instead the "coal-adjusted" carbon tax to estimate tax burdens. Industry's burden would decline by almost $69.5 million, to $295.2 million. Tax burdens would rise for the other three sectors – by $22.5 million, to $213.9 million, for the residential; by $18 million, to $171.5 million, for commerce; and by $33.6 million, to $319.3 million, for transportation.

Table 14 reports the tax effects for key subsectors within industry and transportation. The numbers are derived in a fashion similar to those in Table 13. Within industry, manufacturing in aggregate would pay $331.7 million, or about one-third of the total tax. Areas that would probably be hit particularly hard are iron and steel (tax payments of $130.3 million), pulp, paper, and sawmills ($31.8 million), and chemicals ($29.8 million).

If, however, we assume that the adjusted carbon tax is used, and coal is treated as a feedstock, the tax burden for manufacturing would be $78 million lower ($253.3 million). Iron and steel stand to gain the most – a reduction in taxes of $91 million (to $39.3 million). Except for the cement industry, which would also gain, other industrial subsectors would face relatively small tax increases – for example, $3.7 million for pulp, paper, and sawmills and $2.9 million for chemicals.

Within transportation, the largest burden falls on individuals who operate gasoline-powered automobiles. The carbon tax, which amounts to 1.6 cents per litre on motor gasoline and other petroleum products, would generate almost $208 million from retail pump sales.

TABLE 13
Carbon Tax ($24.68/of Carbon Content) Burden ($ million) by Sector, 1989

Fuels/energy	Residential	Commercial	Industrial	Transportation
Solid				
Canadian bituminous			14.51	
U.S. bituminous			95.22	
Lignite				
Gaseous				
Natural gas	90.21	54.64	127.26	0.16
Liquid				
Motor gasoline		7.80	4.47	194.05
Kerosene	1.69	0.59	0.26	
Aviation gasoline		0.49		0.11
Aviation turbo		2.83		24.68
Diesel oil		12.27	15.46	54.68
Light fuel oil	27.83	7.52	2.32	
Heavy fuel oil	0.07	1.54	20.99	6.91
Petroleum coke			6.08	
Propane	1.59	3.00	5.93	4.48
Electricity	69.95	62.73	77.32	0.58
Total ($ million)	191.35	153.41	359.64	285.66

Sources: Carbon taxes per fuel/energy in $/TJ (Table 11) times fuel/energy use by sector in TJ (Table 5)

Truck operators and urban transit systems would pay about $29 million, primarily for use of diesel fuel.

Domestic airlines could be hit with nearly $20 million in tax payments, while foreign airlines apparently would have paid just under $5 million. U.S.-based carriers could have greater opportunities to avoid the tax. In an "open skies" regime, Canadian carriers, by having greater access to the American market, could attempt to avoid more of the tax, but a carbon tax might further disadvantage them vis-à-vis U.S. carriers. In trucking, domestic operators would face an additional cost disadvantage in the Ontario market against out-of-province truckers, mainly U.S.-based truck firms.

At the industrial level, companies might pursue the following strategies to minimize the tax burden: invest in energy-conservation production technologies and equipment; substitute lower-taxed for higher-taxed fuels; transfer production to plants elsewhere; close down their Ontario operations or do so gradually by not maintaining their investment in the province; or lobby government for exemptions,

TABLE 14
Carbon Tax Burden ($ million), Industry and Transportation, 1989

Sectors and subsectors	Burden	% of totals in Table 13
Industrial		
Agriculture	18.3	1.8
Construction	5.9	0.6
Mining	15.8	1.6
Forestry	0.8	0.1
Manufacturing	331.7	33.2
Chemicals	29.3	2.9
Iron and steel	130.3	13.0
Smelting and refining	6.0	0.6
Cement	16.2	1.6
Pulp, paper, and sawmills	31.8	3.2
Total	369.8	37.0
Transportation		
Rail	13.2	1.3
Domestic airlines	19.9	2.0
Foreign airlines	4.9	0.5
Domestic marine	5.6	0.6
Foreign marine	5.2	0.5
Truck and urban transit	28.8	2.9
Retail pump sales	207.9	20.8
Total	285.7	28.6

Sources: Table 13 and see Table 5.

rebates, or subsidies. The first two strategies are consistent with the environmental objective of a carbon tax, but there is no assurance that either or both would be the preferred strategies.

The sectoral effects of an energy tax and an ad valorem tax are discussed in Appendix C.

Comparative Effects

The three taxes would affect sectors differently – the differences being particularly evident between the carbon/energy taxes and the ad valorem tax. For example, as is apparent in Tables 15 and 16, an ad valorem tax would produce the same relative price increases for the four broad sectors and the industrial and transportation subsectors. The carbon and energy taxes, in contrast, would create the greatest burden for the industrial sector, raising the weighted average prices of its energy inputs by about 8.7 per cent. Within manufacturing, the iron and steel

TABLE 15
Increase (%) in Weighted Average Aggregate Energy Prices Resulting from Taxes,
by Sector, 1989

Sector	Carbon	Energy	Ad valorem
Residential	4.10	4.49	4.79
Commercial	4.13	4.39	4.79
Industrial	8.69	8.62	4.79
Transportation	3.47	3.17	4.79

Source: Calculated by taking tax costs (Tables 13, C1, C3) as proportion of total
expenditures on energy inputs (Table 6), assuming no inter-fuel substitutions. The
quantity weights are the 1989 consumption of inputs (in TJ) as a proportion of total
energy use by each sector.

and the cement industries could be especially hard hit, with weighted
average increases in the costs of energy inputs in the range of 15 to 20
per cent – well above the 4.8 per cent ad valorem tax rate.

Not all industrial subsectors would be worse off with a carbon or
energy tax (Table 16). Agriculture, construction, and forestry would
experience lower price increases with either of these taxes than they
would with an ad valorem tax. Thus there would be both inter- and
intra-sectoral differences in the effects of the various taxes.

Transportation would be least burdened by the carbon and energy
taxes. These taxes would cause energy prices to rise by about 3 to 3.5
per cent on a weighted-average basis – well below the 4.8 per cent
price increase of an ad valorem tax. The residential and commercial
sectors would face larger price increases, but both would be better off,
in total tax burden, than with an ad valorem tax (Tables 15 and 17).

The different sectoral burdens of these taxes suggest that if a provincial environment tax is inevitable, the four major sectors would not
join together in favouring one particular tax. There would be two broad
and competing coalitions. Manufacturing and mining, together with
rail, air, and marine transportation, would probably support an ad
valorem tax. The others (residential, commercial, agriculture, construction, forestry, truck and urban transit, and operators of gasoline-
powered vehicles) would probably back a carbon or energy tax. The
political dilemma would be obvious.

Should the manufacturing sector or select transportation subsectors
bear a larger tax burden? While economic analysis can provide some
assistance for selecting the appropriate trade-off, the choice becomes a
political decision. On the one hand, a carbon or energy tax might
jeopardize the financial health and possibly the survival of the iron

TABLE 16
Increases (%) in Weighted Average Energy Prices Resulting from Taxes, Industry, and Transportation, 1989

Sector	Carbon	Energy	Ad valorem
Industrial			
Agriculture	4.34	4.26	4.79
Construction	4.11	3.71	4.79
Mining	5.06	5.22	4.79
Forestry	3.96	3.53	4.79
Manufacturing	9.45	9.33	4.79
Chemicals	7.10	7.73	4.79
Iron and steel	17.09	14.07	4.79
Smelting and refining	7.86	8.96	4.79
Cement	18.29	15.28	4.79
Pulp, paper and sawmills	6.40	6.96	4.79
Transportation			
Rail	7.43	6.60	4.79
Domestic airlines	5.77	5.11	4.79
Foreign airlines	5.77	5.12	4.79
Domestic marine	8.40	7.22	4.79
Foreign marine	6.99	6.05	4.79
Truck and urban transit	3.46	3.19	4.79
Retail pump sales	3.21	2.96	4.79

Source: Calculated by taking tax costs (Tables 14, C2, C4) as proportion of total expenditures on energy inputs (Table 6), assuming no inter-fuel substitutions. The quantity weights are the 1989 consumption of inputs (in TJ) as a proportion of total energy use by each sector.

and steel industry in Ontario, as well as the cost competitiveness of the chemicals and the pulp and paper industries. On the other hand, an ad valorem tax might renew cross-border shopping, as the gap between gasoline prices in Ontario and adjacent U.S. communities widens. As well, Ontario-based truck operators might become further disadvantaged vis-à-vis their U.S.-based competitors.

Moreover, an ad valorem tax would place a modestly greater burden on residential and commercial users of energy, particularly electricity. An ad valorem tax in the range of 5 per cent, when added to the price increases implemented by Ontario Hydro, could further dampen demand for electricity provided by Hydro. When one combines environmental considerations with concerns about economic effects and competitiveness, and one also factors in the possible implications for

TABLE 17
Tax Burdens ($ million) by Sector for Adjusted and Unadjusted Taxes, 1989

Sector	Carbon	Energy	Ad valorem
Residential			
Unadjusted[a]	191.4	209.5	223.7
Adjusted[b]	213.9	227.1	227.5
Commercial			
Unadjusted	153.4	162.8	177.8
Adjusted	171.5	176.5	180.8
Industrial			
Unadjusted	359.6	366.5	203.7
Adjusted	295.2	313.3	191.0
Iron and steel			
Unadjusted	130.3	107.3	36.5
Adjusted	39.3	41.0	21.9
Transportation			
Unadjusted	285.7	261.1	394.4
Adjusted	319.3	283.1	401.0

Sources: Tables 13, 14 and C1–C4 and calculations by authors
[a] Coal treated as an energy input for the iron and steel industry and the cement industry.
[b] Coal treated as a feedstock.

future demands for Ontario Hydro services, a clear-cut option does not materialize.

The treatment of coal for the iron and steel and the cement industries also poses a problem. A comparison of the sectoral effects of the "coal-adjusted" and non-adjusted taxes (Table 17) reveals that only industry would benefit from following the administrative ruling by Revenue Canada in 1992. Its tax savings would range from $12.7 million with the ad valorem tax to $64.4 million with the carbon tax. The other sectors would see their tax burdens increase. Tax payments by the residential sector would increase by $3.8 million with an ad valorem tax and $22.5 million with a carbon tax. For the commercial sector, the added tax burden would be $3 million (ad valorem) or $18.1 million (carbon). Transportation would face increases of $6.6 million (ad valorem) or $33.6 million (carbon). But as we stated above, an environment tax would encourage both individuals and firms to reduce their tax burdens.

Effects of an Environment Tax

Effects on Energy Conservation and Inter-fuel Substitution

Adjustment Mechanisms

There are several types of adjustments that would take place in response to a tax on fossil fuels and electricity. The tax, whatever its form, would increase the prices of fossil fuels and electricity relative to the prices of all other factors of production. This should encourage firms to conserve energy by installing more energy-efficient equipment and by changing production processes to substitute relatively cheaper factors of production (labour, capital, and materials) for energy. In essence, companies would try to become more energy efficient. Higher energy prices should result in some improvements in energy efficiency which, in turn, should reduce the quantity of carbon dioxide emitted into the atmosphere from direct use of fossil fuels (as an energy input) or indirect use, through electricity (as the energy input).

But these types of adjustments take time, and the scope for substitutions among factors of production might be limited. As Lashof and Tirpak (1990, 41) have pointed out, it takes many years for a cost-effective technology to achieve a large market share, since existing capital stock needs to be replaced.[19] Rapid economic growth, by fostering higher levels of investment, could accelerate replacement of old plants and equipment with more energy-efficient technologies (EPA 1990, VI-5). The adjustment process could also be accelerated by government policies (other than an environment tax) that encourage more rapid replacement of existing buildings and equipment (EPA 1990, VII-10).

A carbon or energy tax would affect differently the prices of the various energy inputs (Table 18). Enterprises directly subject to the tax would attempt to minimize the tax burden by substituting, where possible and feasible – that is, consistent with profit maximization – the least-affected (in terms of relative price impact) energy input(s) for the most-affected energy input(s). For example, focusing on Table 18, we would expect that the industrial sector would switch from coal and natural gas to oil products and electricity. The residential and commercial sectors would also be induced to switch to electricity in the case of either tax. An ad valorem tax, in contrast, would not lead to any inter-fuel substitution.

In the short run, substitution possibilities might be limited. Existing

TABLE 18
Increases (%) in Weighted Average Energy Input Prices Resulting from Taxes, by
Sector, 1989

Sector and fuel	Carbon	Energy	Ad valorem
Residential			
Electricity	2.58	2.52	4.79
Natural gas	6.30	7.93	4.79
Oil products	5.90	5.09	4.79
Commercial			
Electricity	2.89	2.82	4.79
Natural gas	7.56	9.46	4.79
Oil products	4.25	3.78	4.79
Industrial			
Electricity	3.85	3.77	4.79
Natural gas	11.56	14.48	4.79
Oil products	6.58	5.77	4.79
Coal	32.30	23.60	4.79
Transportation			
Oil products	3.48	3.17	4.79

Source: See Tables 15.

facilities (plants, office buildings, single or multiple-unit dwellings) may be built around use of a single energy input. Inter-fuel substitution thus would occur gradually as new facilities and production technologies come "onstream" and existing facilities are refurbished, renovated, or replaced. The long-run scope for substitution might be limited as well.

Even if a carbon or energy tax were to result in some short- and long-term substitution, the substitutions might not necessarily reduce carbon dioxide emissions. A move away from coal would decrease emissions. But the relative price changes produced by these taxes might lead to a switch from natural gas towards oil or electricity – and higher emissions (see Table 3). Any carbon, energy, or ad valorem tax should induce a reduction in energy consumption, but, in the case of the first two taxes, the resulting substitutions and efficiency might do little to lower carbon dioxide emissions.

Even substitution from coal or oil to natural gas might not much affect emissions of carbon dioxide. Lashof and Tirpak (1990, 34) have argued that the advantage of natural gas could be significantly reduced if substantial amounts of methane (another greenhouse gas) reach the atmosphere through leaky transmission. (See as well IEA 1989, 62.)

To lessen further the effects of a tax on costs and competitiveness, companies could switch to suppliers not subject to a tax – those outside Ontario. They could also replace Ontario-based suppliers who attempt to pass on part of the tax with suppliers who absorb the tax. Also, companies with production operations in more than one jurisdiction might transfer production to a subsidiary or facility elsewhere.

Despite these many possible avenues for adjusting to increased energy costs, an environment tax still should lead to relatively higher production costs for energy-intensive products. Under competitive market conditions, the prices of energy-intensive goods and services could increase relative to the prices of goods and services produced using other factors of production more intensively.[20] Consumers would attempt to minimize the indirect effects of the taxes by altering their consumption patterns and substituting the relatively cheaper goods and services – energy-intensive goods and services produced outside Ontario.

The more readily available the external substitutes, the less likely Ontario-based producers subject to the tax would be to pass on higher costs. As a result, substitutions would occur slowly as some producers withdrew from the market because of shrinking profits. Of course, the tax might accelerate the search by these companies for new and cheaper energy-saving production technologies.

In addition, in the case of durable goods, substitutions would take place gradually through addition of more energy-efficient units to the existing stock and replacement of the least energy-efficient and/or most worn-out units in place.[21] Consumers might turn to energy-intensive durable goods produced outside Ontario. However, producers of these types of goods subject to a tax might improve their relative energy efficiency and so maintain or perhaps improve their competitive position.

Substitutions by consumers would help reduce carbon dioxide emissions in two ways. Use of more energy-efficient products would lessen consumers' direct demand for energy and resulting emissions of carbon dioxide. In addition, their substitutions would indirectly decrease aggregate demand for energy by producers. The greater the scope for consumers and firms to substitute, the greater the competitive pressures on firms most affected by a tax. Hence, these companies would be less likely to pass on the tax, and, as a result, their financial performance would deteriorate, leading to their eventual withdrawal from the market.

As more companies reach the stage at which they would need to consider major investments in either additional capacity or new, energy-efficient production technologies, an environment tax would begin to affect location decisions. Enterprises might be spurred to examine alternative locations for these investments. Once a firm decided to begin production outside its home jurisdiction, it would tend to become more comfortable operating in a new location. Therefore, over time, its investment decisions would become more sensitive to tax and other cost considerations. Moreover, its original production facilities could become technologically obsolete and less cost competitive.

The many relative price effects could be moderated or exacerbated over time by non–tax-related movements in the real prices of all factors of production and differential, demand-induced effects on the relative prices of goods and services. Exchange rate movements would also influence the adjustment processes. As a result, the relative, tax-induced price movements for the fossil fuels might be too small to warrant, on the basis of standard net present value, the search for cost-minimizing technologies and/or investments in different technologies.[22] Or the relative price movements might be too small, given the uncertainties regarding future price paths for energy and all other goods and services.

For our purposes, however, we assume away these other changes, because their magnitudes are highly uncertain and our concern is with the marginal effects of an environment tax. Essentially, we are interested in examining the effects of adding an environment tax to whatever other changes might take place.

Short-term Effects on Energy Use

Price elasticities[23] in energy demand are useful tools for estimating the possible effects of carbon, energy, and/or ad valorem taxes on energy consumption and carbon dioxide emissions. Admittedly, elasticities are "summary statistics which conceal long and complicated processes of economic, social and technological change" (Robinson 1987, 19) and are intended to be used to predict the response of demand to small price changes. However, we believe that price elasticities can provide a reasonable, order-of-magnitude estimate of the potential effects of an environment tax, and, as the OECD (1991, 75) pointed out, there is little harm in extrapolating over large price changes.

In this study, we rely on the work of Mahmoud Elkhafif, an economist with Ontario Hydro. His papers (see Elkhafif 1992, for example) have estimated short- and long-term own- and cross-price elasticities of demand by Ontario's residential, commercial, and industrial sectors for electricity, natural gas, oil, and coal.[24] He also estimated short- and long-term own-price elasticities of demand for motor gasoline by the transportation sector. Elasticities provide only a partial estimate of taxes' effects on energy use by the residential, commercial, and industrial sectors and by motor gasoline sales within transportation.[25] Therefore, at best, they indicate a lower limit to the taxes' potential effects on aggregate energy use and subsequently on carbon dioxide emissions.

Shorter- and longer-term effects differ. "In the short run the response will be relatively small since the stock of energy consuming equipment and structures will be relatively constant ... In the medium to long run, the stock of energy consuming equipment and structures will be replaced and the responsiveness of fossil fuel demand to a carbon tax will be much greater" (Gibbons and Valiante 1991, 6, 7).

In this subsection, we are interested in the short run. The estimated short-run (one-year) effects of a tax on energy use are reported in Table 19.[26] The energy tax consistently produces the largest reductions in aggregate use of energy in the residential, commercial, and industrial sectors – 1.4 per cent in all cases. A carbon tax might reduce energy use by 1.0, 1.3, and 1.1 per cent, respectively, in those same sectors. The ad valorem tax would not encourage any inter-fuel substitutions at all.

Not surprising, the ad valorem tax has the largest effect on transportation, because it produces the largest increase in the price of motor gasoline (see Table 12). Demand for motor gasoline would drop by 1 per cent in the short run with an ad valorem tax of 4.8 per cent. Both the carbon and energy taxes would bring about a decline of 0.7 per cent.

In the residential sector, oil consumption would fall the most – ranging from 1.9 per cent with an energy tax to 2.7 per cent with a carbon tax. Use of electricity and natural gas would also decline in this sector under each of the three taxes.

Natural gas would experience the largest and most consistent decreases in use by the commercial sector. An ad valorem tax would reduce its use by 1.2 per cent; an energy tax, by 4.2 per cent. The sharp drop in use of natural gas under an energy tax would be accompanied by greater consumption of both electricity and oil products. In the short run, inter-fuel substitutions seem to predominate in the commercial sector.

TABLE 19
Short-Term Effects (%, TJ) of Taxes on Energy Use by Fuel, by Sector, 1989

Sector	Carbon	Energy	Ad valorem
SHORT-TERM EFFECTS (%)			
Residential			
Electricity	−0.64	−0.50	−1.68
Natural gas	−0.90	−1.81	−0.24
Oil products	−2.71	−1.94	−2.25
Total	−1.04	−1.40	−0.95
Commercial			
Electricity	0.55	1.02	−1.25
Natural gas	−3.12	−4.21	−1.25
Oil products	−0.50	0.28	−1.25
Total	−1.26	−1.43	−1.25
Industrial			
Electricity	−4.09	−1.70	−0.23
Natural gas	0.40	−2.49	−0.23
Oil products	5.10	2.68	−0.23
Coal	−4.61	−0.92	−0.23
Total	−1.07	−1.37	−0.23
Transportation			
Oil products	−0.73	−0.67	−1.01
SHORT-TERM EFFECTS (TJ)			
Residential			
Electricity	−1,040	−815	−2,714
Natural gas	−2,457	−4,949	−655
Oil products	−1,637	−1,171	−1,360
Total	−5,134	−6,935	−4,729
Commercial			
Electricity	801	1,485	−1,808
Natural gas	−5,331	−7,191	−2,126
Oil products	−344	197	−865
Total	−4,874	−5,509	−4,799
Industrial			
Electricity	−7,316	−3,047	−420
Natural gas	1,594	−9,848	−908
Oil products	5,248	2,755	−242
Coal	−8,777	−1,758	−438
Total	−9,251	−11,898	−2,008
Transportation			
Oil products	−4,420	−4,027	−6,085
Total (TJ)	−23,679	−28,369	−17,621
Total (%)	−1.01%	−1.21%	−0.75%

Sources: Short-term price elasticities provided by Mahmoud Elkhafif. These elasticities were combined with price changes (Table 18) and energy use (Table 5).

Each tax produces a significantly different outcome in the industrial sector. A carbon tax would lead to decreases in the use of electricity (4.1 per cent) and coal (4.6 per cent) and to increases in the use of natural gas (0.4 per cent) and oil products (5.1 per cent). An energy tax would lower use of all energy inputs except oil, with natural gas falling the most (2.5 per cent). With an ad valorem tax, there would be a modest decrease of 0.2 per cent in each type of energy.[27]

Aggregating the effects across all energy types and sectors, we find that the taxes would produce cuts in total energy use ranging from 0.8 per cent (17.6 petajoules) for an ad valorem tax to 1.2 per cent (28.4 petajoules) for an energy tax. With the exception of the ad valorem tax, the largest absolute reductions in energy use would occur in the industrial sector (9.3 petajoules with a carbon tax, 11.9 petajoules with an energy tax). An ad valorem tax would spread aggregate reductions more evenly across sectors.

(In Appendix D, we review the short-run effects when the taxes are adjusted for use of coal as a feedstock for the iron and steel and the cement industries.)

Long-term Effects on Energy Use and Carbon Dioxide Emissions

The long-term effects (15 years) presented in Table 20 are estimated using the method discussed in the preceding subsection.[28] Except in the residential sector, the long-term effects are larger than the short-term ones. In industry, the long-term effects are substantially larger, with total energy use declining by 7.6 per cent for a carbon tax, compared to a 1.1 per cent decline in the short run; 7.4 per cent with an energy tax (1.4 per cent in the short run); and 2.7 per cent with an ad valorem tax (0.2 per cent in the short run). For commerce and transportation, the long-run effects are approximately 2.5 times as large as those for the short run.

The larger, long-term effects reflect the greater scope for substitutions over time. Significant inter-fuel and factor substitutions require new investments, which are not likely to be made in the strategic and capital plans of an enterprise at the time an environment tax is introduced. Therefore it is surprising that the long-term effects in the residential sector are uniformly smaller (in absolute terms) than the short-term effects. This suggests that there might be some shortcomings in the empirical procedure used to estimate the long-term elasticities for this sector.

The energy tax no longer consistently produces the largest reduc-

TABLE 20
Long-Term (15 Years) Effects (%, TJ) of Taxes on Energy Use by Fuel, by Sector, 1989

Sector	Carbon	Energy	Ad valorem
LONG-TERM EFFECTS (%)			
Residential			
Electricity	−1.07	−0.78	−3.02
Natural gas	2.15	0.54	2.68
Oil products	−7.96	−6.06	−6.56
Total	−0.13	−0.69	−0.31
Commercial			
Electricity	−1.02	−0.67	−2.97
Natural gas	−5.44	−6.97	−2.97
Oil products	−2.28	−0.94	−2.88
Total	−3.21	−3.51	−2.95
Industrial			
Electricity	−5.45	−2.83	−2.68
Natural gas	−4.91	−9.13	−2.69
Oil products	2.34	0.52	−2.69
Coal	−20.49	−12.22	−2.67
Total	−7.58	−7.36	−2.68
Transportation			
Oil products	−1.88	−1.71	−2.59
LONG-TERM EFFECTS (TJ)			
Residential			
Electricity	−1,728	−1,256	−4,885
Natural gas	5,880	1,478	7,334
Oil products	−4,807	−3,664	−3,965
Total	−655	−3,442	−1,516
Commercial			
Electricity	−1,477	−968	−4,311
Natural gas	−9,285	−11,888	−5,069
Oil products	−1,585	−654	−1,997
Total	−12,347	−13,510	−11,337
Industrial			
Electricity	−9,746	−5,071	−4,800
Natural gas	−19,405	−36,030	−10,610
Oil products	2,407	533	−2,766
Coal	−39,027	−23,269	−5,090
Total	−65,771	−63,837	−23,266
Transportation			
Oil products	−11,367	−10,354	−15,646
Total (TJ)	−90,140	−91,143	−51,805
Total (%)	−3.83%	−3.87%	−2.20%

Sources: See Table 19.

tions in the aggregate use of energy by the residential, commercial, and industrial sectors. The carbon tax appears to be the most effective in reducing aggregate energy use in the industrial sector. The ad valorem tax continues to be the least effective, except for the residential sector; moreover, it has the largest effect on transportation.

Oil continues to suffer the largest decrease in use in the long run in the residential sector, declining 6.1 per cent with an energy tax and 8.0 per cent with a carbon tax. While use of electricity would decrease in the long run, use of natural gas would rise under each of the three taxes. It seems that inter-fuel substitution towards natural gas would offset the effects of energy conservation/efficiency in use of natural gas.

In the commercial sector, however, use of natural gas would fall the most in the long run – by 3 per cent with an ad valorem tax and by 7 per cent with an energy tax. Unlike for the short-run estimates, long-run use of all energy inputs would decline with either a carbon or an energy tax. In the long run, factor substitutions and energy conservation seem to predominate over inter-fuel substitutions.

As with short-run effects, each tax produces a different outcome in industry. Both a carbon and an energy tax would lead to sharp declines in use of coal (20.5 and 12.2 per cent, respectively) and lesser reductions in use of electricity (5.4 and 2.8 per cent, respectively) and natural gas (4.9 and 9.1 per cent, respectively). With both these taxes, use of oil would still increase in the long term, but by smaller amounts than in the short run. An ad valorem tax results in a 2.7 per cent decrease in use of each energy input in the long run.

The long-term effects of each tax on aggregate use of energy by the four sectors appear to be about three to four times greater than theshort-run effects – a 3.8 per cent decrease over time with a carbon tax versus 1 per cent in the short run; 3.9 per cent versus 1.2 per cent for an energy tax; and 2.2 per cent versus 0.8 per cent for an ad valorem tax. The reductions, when measured in natural units of energy, range from 51.8 petajoules with an ad valorem tax to 91.1 petajoules with an energy tax.

As is the short-run experience, the largest absolute long-run reductions in energy use would occur in the industrial sector (65.8 petajoules with a carbon tax; 63.8 petajoules with an energy tax; and 23.3 petajoules for an ad valorem tax). Long-term reductions in use of coal and natural gas would account for much of the aggregate reduction in use of energy.

The estimated long-term effects of the taxes on carbon dioxide emissions are reported in Table 21.[29] A carbon tax, primarily because of its greater relative effect on the price of coal, would probably cut emissions most. According to our calculations and assumptions, a levy of $24.68 per tonne of carbon would reduce emissions over the long run by about 6350 kilotonnes of carbon dioxide per year – roughly 4.3 per cent of the aggregate 1989 level of emissions by the four sectors. If coal for the iron and steel industry is treated as a feedstock, the effect of a carbon tax, and of the other taxes as well, would be much smaller, as can be seen in Appendix E.

The unadjusted energy tax would reduce annual emissions by 3.9 per cent (5755 kilotonnes) from 1989 levels, and an ad valorem tax of 4.8 per cent would produce a 2.4 per cent decline (3481 kilotonnes). The carbon and energy taxes would have the largest effects on industry, producing reductions of 8.6 and 7.4 per cent, respectively, from 1989. These taxes would have the smallest long-run effect in the residential sector – 0.6 and 1.0 per cent, respectively. An ad valorem tax would lead to reductions of between 2.5 and 3 per cent in the other three sectors.

If we accept these various price elasticities and subsequent estimated effects and assume that coal is an energy input for the iron and steel and the cement industries, we then can calculate tax rates to stabilize carbon dioxide emissions in Ontario (at least for the four sectors) at 1989 levels. Use of each energy input by each sector will increase in line with growth of the economy. Consequently, price-induced effects of the taxes and the resulting changes in use of each input must offset growth effects in order to stabilize emission levels. If we assume a linear relationship between reduction in emission levels and tax rates,[30] we can calculate tax rates for various income elasticities of demand combined with different rates of provincial growth over 15 years.

Table 22 examines the products of three assumed average annual growth rates[31] (1, 2, and 3 per cent) and three income elasticities (0.3, 0.6, and 0.9.[32] For example, a 2 per cent average annual rate of growth and a 0.6 income elasticity of demand would raise energy use and carbon dioxide emissions by about 21 per cent. Since an ad valorem rate of 4.8 per cent reduces emissions by 2.4 per cent in the long run, the ad valorem rate would have to reach 42.3 per cent in order for resulting price effects to neutralize growth effects.

As growth rates and/or income elasticities increase, tax levels must rise dramatically in order to stabilize emissions. The most aggressive possibility – 3 per cent average annual growth and an income elasticity

TABLE 21
Long-Term Effects (Kilotonnes, %) of Taxes on Carbon Dioxide Emissions by Sector,
Ontario, 1989

Sector	Carbon	Energy	Ad valorem
LONG-TERM EFFECTS			
(KILOTONNES)			
Residential	−167	−273	−240
Commercial	−677	−707	−684
Industrial	−4,723	−4,062	−1,479
Transportation	−783	−713	−1,078
Total	−6,350	−5,755	−3,481
LONG-TERM EFFECTS (%)			
Residential	−0.59	−0.96	−0.85
Commercial	−2.92	−3.05	−2.95
Industrial	−8.56	−7.36	−2.68
Transportation	−1.88	−1.71	−2.59
Total	−4.28	−3.88	−2.35

Sources: Tables 20 and 3

of 0.9 – would require a carbon tax of almost $290 per tonne (approx-
imately 12 times greater than the tax rate explored in this study); an
energy tax about 13 times greater than the rate used here; and an ad
valorem tax at the exorbitant level of 99 per cent (a 21-fold increase
over the 4.79 per cent rate used above).

The Ministry of Energy assumed income elasticity of 0.6 to forecast
energy use and emissions in the province in 2005 (Ontario Global
Warming Coalition 1991, 6, 7). Williams (1990, 38) has suggested that
such a figure would be consistent with continuing structural shifts
towards less energy-intensive service and light manufacturing industries. Average annual growth of 2.5 per cent would be considered
modest; the ministry used a 3 per cent rate in its projections. Thus,
combining an annual growth rate of between 2.5 and 3 per cent with
an income elasticity of 0.6 to 0.9 results in the need for very high tax
rates to achieve stabilization.[33]

Obviously, the possibility of taking the tax route alone to stabilize
emissions is limited because of economic and political factors. An environment tax would probably have to be part of a larger package of
measures.

TABLE 22
Taxes Required at Various Annual Growth Rates (%) to Stabilize Aggregate Emissions
in Ontario at 1989 Levels, 2004

Elasticities/tax rates	1%	2%	3%
0.3			
Carbon tax ($/tonne)	27.85	59.85	96.53
Energy tax ($/TJ)	526.13	1,130.70	1,823.50
Ad valorem (%)	9.84	21.16	31.12
0.6			
Carbon tax	55.70	119.71	193.06
Energy tax	1,052.27	2,261.40	3,646.99
Ad valorem	19.69	42.32	68.24
0.9			
Carbon tax	83.55	179.56	289.59
Energy tax	1,578.40	3,392.10	5,470.49
Ad valorem	29.53	63.48	99.36

Note: Cumulative rates of growth (1989–2004): for 1 per cent, 16.1 per cent; for 2 per
cent, 34.6 per cent; and for 3 per cent, 55.8 per cent.

Effects of an Environment Tax on Cost Structures
in Manufacturing and Mining

Direct Effects

In this section, we examine the possible effects of an environment tax
on the cost structures of manufacturing and mining industries in
Ontario. Once again, 1989 serves as the base year.

Statistics Canada provides information on expenditures by manufacturing and mining on their inputs – namely, labour, energy, and
intermediate goods and services. We use these figures to estimate the
energy intensities for the major manufacturing industries and mining.
The energy intensity numbers in Table 23 show the proportions of the
total costs (excluding returns on assets) accounted for by use of energy
– fuels and electricity.

Several industries stand out as heavy users of energy: cement (30.2
per cent of total costs are for energy); non-ferrous smelting (almost 20
per cent); mining (8.5 per cent); paper products (6.6 per cent); and
primary steel (5.5 per cent). Carbon, energy, or ad valorem taxes on
energy inputs would probably affect these industries most of all.[34]

Our calculations[35] show that an energy tax consistently would produce the largest increases in energy costs for all industries, followed

TABLE 23
Direct Effects of Taxes on Total Energy Costs (% Increase), by Industry, Ontario, 1989

Industry	Energy intensity[a]	Carbon tax[b]	Energy tax	Ad valorem tax	Carbon tax[c]
Food	1.65	7.6	8.9	4.6	8.5
Beverages	1.89	8.5	10.2	4.7	9.5
Rubber	1.95	7.6	8.9	4.7	8.6
Plastic	2.31	5.1	5.7	4.1	5.8
Leather	1.27	7.4	8.8	4.6	8.3
Primary textiles	4.35	8.6	10.3	4.8	9.6
Textile products	2.07	7.8	9.3	4.4	8.8
Clothing	0.95	5.7	6.5	3.9	6.3
Wood	2.76	5.6	6.3	4.2	6.3
Furniture, fixtures	1.52	6.5	7.5	4.2	7.3
Paper products	6.56	9.7	10.3	4.6	10.9
Printing, publishing	1.12	5.0	5.6	4.0	5.6
Primary metals	5.39	10.1	10.4	4.7	9.8
Primary steel	5.47	17.5	14.4	4.7	9.6
Steel pipe and tubes	1.39	8.7	10.4	4.8	9.8
Non-ferrous smelting	19.95	8.9	9.5	4.7	10.0
Aluminum	2.10	9.1	10.2	4.7	10.2
Other metal rolling	3.08	8.9	10.6	4.7	9.9
Fabricated metal products	1.86	7.0	8.2	4.3	7.9
Machinery, equipment	1.13	6.8	8.0	4.3	7.6
Transportation equipment	0.59	7.9	8.8	4.7	8.9
Electrical, electronic					
products	0.95	6.7	7.8	4.6	7.5
Non-metallic minerals	8.42	12.4	12.5	4.6	8.1
Cement	30.32	24.6	19.9	4.5	4.8
Refined petroleum	2.48	8.2	10.0	4.5	9.2
Chemicals	4.49	7.5	8.6	3.7	8.4
Other manufacturing	1.50	6.2	7.2	4.3	6.9
Mining	8.52	4.9	5.3	4.8	5.4

Sources: Statistics Canada (1984; 1988b; 1989)
[a] Ratio of fuel and electricity costs to total costs, excluding capital. The relative effects of the taxes are measured as the proportionate increases in expenditures on fuel and electricity by each industry.
[b] Based on use of coal as energy input by primary steel and cement industries.
[c] Based on use of coal as feedstock by primary steel and cement industries.

by a carbon tax. Energy costs could increase by between 5.3 per cent (mining) and 19.9 per cent (cement) with such a levy. This tax would increase energy costs by 14.4 per cent for the primary steel industry and by around 10 per cent for the other energy-intensive industries listed above.[36] The carbon tax would increase energy costs by between

4.9 per cent (mining) and 24.6 per cent (cement). An ad valorem tax would increase total energy costs the least.[37]

We also estimate the effects of the carbon tax, adjusted for treatment of coal as a feedstock for the iron and steel and the cement industries. The adjusted tax increases energy costs (compared to the unadjusted case) by more for all industries except primary steel and cement.

Table 24 presents the direct, first-round effects of the taxes on total costs for manufacturing and mining.[38] The results reflect cost increases prior to any passing on of these to customers and incorporation of the resulting higher prices for intermediate goods and services into the costs of these industries. If the higher costs are not passed on, for competitive, contractual, or relationship reasons, then the increases reported here would be the equilibrium increases as well.

For most industries, the direct effects on total costs (or per-unit costs) appear to be trivial – 0.2 per cent or less. Even among industries whose costs we would expect to be sensitive to an environment tax, few would experience increases in their total or per-unit costs of more than 1 per cent. The cement industry could see its costs rise by between 6 per cent (energy tax) and 7.5 per cent (carbon tax), and non-ferrous smelting's costs could grow by about 1.8 per cent with either type of tax. The primary steel industry could see its costs increase by 0.8 and 1 per cent with an energy or carbon tax, respectively, and these taxes could raise the costs of the paper products industry by just under 0.7 per cent. The effects on total costs are even less with an ad valorem tax.

The adjusted carbon tax has a significantly lower effect on costs in the cement industry and does reduce the cost increase for primary steel by almost one-half (from 1 per cent to just over 0.5 per cent). The other industries would suffer marginally greater increases. With the possible exception of the cement and the non-ferrous smelting industries, the cost effects seem modest, possibly inconsequential. However, even modest changes might translate into substantial declines in the "bottom lines" and might suffice to reduce the competitiveness of Ontario as a location for investment.

Direct and Indirect Effects

The cost effects of the taxes would probably be greater than those shown in Table 24. Most industries might pass on part or all of their cost increases to their customers. This, in turn, would further increase their costs, as they would have to pay higher prices for various non-energy inputs. A new cycle of price increases (the passing on of the

TABLE 24
Direct, First-Round Effects[a] of Taxes on Total Costs (% Increase), by Industry, Ontario, 1989

Industry	Carbon tax[b]	Energy tax	Ad valorem tax	Carbon tax[c]
Food	0.13	0.15	0.08	0.14
Beverages	0.16	0.19	0.09	0.18
Rubber	0.15	0.17	0.09	0.17
Plastic	0.12	0.13	0.10	0.13
Leather	0.09	0.11	0.06	0.10
Primary textiles	0.37	0.45	0.21	0.42
Textile products	0.16	0.19	0.09	0.18
Clothing	0.05	0.06	0.04	0.06
Wood	0.16	0.18	0.12	0.18
Furniture, fixtures	0.10	0.11	0.06	0.11
Paper products	0.64	0.68	0.30	0.72
Printing, publishing	0.06	0.06	0.04	0.06
Primary metals	0.54	0.56	0.25	0.53
Primary steel	0.96	0.79	0.26	0.53
Steel pipe and tubes	0.12	0.14	0.07	0.14
Non-ferrous smelting	1.78	1.90	0.94	1.99
Aluminium	0.19	0.22	0.10	0.22
Other metal rolling	0.27	0.33	0.14	0.31
Fabricated metal products	0.13	0.15	0.08	0.15
Machinery, equipment	0.08	0.09	0.05	0.09
Transportation equipment	0.05	0.05	0.03	0.05
Electrical, electronic products	0.06	0.08	0.04	0.07
Non-metallic minerals	1.05	1.05	0.39	0.68
Cement	7.43	6.01	1.36	1.44
Refined petroleum	0.20	0.25	0.11	0.23
Chemicals	0.34	0.39	0.16	0.38
Other manufacturing	0.09	0.11	0.06	0.10
Mining	0.42	0.45	0.41	0.46

Source: Table 23
[a] Direct effects do not factor the influence of taxes on prices of intermediate inputs (materials, supplies). Relative effects are measured as proportionate increases in total costs (excluding capital costs).
[b] See Table 23, note b.
[c] See Table 23, note c.

second round of cost increases) would lead to further cost increases and additional rounds of price increases. Eventually, the ripple effects of the first-round cost/price increases would peter out and an equilibrium would be reached, with the cost effects being much greater than the initial ones.

We attempt to approximate the potential equilibrium effects of these taxes on costs in manufacturing and mining (Table 25).[39] The effects have been labelled quasi-equilibrium because they do not make any allowance for direct effects on the costs of other industries and do not allow for the possibility that the taxes might increase the rates of inflation, nominal wages, and interest. Hence the figures underestimate the equilibrium values when cost increases are fully passed on to customers. We cannot determine the nature of the bias if cost increases are not fully passed on.

As expected, the taxes might lead to much greater increases in total and per-unit costs for manufacturing. Whereas, in the case of the unadjusted carbon tax, the direct or first-round effects among the manufacturing industries range between 0.05 per cent (transportation equipment) and 1.05 per cent (non-metallic minerals), the cumulative direct and indirect effects range between 0.31 per cent (leather) and 1.42 per cent (primary metals). While the effects on costs still appear rather modest, increases in the range of 0.3 to 0.7 per cent are more prevalent.

To gauge the potential effects on industries, it would be necessary to consider the cost increases produced by an environment tax in the context of other changes that also affect costs and competitiveness, among them revaluations of the exchange rate. Alone, an environment tax might not be problematic for most manufacturing industries (there would be some obvious cases where a tax could create serious difficulties, depending on how coal is treated), but when it is added to other factors, the economic consequences might be pronounced. However, a modest depreciation of the Canadian dollar could easily offset any negative effects on cost competitiveness. But, even in this case, industries located in Ontario might be worse off competitively. That is, their cost structures would be higher than they otherwise would be in the absence of any tax.

In order to assess more accurately the potential economic effects of a carbon, energy, or ad valorem tax, we found it necessary to directly survey industries in Ontario. The findings are reported in the following section.

TABLE 25
Quasi-Equilibrium Effects[a] of Taxes on Total Costs (% Increase), by Industry, Ontario, 1989

Industry	Carbon tax[b]	Energy tax	Ad valorem tax	Carbon tax[c]
Food	0.37	0.41	0.30	0.40
Beverages	0.43	0.48	0.30	0.41
Rubber	0.41	0.46	0.30	0.45
Plastic	0.47	0.52	0.34	0.52
Leather	0.31	0.35	0.23	0.34
Primary textiles } Textiles products	0.58[d]	0.67	0.37	0.64
Clothing	0.31	0.36	0.22	0.34
Wood	0.47	0.50	0.45	0.51
Furniture, fixtures	0.37	0.41	0.28	0.39
Paper products	0.98	1.03	0.58	1.08
Printing, publishing	0.37	0.40	0.28	0.41
Primary metals	1.42	1.41	0.62	0.94
Fabricated metal products	0.50	0.55	0.35	0.52
Machinery, equipment	0.35	0.39	0.26	0.36
Transportation equipment	0.36	0.40	0.28	0.37
Electrical, electronic products	0.32	0.36	0.24	0.33
Non-metallic minerals	1.39	1.40	0.63	0.89
Refined petroleum	0.33	0.38	0.22	0.36
Chemicals	0.62	0.70	0.39	0.69
Other manufacturing	0.34	0.38	0.27	0.37
Mining	0.53	0.57	0.52	0.58

Sources: Table 23 and Statistics Canada (1988[a])
[a] The influence of taxes on prices of intermediate inputs (materials, supplies). Relative effects are measured as proportionate increases in total costs (excluding capital costs).
[b] See Table 23, note b.
[c] See Table 23, note c.
[d] Input-output data available for the aggregate textiles industry, which combines primary textiles and textile products.

A Survey of the Effects of a Carbon Tax on Manufacturing and Resources

The Questionnaire

We prepared a questionnaire that we distributed to 75 divisions in 60 companies in order to probe further into the many possible adjustments that might occur in response to a tax of $25 per tonne of carbon content. We targeted the following industries: mining, forestry, petrochemicals, primary metals, pulp and paper, autos and parts, cement, food products, appliances, industrial equipment, plastics, and truck transport. These were selected because they are either intensive users of energy or employ large numbers of workers. Approximately the same number of companies was selected in most of these industries. In some cases, we restricted our potential sample population to firms with significant Ontario operations and aggregate Canadian sales in excess of $35 million. Therefore, there were ten industries in which fewer companies were contacted, although they did represent a much larger proportion of the sample population in these industries than in the others.

Each company was requested to provide information on its probable response, assuming that a tax had been introduced in 1989 (when the Ontario economy was at the peak of the last business cycle), and assuming also that the tax was introduced in 1992 (when the economy was beginning to recover from the recession). We chose both years, since we believe that it is important to examine the effect of general economic conditions on these adjustments.

The questionnaire was divided into five sections. The first collected background information on operations (usually a specific division was emphasized either in the covering letter or in conversation with officials). The second focused on the direct, short-term effects of a carbon tax. The companies were required to consider only the initial and direct effects of the tax on the costs of their energy inputs and to disregard the effects on the costs of their suppliers. We asked them to estimate the effects of the tax on their cost structure and whether they might have been able to pass on any or all of the increase in their unit costs to their domestic and/or foreign customers in either 1989 or 1992. They had to estimate the possible repercussions on demand of higher prices for the customers.

In the third section, companies evaluated indirect, short-term effects of the carbon tax on their suppliers' costs and the abilities of their suppliers to pass on part or all of the higher costs to them. In responding to higher prices from their suppliers, each firm was asked whether it would try to minimize the indirect effect by switching to suppliers based outside Ontario, which would be exempt from the tax.

The potential longer-term effects (defined in the questionnaire as three to five years, to correspond with the general planning horizon of a company) were explored in the fourth section. Each firm estimated longer-term effects on unit costs, prices, sales volume (both within and outside Ontario), energy costs, and investment commitments within the province. Each was asked to provide specific details of inter-fuel substitutions that might be technologically and financially feasible and whether it might consider shifting production out of Ontario as a result of a carbon tax. If the levy of $25 per tonne would not lead to any significant adjustments, the companies estimated the tax level that would begin "to bite" and make adjustments necessary in order for it to survive.

In the fifth section, firms could offer their suggestions on how the revenues generated by the tax should best be used in order to make the tax revenue neutral. The options ranged from various types of tax cuts/subsidies for corporations to personal income tax cuts to additional government expenditures on infrastructure. In addition, each company was asked whether Queen's Park should allow exemptions to the carbon tax, to whom, and how much.

Survey Results

Twenty companies responded to the survey. There were no responses from the food products, appliances, plastics, or truck transport industries. In order to minimize any biases that could arise as a result of companies' responding strategically to the questionnaire, we reviewed the survey, either by phone or personal interview, with each respondent. During these follow-up interviews, we expanded upon the questionnaire and asked other questions that allowed us to test for consistency and bias. By and large, we found that, although the respondents were not supportive of the NDP government and several of its regulatory initiatives, they did approach the questionnaire objectively and they all made every effort to answer the many questions with a minimum of bias.

The companies that did respond had sales ranging between $100 million and $10 billion. All experienced a decline in sales between 1989 and 1992. Only two did not sell abroad; the others had export sales that averaged between 5 and 35 per cent of the total sales of their Canadian operations. Ontario-based operations accounted for 30 to 100 per cent of total sales of Canadian operations. This ratio was below 50 per cent for only three companies. Seventeen firms were familiar with Ottawa's discussion paper (Environment Canada 1990).

Most companies (60 per cent) estimated that a $25-per-tonne carbon tax would increase their costs in the short run by less than 1 per cent. The maximum effect was 6 per cent.[40] The estimated long-run effects were about 10 to 30 per cent smaller, reflecting continual improvements in energy efficiency and ongoing investments in more energy-efficient technologies. However, the recent recession appears to have reduced the funds available for these types of investment, as firms focus on survival in an increasingly cost-competitive environment. With energy costs expected to remain relatively stable over the next three to five years, pay-offs to investments in energy efficiency have declined.

The carbon tax would affect the costs and possibly the prices of Ontario-based suppliers of various products and services to these 20 companies. The respondents estimated that if these costs could be passed on to them, the "indirect" effects of the carbon tax would add between 1 and 3 per cent to their costs. However, they did not expect that their Ontario-based suppliers would be able to pass on the higher costs, and so the indirect cost effects were anticipated as negligible.

Only one company believed that the carbon tax would accelerate its search for and investment in energy-efficient technologies. Two answered that the tax would slow this process, since it would reduce cash flows. The remaining firms did not believe that the tax would have any effect, because there are no further energy-efficient technologies foreseeable during the next three to five years, the level of the tax is too small to influence these investment decisions, or other investments are much more critical. Several companies noted that new investments did improve energy efficiency, even when this was not the principal objective.

None of the firms would be able to pass on any part of their higher costs to foreign customers. Competition outside Canada would force them to absorb the tax. This response appeared to be independent of general economic conditions. In the short run, very few companies would be able to pass on part of the higher costs to their Ontario customers. Indeed, in the long run, only one would raise domestic prices in order to pass on part of its higher energy costs. Competition in Ontario would protect customers against price increases. These responses suggest that the estimates in Table 24 (direct first-round effects) would be more indicative of an environment tax than those in Table 25 (quasi-equilibrium effects).

If a carbon tax were introduced in every province, none of these companies would shift production to any facilities that they operate in other provinces or relocate elsewhere in Canada. At least, this would be the case if they had to consider only the carbon tax and not other government initiatives. If a carbon tax were implemented in all provinces and every U.S. state, only two companies would look to relocate out of Ontario and outside Canada and the United States. In both cases, Mexico and Southeast Asia were mentioned.

Among factors important for a company's competitive position, tax policies and government regulations ranked high (within the top four) for 70 and 80 per cent of respondents, respectively. Trade barriers ranked high for half of the companies, and 40 per cent listed competitors' strategies and the carbon tax among the four most significant factors.

For policy alternatives, 60 per cent of respondents ranked cuts in corporate income tax and/or subsidies for companies most hurt by a carbon tax among the top four in priority if Queen's Park intended to make the carbon tax revenue neutral. Grants to businesses for purchases of energy-conservation equipment and new investment tax credits were ranked just as high by 40 per cent of the firms. No company ranked new spending on capital projects as a high priority. In light of the recession's impact on financial performance, it is not surprising that respondents favoured offset programs that would tend to mitigate the cash-flow effects of a carbon tax on their operations.

Sixty per cent favoured a five-year phase-in of the carbon tax so that they could adjust to the tax and recover from the recession. All but two wanted some form of exemption from the tax for energy-intensive industries; about half supported permanent exemptions.

To understand better the nature of the responses, we separate companies into three groups – (1) those that manufacture the same product or line in Ontario as in other jurisdictions; (2) those that have production facilities only in Ontario but compete on the basis of cost and price; and (3) those that operate in Ontario only, but either do not compete solely on the basis of cost and price and/or are insulated from external competition. Most of the firms fall into groups 1 and 2. They generally face the same competitors in the domestic and foreign markets. For about 30 per cent, the principal competitor is the U.S. parent or a U.S.-based subsidiary. Each of the three groups must also be disaggregated with two parts on the basis of energy intensity, which depends critically on whether certain fossil fuels are treated (A) as energy inputs or (B) as feedstocks – important distinctions for the petrochemicals, cement, and primary metals industries.

Classification into one of the six resulting sub-groups appears more meaningful for interpreting results than the standard industrial classification. Firms with multiple production facilities (group 1) have a ready option available in the short run – to shift production outside Ontario, especially if they have excess capacity. As well, since these businesses contract with a number of suppliers, they might find it easier to switch to sources outside the province to avoid the tax. They would not need to search for new suppliers and to test their materials or parts and their reliability. Indeed, suppliers could possibly fill Ontario customers' orders from their plants located outside the province.

This group of companies did include switching production among short-run options to minimize the impact of an Ontario carbon tax. Over the long term, the carbon tax would be added to the list of cost factors that would affect investment/location decisions. For energy-intensive businesses with multiple production facilities (sub-group 1A), such a levy would make Ontario a less attractive investment location if other jurisdictions in North America did not introduce a similar tax. Conceivably, Ontario plants could be shut down well before they were fully depreciated. All the members of this sub-group responded that a carbon tax would significantly reduce investment plans for their Ontario-based operations during the next three to five years.

Companies that operate energy-intensive plants only in Ontario and compete on cost and price (sub-group 2A) would be hard hit by a carbon tax, even at the rather modest level of $25 per tonne. Such firms would be more likely to search for more energy-efficient technologies than comparable businesses that have multiple production facilities. But all respondents are searching for more energy-efficient and cost-effective technologies. One commented that many pollution abatement technologies reduce energy efficiency, and so the burden of a carbon tax would be greater for companies that are also subject to environmental regulations that require reductions in emissions of other gases or wastes.

Companies in group 2 would also begin to explore alternative locations for future investments. But given their lack of experience and knowledge in other markets (at least from the production side), the tax might have to be higher for them to launch such an endeavour. All the industries in our survey are currently experiencing excess capacity on a global basis. An Ontario-only carbon tax might result in Ontario-based facilities being disproportionately disadvantaged in the ongoing restructuring and phasing out of excess capacity in these industries. The U.S. trade actions in the steel industry in 1991 may be just the first step of an American strategy to force other countries to bear the brunt of the costs of restructuring across a broad spectrum of industries. If the United States targets other industries for trade actions, then a carbon tax in Ontario would compound the problems for Ontario-based companies.

Companies in groups 1 and 2, regardless of the energy intensity of production, seem reluctant to switch to suppliers outside Ontario. Both groups value a continuing relationship with their suppliers. Obviously, Ontario-only producers (groups 2 and 3) might be constrained by their lack of knowledge about suppliers who do not operate in the province. Multiple-location firms might not need to search for suppliers elsewhere. As suggested above, domestic suppliers might switch for them, but only if "just-in-time" inventory deliveries are not an integral part of the production process – that is, if suppliers do not need to provide inputs on a demand basis. In such a case, production costs for sub-group 3A would outweigh transportation and inventory costs. If, however, just-in-time deliveries *are* critical, production costs would become less important than suppliers' ability to provide materials, components, or other inputs in a timely and reliable manner.

Companies that compete on cost and price (group 2) would probably not pass on any increase in per-unit costs unless they had some market power. In most industries that we surveyed, the Ontario-based divisions or firms did not possess such power. Even those that had some had long-term contracts or ongoing relations with key customers that would preclude an increase in prices, and they would probably press suppliers to absorb some of the cost increases.

For the less energy-intensive companies that do not compete primarily on the basis of cost and price and/or are insulated from foreign competition (sub-group 3B), the carbon tax would not present a problem. They would not be likely to explore marginal adjustments that would reduce the effects of the tax. Energy-intensive firms (sub-group 3A) would continue looking for energy-conserving investments. A carbon tax would have little effect at all on this strategy. As well, these types of businesses could pass on the tax in higher prices if they so desired. But because of long-term relationships with major customers, they would not fully pass the tax through in higher prices.

In all cases, unless the carbon tax pushed costs beyond a critical threshold, it would be largely ignored in pricing and energy-efficiency investments. In fact, there could be several thresholds, each one leading to a more dramatic adjustment. For some companies, a tax of $25 per tonne of carbon would not move them past the first threshold; for others, this tax could result in costs pushing through a few threshold levels. But unlike traditional theory, in which marginal adjustments are likely, the general tenor of answers to our questionnaire suggests that there would be no response until a threshold were passed. However, once it were passed, the adjustment might be quite substantial.[41] This behaviour is reasonable in light of uncertainties regarding future energy prices.

There appears to be a consensus that the carbon tax has to be considered in the context of continual changes in costs and government policies. The cumulative effect of these changes can affect a company's strategic decision making. Thus the carbon tax in isolation from other factors and events might not precipitate any significant shift in corporate behaviour. But within the context of other changes, it might warrant dramatic alterations in investment, location, and other strategic decisions. A seemingly low tax rate with little influence on cost might, because of its timing, be the proverbial "straw that breaks the camel's back."

Finally, several companies are planning to invest in co-generation technologies (for their own use) in order to reduce or eliminate use of electricity sold by Ontario Hydro. The rate increases during the past two years seem to have been extrapolated well into the future and so have tilted investment decisions towards co-generation. We suspect that if Hydro's rates continue to increase in real terms, many businesses might begin committing themselves to this type of investment. At this time, the key factors holding up these investments are the state of the economy, the conservative lending practices of the banks, and the high prices that Ontario Hydro is quoting firms for providing back-up service. Of course, the only companies and industries in a position to switch to co-generation are those whose production processes generate sufficient quantities of heat.

Conclusion

Introduction of a carbon, energy, or ad valorem tax by Queen's Park could indicate the potential climatic effects of the accumulation of greenhouse gases in the Earth's atmosphere and convince individuals and companies to change their behaviour so as to reduce the stock of such gases in the atmosphere. It could also generate revenue for the government. In deciding whether to set up any one of these taxes, government should consider as well administrative costs (on both the public and private sectors) of a tax, its political acceptability, and its effect on domestic industry.

Ottawa (Environment Canada 1992, 21) has stated that administrative costs may be significantly lower for one type of economic instrument and so tilt the scales in that tax's favour: "Administrative costs tend to be reduced to the extent that there is an existing administrative structure on which it is possible to 'piggyback.' " An ad valorem tax that could be incorporated into the existing provincial tax system appears to have an administrative cost advantage over a new carbon or energy tax.

Administrative procedures would have to be established to support either a carbon or an energy tax. For petroleum products, natural gas, and electricity, a carbon or energy tax could be collected by suppliers in Ontario, who would then add the tax to the prices that they charged to their customers.[42] For coal, industrial users would have to keep records of their use and pay the appropriate tax directly to the government. If either tax permits exemptions for use of fossil fuels as a feedstock, then industrial users would have to keep track of their use of these fuels as feedstocks and submit a request for a tax credit or rebate. In transportation, companies could be required to pay the tax on their use in Ontario of fossil fuels purchased in the United States, creating obvious problems.

A tax would be more politically acceptable if it were linked directly to the environmental objective and were not seen as a revenue grab. This implies that the tax be revenue neutral and that the revenues be used principally to finance energy conservation by industry, government, and individuals. Furthermore, political acceptability might be enhanced if it had limited adverse effects on industry and employment in the province; if it were part of a larger package aimed at reducing greenhouse gases; and if it were part of a wider, multilateral effort in this direction. The last factor is extremely important, because a unilateral tax by Ontario would have a negligible effect on global emissions of carbon dioxide. The U.S. Environmental Protection Agency (1990, VII–2) has emphasized that "from any country's viewpoint, costs of controlling emissions exceed the benefits since, without international agreement, reductions achieved by one nation may be offset by another."[43]

In the absence of a multilateral agreement, a tax whose sole objective is to induce changes in behaviour in order to stabilize emissions of carbon dioxide in Ontario would encounter serious difficulties. The combination of a tax and one or more of the following measures – investment tax credits for acquisition of energy-efficient machinery and equipment; increases in capital consumption allowances for energy-efficient machinery and equipment; and/or grants for the purchase of energy-efficient machinery, equipment, or appliances – might, in theory, accelerate investments to keep Ontario firms cost competitive and reduce emissions. But, although one of our respondents did point out the possible value of a tax as a signal to Ontario companies and residents, our survey results indicate that the combination of a tax and investment incentives would do little to change the timing or magnitude of investments in energy-efficient technologies and processes.

Moreover, the cumulative effects of a tax (even if set at a modest level) in combination with other policies and market developments might be large enough to pierce through one or more of the critical thresholds cited by respondents and thus precipitate dramatic adjustments. In other words, Queen's Park might seriously affect the international competitiveness of domestic industry, especially since it has no direct influence over exchange rates for the Canadian dollar. Hence, solitary action by Ontario might accomplish little towards the domestic goal, let alone noticeably affecting the global problem. At the same time, Ontario could become an extremely undesirable location for most types of investment.

Porterba (1991, 90) has argued that unilateral actions "could be unattractive both because they create production inefficiencies, distorting production of these intermediate goods away from domestic locations, and because the opportunities for offshore production reduce the revenue potential of the tax." In addition, Gibbons and Valiante (1991, 46, 47) have commented that "if Ontario's carbon intensive industries lose market share to foreign competitors, because our carbon dioxide reduction targets are more ambitious than our competitors', the cost of reducing our carbon dioxide emissions will be greater than the rise in our energy services bill. In addition, under the latter scenario, the fall in output in Ontario's carbon intensive industries will not necessarily lead to a reduction in global dioxide emissions."

Not surprising, discussions of carbon or energy taxes have focused on their effects on the competitiveness of domestic industries. Sweden has exempted its energy-intensive industries from the carbon tax. While exemptions mitigate adverse effects on cost competitiveness, they also lessen a tax's potential to achieve emission targets. Moreover, the Canadian constitution prevents Ontario from providing rebates to domestic producers on their shipments outside the province and taxing imports of competing goods and services into the province. Such options are possible at the national level.[44]

Therefore, the government might wish to consider, either as an alternative strategy or as a complement to a revenue-neutral tax, regulations that encourage energy conservation.[45] If a tax is to be part of the package, an ad valorem tax might be the best choice initially, as long as stabilization of emissions of carbon dioxide at some target level is not the overriding objective. An ad valorem tax has an administrative cost advantage; it would have a smaller direct effect on the cost-competitive position of manufacturing and resource industries in Ontario.[46]

If regulations are to play a role in a comprehensive strategy to reduce or control emissions, the province might wish to examine the feasibility of changing energy-efficiency standards for appliances, automobiles, machinery, and building codes. Reinforcing these regulatory changes with aggressive initiatives by Ontario Hydro might be more effective than a tax in reducing emissions over the long term. And there might be positive industrial policy spin-offs from this approach. Instead of harming industry in pursuit of stabilizing emissions, Queen's Park should search for a policy package that mitigates negative effects on industry and assists in creating or strengthening competitive advantages for Ontario-based industry.

Given the primary motivation for this study and our findings regarding the potential effects on competitiveness, we would support a combination of a modest tax (preferably ad valorem, with or without exemptions) and new regulations, as recommended by the Ontario Global Warming Coalition (1991). A similar recommendation has been proposed by others – Bierbaum (1991) and the Environmental Protection Agency (1990) for the United States, and Australia's Industry Commission (1991, chap. 10). A tax, even a shift to a carbon tax, could assume a more prominent role in the strategy when one or more international agreements on implementing a carbon tax have been negotiated. A carbon tax for Ontario, phased in over five to ten years, as part of a global effort to stabilize emission levels, might begin to make sense.

In the mean time, while we agree with Queen's Park's desire to display leadership in the environmental area and we share the concern for the potential long-term harm to the environment caused by current levels of carbon dioxide emissions, we caution against unilateral introduction of a carbon or energy tax, and especially against relying solely on either one to stabilize emissions. Leadership can be demonstrated by developing and implementing a mix of regulatory and tax (including grants and subsidies) initiatives, with the environment tax restricted to modest levels. An ad valorem tax of 2 to 4 per cent phased in over 18 to 24 months could be one component of the package. An ad valorem tax could be replaced by a carbon or energy tax when other jurisdictions have introduced a similar levy. But more rapid economic growth, accompanied by higher levels of investment, could be even more helpful in improving the energy efficiency and cost competitiveness of Ontario industry, and it may be even more important for Queen's Park to show leadership in spurring growth.

Appendices

Appendix A: Environment Taxes on Per-Unit Basis

To derive the data in Table A1 – the carbon, energy, and ad valorem taxes per basic unit for each of the fuels and for electricity – we multiplied the retail prices reported in Table B1 below by the percentage increases in Table 12 in the text. For natural gas, the resulting price changes range from 0.5 cents per cubic metre (ad valorem tax, natural gas used for industrial use) to 1.6 cents (energy tax). The price increases generally are between one and three cents per litre for refined petroleum products. For electricity, the taxes tend to increase prices by about 0.2 cents per kilowatt hour. Coal prices rise by between 44 cents per tonne (lignite, ad valorem tax) to just under $17 per tonne (Canadian bituminous, carbon tax).

Appendix B: Energy Input Prices, 1989

Table B1 presents the average retail prices in Ontario in 1989 for various types of fuels and electricity. The prices are reported per terajoule of energy and per tonne, megalitre, kilolitre, and megawatt hour for solid fuels, gaseous fuels, liquid fuels, and electricity, respectively.

With natural gas, propane, and electricity, residential users faced the highest prices and industrial users the lowest, with differences ranging up to approximately $9000 per terajoule for propane. On a dollar-per-terajoule basis, coal is the cheapest energy input and electricity and motor gasoline are among the most expensive. For industrial users, natural gas costs between 50 and 200 per cent more than bituminous coal. However, the cost of natural gas is roughly on a par with that of heavy fuel oil and only about 25 per cent of the cost of electricity.

Table B2 combines the data in Tables 4 (in the text) and B1 to show the carbon content (in kilograms) per dollar cost for each of the fuels. The carbon intensity has been standardized so that readers can directly compare it with natural gas for industrial use. The first column is derived by dividing the carbon content of each fuel (expressed in

TABLE A1
Taxes ($/Basic Unit), 1989

Fuels/energy	Carbon	Energy	Ad valorem
Solid: Coal (tonne)			
Canadian bituminous	16.98	12.81	1.52
u.s. bituminous	16.78	12.26	2.64
Lignite	10.04	6.34	0.44
Gaseous (cubic metre)			
Natural gas			
Residential	0.013	0.016	0.009
Commercial	0.013	0.016	0.008
Industrial/transportation	0.013	0.016	0.005
Liquid (litre)			
Motor gasoline	0.016	0.016	0.024
Kerosene	0.017	0.016	0.018
Aviation gasoline	0.016	0.014	0.014
Aviation turbo	0.017	0.015	0.014
Diesel oil	0.018	0.016	0.023
Light fuel oil	0.019	0.016	0.015
Heavy fuel oil	0.021	0.018	0.005
Petroleum coke	0.019	0.018	0.007
Propane			
Residential/transportation	0.010	0.011	0.017
Commercial	0.010	0.011	0.015
Industrial	0.010	0.011	0.006
Electricity (KwH)			
Residential	0.002	0.002	0.003
Commercial	0.002	0.002	0.003
Industrial	0.002	0.002	0.002

Sources: Table 12 and calculations by authors

tonnes per terajoule, Table 4) by the price per terajoule for each fuel
(Table B1). When carbon content is expressed in this manner, the carbon intensity of natural gas (that is, the quantity of carbon in one
dollar's worth of purchased natural gas) for industrial use exceeds that
of electricity and most liquid fuels (except heavy fuel oil and petroleum
coke). The carbon intensity of coal, in contrast, far exceeds that of
natural gas. One dollar's worth of Canadian bituminous coal contains
roughly 22 kilograms of carbon, compared to the nearly five kilograms
of carbon in one dollar's worth of natural gas purchased by industrial
users.

TABLE B1
Fuel/Energy Prices, Ontario, 1989

Fuels/energy	$ NU[a]	NU	$/TJ[b]
Solid: Coal			
Canadian bituminous	31.69		1,045.90
U.S. bituminous	55.11	tonnes	1,900.30
Lignite	9.24		616.00
Gaseous			
Natural gas			
Residential	196.50		5,200.10
Commercial	155.70	megalitres	4,119.90
Industrial/transportation	106.90		2,829.50
Liquid			
Motor gasoline	501.70		14,474.90
Kerosene	386.30		10,252.10
Aviation gasoline	296.80		8,854.40
Aviation turbo	296.80		8,260.50
Diesel oil			
Road	488.00		12,616.30
Rail	247.60		6,401.20
Light fuel oil	317.00		8,195.40
Heavy fuel oil	113.00		2,707.90
Petroleum coke	139.30		3,286.90
Propane			
Residential/transportation	361.70		14,167.60
Commercial	307.20		12,032.90
Industrial	132.80		5,201.70
Electricity			
Residential	60.30		16,750.00
Commercial/transportation	53.90		14,972.20
Industrial	40.40		11,222.20

Source: Ontario Ministry of Energy
[a] NU = natural unit of fuel.
[b] TJ = terajoule of energy.

Appendix C: Sectoral Effects of an Energy Tax and an Ad Valorem Tax

The data in Table C1 are estimated in a manner similar to that used in calculating the figures in Table 13 in the text. In determining the sectoral effects of a $422.65-per-terajoule energy tax, we assume, as with the carbon tax, that the levy would not be treated as a deductible expense for tax purposes. Once again, if the tax is allowed as a deduct-

TABLE B2

Carbon Content (Kilograms) per Dollar Cost (Retail) of Fuel, Ontario, 1989

Fuels	kg/$	Relative to natural gas
Solid: Coal		
Canadian bituminous	21.71	452.9[b]
U.S. bituminous	12.34	257.4
Lignite	44.05	918.8
Gaseous		
Natural gas		
Residential	2.61	54.5
Commercial	3.29	68.7
Industrial/transportation	4.79	100.0
Liquid		
Motor gasoline	1.28	26.7
Kerosene	1.80	37.5
Aviation gasoline	2.14	44.6
Aviation turbo	2.34	48.8
Diesel oil		
Road	1.53	31.9
Rail	3.02	63.0
Light fuel oil	2.43	50.8
Heavy fuel oil	7.45	155.5
Petroleum coke	5.65	117.9
Propane		
Residential/transportation	1.15	24.1
Commercial	1.36	28.4
Industrial	3.14	65.4

Sources: Tables 4 and B1

ible expense, the rate would have had to be higher in order to produce a net revenue of $1 billion for Ontario.

An energy tax would result in slightly higher tax payments, as compared to the carbon tax, for the industrial sector ($366.5 million versus $359.6 million); the residential sector ($209.5 million versus $191.4 million); and the commercial sector ($162.8 million versus $153.4 million). Transportation's tax burden would fall by almost $25 million to $261.1 million. (The energy tax has a larger relative effect on the price of natural gas and a smaller one on the prices of refined petroleum products, and the non-transportation sectors use more natural gas than the transportation sector.)

Again, the largest single source of tax revenues would be motor gasoline used in transportation ($179 million). Next would be the

TABLE C1
Energy Tax ($422.65 per Terajoule) Costs ($ million), by Sector, 1989

Fuels/energy	Residential	Commercial	Industrial	Transportation
Solid				
Canadian bituminous			10.95	
U.S. bituminous			69.54	
Lignite				
Gaseous				
Natural gas	113.90	68.99	160.66	0.20
Liquid				
Motor gasoline		7.21	4.13	179.24
Kerosene	1.57	0.54	0.24	
Aviation gasoline		0.44		0.10
Aviation turbo		2.51		21.88
Diesel oil		10.90	13.73	48.57
Light fuel oil	23.90	6.46	1.99	
Heavy fuel oil	0.06	1.30	17.81	5.87
Petroleum coke			5.61	
Propane	1.67	3.15	6.22	4.70
Electricity	68.41	61.35	75.62	0.57
Total	209.52	162.85	366.51	261.13

Sources: Energy taxes per fuel/energy (expressed in $/TJ, Table 11) times fuel/energy use by sector (in TJ, Table 5)

industrial sector, for natural gas ($160.7 million, or nearly $33 million more than with a carbon tax). The residential sector would face a substantial tax for natural gas ($113.9 million – approximately $24 million more than with a carbon tax). Industry's tax outlays for coal, while still substantial ($80.5 million), would be $29 million lower than with a carbon tax. Tax payments ranging between $60 and $75 million would be made by the residential, commercial, and industrial sectors for use of electricity and by the commercial sector for natural gas.

Table C2 is the energy-tax counterpart to Table 14. It reports the energy tax's effects on key subsectors within industry and transportation. We calculated the data using the same procedures as for Table C1. Total manufacturing bears the greatest burden, with potential tax liabilities of $327.5 million, a modest improvement from the carbon tax. Once more, within manufacturing the areas that appear particularly hard hit are iron and steel (tax payments of $107.3 million – a slight improvement because of the smaller effect of an energy tax on coal); pulp, paper, and sawmills ($34.6 million in taxes); and chemicals

TABLE C2
Energy Tax Costs, Industry and Transportation, 1989

Sectors and subsectors	$ million	% of totals in Table C1
Industrial		
Agriculture	18.0	1.8
Construction	5.3	0.5
Mining	16.3	1.6
Forestry	0.7	0.1
Manufacturing	327.5	32.8
Chemicals	31.8	3.2
Iron and steel	107.3	10.7
Smelting and refining	6.9	0.7
Cement	13.5	1.4
Pulp, paper, and sawmills	34.6	3.5
Total industrial	366.5	36.7
Transportation		
Rail	11.8	1.2
Domestic airlines	17.6	1.8
Foreign airlines	4.3	0.4
Domestic marine	4.8	0.5
Foreign marine	4.5	0.4
Truck and urban transit	26.6	2.7
Retail pump sales	191.4	19.1

Sources: Table C1 and see Table 5.

($21.8 million). Within transportation, retail pump sales would generate taxes of $191 million and truck operators and urban transit systems would pay about $27 million, primarily for diesel fuel. The effect on domestic airlines would be somewhat smaller ($18 million) than with a carbon tax, but the competitive-cost disadvantage relative to U.S. carriers would still be present.

An ad valorem tax affects the sectors differently. Since this type of tax has a greater relative effect on the prices of refined petroleum products and electricity than either of the other two types of taxes, and hence a relatively smaller effect on natural gas and coal, transportation would be most vulnerable (see Table C3). Its tax burden would rise to almost 40 per cent ($394.4 million) of the aggregate $1 billion in revenues generated by this tax. Its burden would be roughly $108 million greater than with a carbon tax, and $133 million more than with an energy tax.

The industrial sector would benefit the most from an ad valorem

TABLE C3
Ad Valorem Energy Tax (4.79%) Burden ($ million), by Sector, 1989

Fuels/energy	Residential	Commercial	Industrial	Transportation
Solid				
Canadian bituminous˙			1.30	
U.S. bituminous			14.98	
Lignite				
Gaseous				
Natural gas	67.12	32.21	51.52	0.06
Liquid fuels				
Motor gasoline		11.82	6.77	294.04
Kerosene	1.83	0.63	0.28	
Aviation gasoline		0.45		0.10
Aviation turbo		2.35		20.48
Diesel oil		15.59	19.64	69.44
Light fuel oil	22.20	6.00	1.85	
Heavy fuel oil	0.02	0.40	5.47	1.80
Petroleum coke			2.09	
Propane	2.68	4.30	3.67	7.53
Electricity	129.87	104.10	96.18	0.97
Total	223.72	177.84	203.74	394.45

Sources: Ad valorem taxes per fuel/energy (in % Table 11) times fuel/energy
expenditures by sector (in $ million, Table 6)

tax, compared with either of the other taxes. The tax burden would
exceed $203 million, which is well below the $360 million for both the
carbon and the energy taxes. The reduction would result from the sharp
decline in tax payments for use of natural gas ($51.5 million, compared
with $160.7 million under an energy tax) and coal ($16.3 million, down
from $109.7 million with a carbon tax). The residential and commercial
sectors would face higher tax payments (about 10 per cent greater)
than with an energy tax.

An ad valorem tax would generate 29 per cent of the aggregate
revenue from the 2.4-cents-per-litre tax on motor gasoline used in
transportation. The next largest sources of revenue would be use of
electricity by the residential ($129.9 million), commercial ($104.1
million), and industrial ($96.2 million) sectors.

The tax burden on use of natural gas and coal would decline sharply
with an ad valorem tax. For example, for the residential, commercial,
and industrial sectors, total tax payments for use of natural gas would

be $150.8 million with an ad valorem tax, compared with $272 million with a carbon tax and $343.6 million with an energy tax.

In Table C4, with subsectoral breakdowns for industry and transportation, we find that an ad valorem tax on retail pump sales in transportation would produce approximately 31 per cent of the total revenues. The aggregate tax burden on manufacturing ($168.1 million) would be about 50 per cent smaller than with either an energy tax ($327.5 million) or a carbon tax ($331.7 million). The iron and steel industry would gain the most from a shift from either a carbon tax (tax payments of $130 million) or an energy tax ($107 million) to a carbon tax ($36 million), primarily because of the sharp drop in the tax on coal.

Appendix D: Short-Run Effects of an Adjusted Environment Tax on Energy Use

To obtain data in Table D1, we repeated the exercise used in deriving Table 19, but assuming that coal is a feedstock for the iron and steel and the cement industries. Since this adjustment generates higher tax levels or rates and, correspondingly, larger increases in the prices of the various energy inputs, we find marginally greater effects (in absolute terms) for the residential, commercial, and transportation sectors than is the case in Table 19, where unadjusted tax rates are used.

The results for the industrial sector, however, change significantly for the carbon and energy taxes. Inter-fuel substitutions become even more pronounced with the adjusted tax rates. With the carbon tax, aggregate use of energy might increase in the short run, as a consequence of the dramatic switch from electricity to natural gas and petroleum products. While the percentage decline in use of coal is very large, the base has been sharply cut and so the resulting decline in use of coal is about one-tenth (0.9 petajoules) of that reported in Table 19 (8.8 petajoules).

The energy tax appears to lead to a net short-term decrease of 1.8 petajoules in this sector's aggregate use of energy. This figure is well below the reduction of 11.9 petajoules shown in Table 19, where the energy tax is not adjusted. The adjusted energy tax does not seem to reduce industry's use of natural gas; there is a modest increase of 0.2 per cent.

The aggregate reductions in use of energy are smaller (in absolute terms) with a carbon and an energy tax (0.2 and 1.0 per cent, respectively) than in the case where the effects of these taxes are estimated while treating coal as an energy input for all manufacturing industries (1.0 and 1.2 per cent, respectively). The adjusted ad valorem tax pro-

TABLE C4
Ad Valorem Tax Burden, Industry and Transportation, 1989

Sectors and subsectors	$ million	% of totals in Table 13
Industrial		
Agriculture	20.2	2.0
Construction	6.8	0.7
Mining	14.9	1.5
Forestry	1.0	0.1
Manufacturing	168.1	16.8
Chemicals	19.8	2.0
Iron and steel	36.5	3.7
Smelting and refining	3.7	0.4
Cement	4.2	0.4
Pulp, paper, and sawmills	23.8	2.4
Total	203.7	20.4
Transportation		
Rail	8.5	0.9
Domestic airlines	16.5	1.7
Foreign airlines	4.0	0.4
Domestic marine	3.2	0.3
Foreign marine	3.6	0.4
Truck and urban transit	40.0	4.0
Retail pump sales	310.3	31.0
Total	394.4	39.4

Sources: Table C3 and see Table 6.

duces a marginally larger cutback in use of energy by all four sectors in the short run.

We caution against accepting at face value the results for the industrial sector with the adjusted tax rates because the elasticity estimates were derived from data that counted coal as an energy input for the iron and steel and the cement industries. We suspect that if the elasticities were re-estimated with use of coal as a feedstock removed from the data, the results would not be as dramatically different and there would not be the anomalous outcome for the carbon tax – that is, an increase in industry's aggregate use of energy.

Appendix E: Long-Run Effects of an Adjusted Environment Tax on Energy Use

If we perform the same exercise employed in deriving Table 20, using instead the adjusted tax rates and treating coal as a feedstock for the

TABLE D1
Short-Term Effects (%, TJ) of Taxes (Adjusted for Treatment of Coal as a Feedstock) on Energy Use by Fuel, by Sector, 1989

Sector	Carbon	Energy	Ad valorem
SHORT-TERM EFFECTS (%)			
Residential			
Electricity	−0.7	−0.5	−1.7
Natural gas	−1.0	−2.0	−0.2
Oil products	−3.0	−2.1	−2.3
Total	−1.2	−1.5	−1.0
Commercial			
Electricity	0.6	1.1	−1.3
Natural gas	−3.5	−4.6	−1.3
Oil products	−0.6	0.3	−1.3
Total	−1.4	−1.6	−1.3
Industrial			
Electricity	−9.5	−5.6	−0.2
Natural gas	4.3	0.2	−0.2
Oil products	12.0	7.7	−0.2
Coal	−12.2	−6.3	−0.2
Total	1.7	−0.3	−0.2
Transportation			
Oil products	−0.7	−0.7	−1.0
SHORT-TERM EFFECTS (TJ)			
Residential			
Electricity	−1,160	−888	−2,759
Natural gas	−2,749	−5,371	−666
Oil products	−1,828	−1,266	−1,383
Total	−5,737	−7,525	−4,808
Commercial			
Electricity	896	1,609	−1,838
Natural gas	−5,959	−7,799	−2,161
Oil products	−384	214	−880
Total	−5,447	−5,976	−4,879
Industrial			
Electricity	−16,948	−9,982	−427
Natural gas	16,814	763	−923
Oil products	12,307	7,891	−246
Coal	−863	−450	−17
Total	11,310	−1,778	−1,613
Transportation			
Oil products	−4,484	−4,027	−6,186
Total (TJ)	−4,358	−19,306	−17,486
Total (%)	−0.2%	−1.0%	−0.9%

iron and steel and the cement industries, we find that the long-term effects on aggregate energy use and carbon dioxide emissions would be substantially smaller. The long-term effects of the adjusted and unadjusted taxes are compared in Table E1.

The adjusted taxes produce larger cuts in energy use by the residential, commercial, and transportation sectors (motor gasoline) than do the unadjusted taxes. This follows from the higher tax rates that are required to offset lost revenues from taxation of coal as a feedstock. But the reduction in industry's energy use is much smaller, anywhere from 4.6 petajoules lower for the ad valorem tax to 46.6 petajoules lower for the carbon tax. Consequently, aggregate use of energy does not decline as much with the adjusted taxes as with the unadjusted ones. The decrease is 92 per cent of the level of the reduction in the case of the ad valorem tax (47.7 petajoules versus 51.8 petajoules); 70 per cent for the energy tax (64.3 versus 91.1 petajoules); and 50 per cent for the carbon tax (45.3 versus 90.1 petajoules).

Industry's smaller decline in energy use translates into proportionately smaller cutbacks in carbon dioxide emissions. Even allowing for this sector's lower emission base (39,700 kilotonnes versus 55,200 kilotonnes) when coal is treated as a feedstock, the percentage reductions in emissions from the 1989 base levels would be significantly smaller under a carbon and an energy tax. The same story unfolds at the aggregate level. Obviously, the treatment of coal for tax purposes plays a key role in terms of both economic and environmental effects.

Appendix F: Tax Rates to Generate Net Revenues of $1 Billion

We use data in Tables 19 and 20 in the text to estimate the tax savings for each sector resulting from inter-fuel and factor substitutions (Table F1). We multiply the changes in the use of each type of energy resulting from a specific tax by the appropriate tax rate (Table 11). In the short run, each sector would pay approximately 1 per cent less in environment tax than the figures reported in Tables 13, C1, and C3. In total, tax payments would be $10.8 million less than the $1-billion figure for the carbon tax; $11.9 million less for the energy tax; and $9.5 million less for the ad valorem tax. Thus, for the various environment taxes to generate net revenues of $1 billion in the short run, they would have to be approximately 1 per cent higher than those used in this study – approximately $24.95 per tonne for the carbon tax; $427.74 per terajoule for the energy tax; and 4.84 per cent for the ad valorem tax.

In the long run, the aggregate reductions in the tax payments would

TABLE E1

Long-Term Reductions (Terajoules [%]) in Energy Use and Carbon Dioxide Emissions Resulting from Adjusted and Unadjusted Taxes, with Base Year 1989

Sector	Carbon	Energy	Ad valorem
REDUCTIONS IN ENERGY USE			
Residential			
Unadjusted	655(0.1)	3,442(0.7)	1,516(0.3)
Adjusted	734(0.1)	3,750(0.8)	1,540(0.3)
Commercial			
Unadjusted	12,347(3.2)	13,510(3.5)	11,377(3.0)
Adjusted	13,801(3.6)	14,653(3.8)	11,566(3.0)
Industrial			
Unadjusted	65,771(7.6)	63,837(7.4)	23,266(2.7)
Adjusted	19,195(2.8)	35,544(5.2)	18,674(2.7)
Transportation			
Unadjusted	11,367(1.9)	10,354(1.7)	15,646(2.6)
Adjusted	11,530(1.9)	10,354(1.7)	15,907(2.6)
Total			
Unadjusted	90,140(3.8)	91,143(3.9)	51,805(2.2)
Adjusted	45,260(1.9)	64,301(2.7)	47,687(2.0)
REDUCTIONS IN CARBON DIOXIDE EMISSIONS			
Industrial			
Unadjusted	4,723(8.6)	4,062(7.4)	1,479(2.7)
Adjusted	1,116(2.8)	1,885(4.8)	1,083(2.7)
Total			
Unadjusted	6,350(4.3)	5,755(3.9)	3,481(2.4)
Adjusted	2,853(2.1)	3,662(2.7)	3,112(2.4)

Sources: Tables 17, 20, and 21

TABLE F1

Reductions ($000 [%]), in Revenue from Taxes on Energy Inputs Resulting from Effects of Taxes on Energy Use, Short Term and Long Term, by Sector, 1989

Sector	Carbon	Energy	Ad valorem
Short-term effects	2,082.7(1.1)	2,833.4(1.4)	2,874.2(1.3)
Residential			
Commercial	1,605.0(1.0)	2,330.3(1.4)	1,974.6(1.1)
Industrial	5,066.5(1.4)	5,032.8(1.4)	481.3(0.2)
Transportation	2,033.2(1.0)	1,703.4(0.9)	4,216.9(1.4)
Total	10,787.4	11,899.9	9,547.0
Long-term effects			
Residential	1,156.2(0.6)	1,456.0(0.7)	3,649.8(1.6)
Commercial	4,509.4(2.9)	5,714.7(3.5)	4,688.7(2.6)
Industrial	31,605.9(8.6)	29,329.9(8.0)	5,539.0(2.7)
Transportation	5,228.8(2.5)	4,379.7(2.3)	10,842.7(3.5)
Total	42,500.3	40,880.3	24,720.2

Sources: For short term, Tables 19 and 11; for long term, Tables 20 and 11

range from 2.5 per cent ($24.7 million) for the ad valorem tax to 4.2 per cent ($42.5 million) for the carbon tax. To generate $1 billion in net revenues in the long term, each of the tax levels would have to be increased marginally, to $25.78 for the carbon tax, $440.66 for the energy tax, and 4.91 per cent for the ad valorem tax.

Notes

1 Multilateral negotiations, held under the auspices of the United Nations Environment Programme (UNEP), produced in 1985 a framework (the Vienna Convention) for the protection of the ozone layer. Signatories agreed to take the necessary actions to protect the environment against further modifications of the ozone layer (UNEP 1989, 8). Another conference convened by the UNEP to build upon the Vienna Convention was held in Montreal in 1987. The resulting Montreal Protocol called for reduction and eventual elimination of ozone-damaging chlorofluoro-carbons and halons. The protocol was initially signed by 29 countries (including Canada) and the European Community, and by the end of 1990 another 27 countries had ratified the agreement.
2 The United States finally may be addressing this issue in light of President Clinton's proposed energy tax.
3 In order to make the project manageable, given time and budgetary constraints, we were not asked to consider tradeable permits or command and control regulations as alternative or complementary policy initiatives.
4 Some form of input tax would have similar advantages over tradeable permits based on carbon dioxide emissions, since the residential sector and drivers using motor gasoline accounted for approximately 26 per cent of all such emissions in Ontario in 1989.
5 Tonnes are metric tonnes, which are the equivalent of 1000 kilograms. One British thermal unit (BTU) is equal to 1054.6 joules. One terajoule is equal to 10^{12} joules, and one petajoule equals 10^3 terajoules. One kilolitre (kilotonne) equals 1000 litres (tonnes), and one megalitre (megawatt hour – MwH) equals 1000 kilolitres (kilowatt hours – KwH). See Statistics Canada (1992).
6 The residential sector contains single and multiple-dwelling units, which are owned or rented. The commercial sector covers schools, religious institutions, hospitals, retail stores, offices, hotels, restaurants, warehouses, government buildings, and street lighting. The industrial sector consists of agriculture, construction, mining, forestry, and manufactur-

ing. Included in the transportation sector are rail, airlines, marine services, truck operators, urban transit, and personal use of automobiles.

7 According to the Canadian Portland Cement Association, natural gas also can be used as a feedstock by the cement industry. Adopting this assumption instead results in a sharp decline in industry's use of coal as an energy input – from 190.4 petajoules (as reported in Table 5) to 7.1 petajoules.

8 If we adjust expenditure figures for industry to exclude use of coal as a feedstock, expenditures on coal by this sector fall by $332.4 million. Industry's total expenditures for energy inputs decline from $4.2 billion to $3.9 billion.

9 The carbon contents of the fossil fuels used by each of these sectors are estimated by multiplying the energy use (in terajoules) of each of the fuels (Table 5) by the carbon content (expressed in tonnes per terajoule of energy, Table 4) of each fuel. A different procedure is used for estimating the carbon content of electricity. The total carbon content of the fuels used in electricity generation by Ontario Hydro is prorated over the primary electricity consumed by these four sectors. The implicit carbon content for electricity consumed in the province in 1989 was 17.51 tonnes per terajoule, or 63.04 tonnes per gigawatt hour (GwH) of electricity. Hence, the carbon content in electricity generation by Hydro is allocated to the sectors using electricity as an energy input. The authors and the FTC agreed to assume that Hydro would be exempt from an energy or ad valorem tax and, in the case of a carbon tax, would fully pass on the tax to its customers. Moreover, it was agreed to assume that a carbon tax and the carbon content of the fossil fuels used by Hydro would be fully allocated to direct users of Hydro-provided electricity as an energy input.

10 The carbon dioxide emissions are calculated in a manner similar to that used for estimating carbon contents. Energy use (in terajoules) of each of the fuels (Table 5) is multiplied by the respective carbon dioxide emission factors (expressed in tonnes per terajoule of energy, Table 3) for each fuel. As above, a different procedure is employed for electricity, since its use as a primary energy source does not result in emission of carbon dioxide into the atmosphere. Carbon dioxide is emitted when electricity is generated using fossil fuels, most notably coal. The carbon dioxide emitted in electricity generation is prorated over the electricity consumed by these sectors in Ontario. The implicit emissions for electricity consumed in Ontario in 1989 were 63.93 tonnes per terajoule. The carbon dioxide emitted in electricity generation was allocated to the sectors using electricity as an energy input.

11 Actual emissions by this industry would still remain in the 19,000-kilotonne range, but only a fraction would be recorded as resulting from use of coal as an energy input.

12 According to the calculations discussed in Appendix F, the behavioural responses to an environment tax would not result in more than a 1 per cent decrease in our $1-billion revenue assumption.

13 This figure is derived by dividing the $1-billion revenue target by the aggregate carbon content of the fuels and electricity used by the residential, commercial, industrial, and transportation sectors in 1989 (see Table 8). This tax is translated into one dollar per terajoule of energy for each fossil fuel by multiplying by the respective carbon content factors for the fuels (tonnes per terajoule reported in Table 4). The carbon content of electricity is estimated by prorating the carbon content of fossil fuels used by Ontario Hydro in generating electricity over the total electricity used by residential, commercial, industrial, and transportation sectors as a primary energy input. In the calculations, it is assumed that Hydro acts as a conduit with respect to the carbon tax, passing on fully to its customers in these four sectors any carbon taxes that it pays. Hydro received one of our questionnaires and its response to the question regarding the extent to which a carbon tax would be passed on to customers supported our assumption. Hydro would pass on fully a carbon tax.

14 This tax rate is calculated in a manner similar to that used for the carbon tax. That is, the $1-billion target is divided by aggregate use of energy (measured in terajoules, Table 5) by the four sectors. In this case, electricity is subject to the same tax as are the fossil fuels, and no separate calculations were necessary. Moreover, Ontario Hydro is assumed to be exempt from this tax. In other words, the energy tax is levied directly on end-users in the four sectors.

15 In this case as well, Ontario Hydro is assumed to be exempt.

16 The relative effects of the carbon, energy, and/or ad valorem taxes (derived by treating coal as a feedstock) on the prices of fossil fuels and electricity can be derived in a relatively straightforward manner from the data in Table 12. For the carbon tax, the corresponding figures in this table should be increased by 11.8 per cent. Thus, for example, the increase in the price of Canadian bituminous coal would be 59.9 per cent with the higher carbon tax. Natural gas prices for residential, commercial, and industrial users would rise by 7.2, 9.1, and 13.2 per cent, respectively. Electricity prices would be 2.9, 3.2, and 4.3 per cent higher for residential, commercial/transportation, and industrial users, respectively. With the "coal adjusted" energy tax ($458.15 per terajoule), the

price increases in Table 12 should be marked up by 8.4 per cent. For a
similarly adjusted ad valorem tax, the rate in the ad valorem tax column
in Table 12 would become 4.87 per cent.

17 Gibbons and Valiante (1991, 42) noted these same observations: "a relatively high proportion of the [energy prices for residential, commercial,
and transportation users] consist of taxes (e.g., the federal and provincial
gasoline taxes) and/or delivery and administration mark ups."

18 In deriving the carbon tax and tax effects by sector, we assume that the
tax would not be treated as a business expense for tax purposes. If it
were so treated, the carbon tax rate would have to be greater in order
to generate a net revenue of $1 billion, and the relative effects of this
adjusted tax would be different from those reported in Table 13. More of
the burden would be borne by the residential sector, since the tax would
not be a business expense for most residential consumers of energy.

19 The U.S. Environmental Protection Agency (EPA) (1990, VII-10) has
pointed out that the existing automobile fleet is replaced over an 8- to 12-
year period, major home appliances and space heating and cooling systems over a 10- to 20-year period, and industrial equipment over a 10- to
25-year period; buildings are in use for 40 or more years.

20 Factor intensity is a relative concept. One production technology uses
one factor of production more intensively than another relative to
another production technology if the former uses a greater proportion of
this factor in the production of one unit of output than does the other
technology. In comparing the energy intensities of industries, we can say
that one industry uses energy more intensively than another if energy
accounts for a larger proportion of its total costs than in the case of the
other industry.

21 The EPA (1990, VII-10) commented that the process might be accelerated if
government policies encouraged faster turnover of the existing stock of
consumer durables. Since there is much uncertainty regarding future
energy savings, and consumers have limited access to capital, consumers' decisions are more sensitive to policies that reduce "up-front"
costs of durable goods.

22 Companies will invest in searching for or adopting new production technologies if expected returns warrant. If the potential savings from minimizing the effects of an environment tax are small, the investment in
more energy-efficient production technologies might not be made.

23 The own-price elasticity of demand measures the percentage change in
the quantity demanded of a product resulting from a small percentage
change in its own price.

24 The cross-price elasticity measures the percentage change in the quantity

demanded of a product caused by a small percentage change in the price of another product. If the figure is positive, the two commodities are complements; if it is negative, they are substitutes.

25 They combine the effects of inter-fuel substitutions (except for motor gasoline sales) and energy conservation/efficiency (substitution by producers of other factors of production for energy and replacement of existing energy-inefficient durable goods by new, energy-efficient goods). But they do not factor in the product substitutions by consumers on the product mix and resulting energy demands in the industrial sector. Nor do they directly measure the effects of switching to suppliers and/or production facilities located outside Ontario.

26 The estimates are obtained by using the appropriate relative price effects for the various energy inputs (in Table 18), together with the appropriate price elasticities. For example, to estimate the potential short-run effect of a carbon tax on industry's use of electricity, we combine the price increases for electricity, oil, natural gas, and coal that would result from a carbon tax (3.8, 6.6, 11.6, and 32.3 per cent, respectively; Table 18) with the own-price elasticity of demand for electricity by the industrial sector (-0.147) and the cross-price elasticities of demand for electricity with respect to oil, natural gas, and coal (0.227, 0.077, and -0.206, respectively) as follows: % change in use of electricity by industry = $-0.147*0.038 + 0.227*0.066 + 0.077*0.116 - 0.206*0.323 = -0.041$. These effects are translated into actual changes in use of various types of energy by sector by multiplying the energy use data in Table 5 by the corresponding percentage changes in the upper half of Table 19.

27 The reported effects of an ad valorem tax are the same for each energy type in both commerce and industry (an across-the-board decrease of 1.2 per cent in the former and of 0.2 per cent in the latter). The similar effects are what one should expect with an ad valorem tax, because there would be no inter-fuel substitutions. The results for the residential sector do not follow this pattern, because the elasticities were estimated using a different procedure, which did not allow for consistency in outcomes.

28 The appropriate relative-price effects for the various energy inputs (in Table 18) are combined with the appropriate long-term, own- and cross-price elasticities estimated by Elkhafif. The potential long-run effect of a carbon tax on industry's use of electricity is estimated by using the relative price increases for electricity, oil, natural gas, and coal that would result from a carbon tax (3.8, 6.6, 11.6, and 32.3 per cent, respectively; Table 18), together with industry's long-term, own-price elasticity of demand for electricity (-0.697) and the cross-price elasticities of demand for electricity with respect to oil, natural gas, and coal (0.297, 0.040, and

− 0.200, respectively) as follows: % change in long-term use of electricity by industry =

− 0.697*0.038 + 0.297*0.066 + 0.040*0.116 − 0.200*0.323 = − 0.054.

As above, the effects are translated into actual changes in use of various types of energy by sector by multiplying the energy use data in Table 5 by the corresponding percentage changes in the upper half of Table 20.

29 For each sector, the long-run reductions (measured in terajoules) in use of each fossil fuel and electricity are multiplied by the corresponding carbon dioxide factor (Table 3) to yield the resulting cutbacks in emissions (measured in kilotonnes).

30 We assume, for example, that if the tax rate doubles, so too would the estimated effect on emissions.

31 The assumption of a particular average annual growth rate does not require that the growth rate be equal to this value each year. Over the 15-year period, cumulative growth is equivalent to what the average annual growth rate would produce. Thus, even though we have experienced growth in Ontario since 1989 that is well below an average of 1 per cent per year, it is conceivable that by the year 2004 growth could pick up sufficiently so that the average rate might exceed 1 per cent.

32 Income elasticity measures the effect on the quantity demanded of a product as a result of a small change in real income or real gross domestic product.

33 Hoeller, Dean, and Nicolaisen (1991), in reviewing a number of the more important empirical studies of the effects of carbon taxes on emissions, found that most of the studies concluded that carbon taxes would have to far exceed u.s.$50 per tonne to achieve stabilization. Only Jorgenson and Wilcoxen (1991) found that a relatively low tax rate (u.s.$15 – $20) would achieve this goal.

34 The Congressional Budget Office (1990, xii, xiii) stated that the following industries would be most hurt by a carbon tax: steel, clay, glass, rubber, plastics, and chemicals. Other studies have added the pulp and paper and cement industries to this list.

35 While we are able to calculate aggregate energy intensities for 1989, we have to rely in Table 23 on Statistics Canada (1984) in order to estimate the effects of the taxes on the weighted average costs of energy for the listed industries. Indeed, 1984 was the last year for which Statistics Canada disaggregated total energy expenditures by industries into spending on each of the various types of fossil fuels and electricity. To estimate the energy cost effects of the taxes, we assume that the distributions of expenditures on specific fuels and electricity are identical in 1989 and 1984. Thus we calculate the effects for 1989 by taking a weighted average

of the percentage increases in the prices of the various energy inputs, where the weights are the 1984 expenditures shares. Obviously, these weights changed between 1984 and 1989, but there are no data publicly available that we could have used to estimate the direction and magnitude of the changes. We suspect that if we had the actual 1989 weights, the revised estimates would be within a very small range of the numbers reported in Tables 23 and 24.

36 In this study, we define energy-intensive industries to be those for which energy costs exceed 5 per cent of total costs.

37 In Table 23, an ad valorem tax of 4.8 per cent generates energy-cost increases of less than 4.8 per cent for many industries because some of the energy inputs used would not be subject to the tax.

38 The data in this table are obtained by multiplying together the energy intensities and the energy-cost increases produced by the respective taxes.

39 To do so, we use the input-output data published by Statistics Canada. The last year for which these data are available is 1988, and the data relate to the input-output relationships at the national level. We did not use the 1984 input-output table for Ontario for several reasons: provincial input-output tables are less reliable than national data; 1988 was near the peak of economic activity, while the economy was in the early stages of a recovery in 1984; and since Ontario is the "industrial heartland" of Canada, the input-output relations for manufacturing probably provide a reasonable approximation for the corresponding relations in Ontario. We incorporate two additional assumptions into the exercise for estimating the longer-term, equilibrium effects on costs. First, for the industries and services for which we do not have any data on expenditures on energy inputs, we assume that the first-round effects on their costs would be zero. Second, we assume that at each stage the entire cost increase would be fully passed on by each industry. At each stage, we estimate the weighted average increase in costs for the non-energy inputs of each industry. The incremental effects are added to the direct effects caused by the tax, and a new iteration follows. We repeat these steps until the incremental effects for each manufacturing industry and for mining fall below a specified threshold.

40 All the companies were informed that the tax would not apply to use of fossil fuels as non-energy inputs.

41 To put this into the context of own- and cross-price elasticities, for a certain range of price increases the elasticities might be zero. For a marginally higher range, they might be very large. In other words, we are looking at discontinuous rather than continuous relationships at the firm

level. Of course, aggregating over a large number of companies might produce a continuous relationship.

42 In essence, we have assumed throughout this study that Ontario consumers of fossil fuels face a perfectly elastic supply curve, so that any environment tax would be passed on fully to them.

43 The federal government also has commented on the limited effectiveness of a unilateral tax initiative: "Production of imported goods will presumably cause more emissions than domestic production because the foreign competition will not have to pay the tax. Environmental consequence of the unilateral tax may therefore be quite small" (Environment Canada 1992, 83).

44 A GATT panel has upheld the U.S. government's right to impose a superfund levy on imported as well as domestic products.

45 Tradeable permits would face higher administrative costs than a tax scheme. In addition, enforcement and monitoring would be expensive. A system of tradeable permits merits serious consideration when there are only a few polluters. For carbon dioxide emissions, the number of sources is too large to warrant experimentation with such a scheme. Moreover, as we have already pointed out, there are no obvious incentive advantages, in the short run, for an output tax over an input tax. Tradeable permits are analogous to an output tax.

46 Although, by itself, it will have the smallest effect in reducing emissions, new regulations and investment incentives could render this disadvantage relatively insignificant. If exemptions are to be provided for the iron and steel and the cement industries, then our findings show that an ad valorem tax would reduce emissions more than would a carbon tax. The energy tax would still be 25 per cent more effective in reducing emissions in Ontario.

Bibliography

Australia, Industry Commission. 1991. *Costs and Benefits of Reducing Greenhouse Gas Emissions, Volume 1: Report.* Canberra: Australian Government Publishing Service

Bergman, Lars. 1991. "Comments." In *Global Warming: Economic Policy Responses*, ed. Rudiger Dornbusch and James M. Porterba, 105–8. Cambridge, Mass.: MIT Press

Bierbaum, Rosina. 1991. "Prepared Statement." In *Hearing before the Subcommittee on Environmental Protection of the Committee on Environment and Public Works*, U.S. Senate, 222–32. Washington, DC: U.S. Government Printing Office

Bye, B., T. Bye, and L. Lorentsen. 1989. *SIMEN: Studies of Industry, Environment*

and Energy towards 2000, Discussion Paper No. 44. Oslo: Central Bureau of
Statistics

Congressional Budget Office (CBO). 1990. *Carbon Charges as a Response to
Global Warming: The Effects of Taxing Fossil Fuels.* Washington, D.C.: U.S.
Congress

Elkhafif, Mahmoud A.T. 1992. "Estimating Disaggregated Price Elasticities in
Industrial Energy Demand." *Energy Journal,* 13: 1–9

Environment Canada. 1990. *Canada's Green Plan for a Healthy Environment.*
Ottawa: Government of Canada

– 1992. *Economic Instruments for Environmental Protection, Discussion Paper.*
Ottawa: Government of Canada

Environmental Protection Agency (EPA). 1990. *Policy Options for Stabilizing
Global Climate, Report to Congress.* Washington, D.C.: U.S. EPA

Gibbons, Jack, and Marcia Valiante. 1991. *Carbon Taxes and Tradeable Carbon
Quotas: A Least Cost Strategy to Reduce Ontario's Carbon Dioxide Emissions.*
Toronto: Canadian Institute for Environmental Law and Policy

Hoeller, Peter, and Markku Wallin. 1991. "Energy Prices, Taxes and Carbon
Dioxide Emissions." *OECD Economic Studies,* 17:92–105

Hoeller, Peter, Andrew Dean, and Jon Nicolaisen. 1991. "Macroeconomic
Implications of Reducing Greenhouse Gas Emissions: A Survey of Empirical Studies." *OECD Economic Studies,* 16:46–77

Homung, Robert. 1990. "The Carbon Dioxide Report for Ontario." In *The
Carbon Dioxide Report for Canada,* ed. Friends of the Earth, 32–35. Ottawa:
Friends of the Earth

International Energy Agency (IEA). 1989. *Energy and the Environment: Policy
Overview.* Paris: OECD

Jacques, A.P. 1992. *Canada's Greenhouse Gas Emissions: Estimates for 1990.*
Ottawa: Environment Canada.

Jorgenson, Dale W., and Peter J. Wilcoxen. 1991. *Reducing US Carbon Dioxide
Emissions: The Cost of Different Goals,* Harvard Institute for Economic
Research Discussion Paper No. 1575. Cambridge, Mass.: Harvard Univer-
sity

Lashof, Daniel A., and Dennis A. Tirpak. 1990. *Policy Options for Stabilizing
Global Climate, Report to Congress.* Washington, DC: U.S. Environmental Protection Agency

Ontario. 1990. Ministry of Energy. *Global Warming: Towards a Strategy for
Ontario.* Toronto: Queen's Printer for Ontario

Ontario Global Warming Coalition. 1991. *Degrees of Change: Steps towards an
Ontario Global Warming Strategy.* Toronto: Coalition

Organisation for Economic Cooperation and Development (OECD). 1991.
Responding to Climate Change: Selected Economic Issues. Paris: OECD

Porterba, James M. 1991. "Tax Policy to Combat Global Warming: On

Designing a Carbon Tax." In *Global Warming, Economic Policy Responses*, ed.
Rudiger Dornbusch and James M. Porterba, 71–97. Cambridge, Mass.: MIT
Press

Robinson, Colin. 1987. "Opening Address to IEA Energy Demand Analysis
Symposium." In *Energy Demand Analysis Symposium, Proceedings*, 12–22.
Paris: IEA

Statistics Canada. 1984. *Consumption of Purchased Fuel and Electricity, 1984*.
Cat. 57-208. Ottawa: Supply and Services

– 1988a. *The Input-Output Structure of the Canadian Economy, 1988*. Cat. 15-
501. Ottawa: Supply and Services

– 1988b. *Manufacturing Industries of Canada: National and Provincial Areas,
1988*. Cat. 31-203. Ottawa: Supply and Services

– 1989. *General Review of the Mineral Industries, 1989*. Cat. 26-201. Ottawa:
Supply and Services

– 1990. *Quarterly Report on Energy Supply-Demand in Canada, 1989-IV*.
August. Cat. 57-003, Vol. 14, No. 4. Ottawa: Supply and Services

– 1992. *Energy Statistics Handbook*. Cat. No. 57-601. Ottawa: Government of
Canada Printing Office

United Nations Environment Programme (UNEP). 1989. *Action on Ozone*. New
York: United Nations

Williams, Robert H. 1990. "Low-Cost Strategies for Coping with CO_2 Emission Limits." *Energy Journal*, 11:35–59

4 Ontario Tax Expenditures

SHEILA M. BLOCK and ALLAN M. MASLOVE

Introduction[1]

Information about tax expenditures is useful to governments and legislatures alike. For governments, it is a major component of effective fiscal management; for legislatures, it is a prerequisite to maintaining control of the budget and to making government accountable both to the legislature and, ultimately, to the electorate.

To evaluate the effectiveness of existing tax expenditures, it is necessary to identify which provisions in the tax system are tax expenditures, explain why they exist, and determine how much they cost. This paper serves as input into this exercise by identifying the major tax expenditures currently provided by the Ontario government (Queen's Park) through its taxing statutes – personal income tax, corporate taxes (corporate income tax, capital tax, employer health tax, and mining tax), and the retail sales tax. Where possible, the most recent available cost estimate of each tax expenditure is also reported.

Discussion of tax expenditures often focuses on three sets of issues: identification and quantification, effectiveness, and process.

Identification and Quantification

It is essential to distinguish between two types of tax provisions – those that define the base, the rates, the tax unit, and the accounting period, in order to achieve the desired properties of the tax system, and those intended to promote certain types of behaviour or to support certain groups. The former are part of the "benchmark" tax system, while the latter are tax expenditures. To illustrate, there are provisions within any tax statute that define a fair measure of the tax base and that also (incidentally) reduce taxes. For example, provisions that allow for deduction of expenses incurred to earn business income are necessary to calculate net income and, therefore, should be characterized as an integral part of any business income tax system, not as a tax expenditure. Similarly, provisions designed to compensate for failure of the tax system to adjust for inflation, such as indexation of exemptions and brackets in personal income tax, and provisions intended to avoid double taxation of income, such as the foreign tax credit, should not be considered tax expenditures.

Effectiveness

We can compare the relative merits and effectiveness of pursuing policy goals by means of tax expenditures or by direct grants and subsidies (or potentially direct provision by government). On a case-by-case basis, which type of instrument is more effective in attaining social objectives? Which offers government better fiscal control? Which embodies better potential for public accountability? For example, how does the existence of tax expenditures affect the equity properties of a single tax and of the overall tax system? In particular, do tax expenditures tend to erode the progressivity of tax systems?

Process

Issues of process and tax policy include the relationship between making of tax policy and policy making in other areas that involve tax instruments. Can budget processes be improved with respect to treatment of these tax measures?

Structure of This Paper

This paper addresses primarily the first set of issues and, to a lesser extent, the second; the third set is treated in a separate study (see Lindquist 1994). The structure of the paper is as follows. The first section introduces the concept of tax expenditures; the second, issues of identification. The third section considers the choice between tax expenditures and direct government spending. In the fourth section, we discuss measurement of tax expenditures. The fifth, and final section estimates revenue costs for tax expenditures in personal and corporate income tax, the capital tax, the employer health tax, the mining tax, and the retail sales tax.

The Concept of Tax Expenditures

Taxes and tax systems serve two broad sets of goals. The most widely recognized is to raise revenues to finance government operations. We demand that our governments provide a range of goods and services, such as education, child care, road construction and maintenance, protection of people and property, health care, and safety inspections of restaurants and worksites. The provision of these services requires governments to raise revenues, and taxes are, by far, the largest sources of revenue.

In the designing of taxes to raise revenues, certain criteria are desirable. Tax revenues should be raised equitably – in accordance with societal norms of fairness. In most circumstances, the tax system should strive for neutrality – tax considerations should not affect private decisions about work, investment, and consumption. To the extent that such effects are unavoidable, they should at least be minimized. The tax system should also be simple and transparent – it should be readily understandable, and the tax implications of various courses of action should be clear to taxpayers. Finally, the tax system should generate a stable and predictable flow of revenue. Otherwise, government planning becomes extremely difficult, and provision of public services may become unreliable.

Individual taxes and overall tax systems can be crafted to achieve these criteria, or a balance among them when they are in conflict. These criteria enter into the design of the elements of a tax: definition of tax base, specification of rate or rate structure, designation of taxpayers, and accounting period. Such considerations produce what the tax expenditure literature refers to as the "benchmark tax system."

The other goal of the tax system is much less recognized. It is to pursue specific policy objectives that are not necessary to the raising of revenue. Governments sometimes use tax measures to deliver benefits to particular groups (for example, the elderly, single parents, and families incurring large medical expenses) or to provide incentives for individuals and businesses to undertake particular activities. For example, governments may offer tax incentives to encourage people to save for retirement, to donate to charities, or to invest in domestic corporations; they may use tax measures to spur businesses to increase spending on research and development or to establish facilities in designated regions. They may design tax instruments to lead individuals and firms to act in ways less harmful to the natural environment.

Sometimes these tax measures take the form of tax penalties to discourage undesirable activities. More often, however, they are in the form of tax benefits delivered through exemptions, deductions, credits, refundable credits, or preferential tax rates. Such provisions, or tax expenditures, reduce taxes.

The term "tax expenditure" captures the sense in which governments choose to "spend" money by deciding not to collect what would otherwise be paid.[2] Also, virtually all the purposes to which tax expenditures are directed could be pursued though direct spending. In theory, as an alternative to tax expenditures, a government could collect all the revenue that would have accrued through the normal operation of the benchmark tax system and then direct a portion to these desired activities or to the targeted groups by means of direct grants or subsidies.

Tax expenditures are thus departures from the benchmark tax system. As becomes clear below, however, the distinction between provisions that are part of the benchmark tax system and tax expenditures is not always obvious.

A Benchmark Tax System

Determination of a benchmark tax system requires definitions of the base, the unit, the rate structure, and the accounting period for each tax. After each element has been defined, much of the work of tax expenditure analysis is in determining whether individual tax provisions meet this definition or should be considered tax expenditures.

In the case of personal income taxation, a broad definition of income – for example, net accretion of purchasing power from all sources over the accounting period – is generally adopted as the base. For corporate income taxation, benchmark income is generally defined as book profit before both current and deferred income taxes, as well as other taxes. Benchmark income excludes intercorporate dividends, to prevent double counting of income arising in the corporate sector.

Ontario's retail sales tax (RST) is levied on the final consumption of "tangible personal property and selected services only." This definition is relatively straightforward for individuals as consumers, but rather complex for businesses as consumers. Businesses purchase various types of "tangible personal property" and services that they use as inputs in the production process and machinery and equipment to facilitate production of a finished product or service or to help support their business activities. Tangible personal property used as an input is excluded from the retail sales tax base for constitutional reasons.[3] However, many of the other purchases, such as building materials, office equipment and supplies, and telecommunications are taxable under the RST.

As a result, the benchmark tax base for the RST can be defined in two ways: either by product or by use. If the benchmark base is defined as all tangible personal property, those business purchases that are exempted or excluded from the RST base could be considered tax expenditures. However, in this paper, the benchmark, defined by use, is the total consumption expenditure by households. This base is consistent with general presumptions in favour of broad neutral bases for general sales taxes. Since all business purchases are intermediate consumption, exemptions for business inputs are not tax expenditures, but rather a normal part of the tax system. As a result, the RST paid on business inputs should be characterized as negative tax expenditure.[4]

Another step in defining the benchmark tax system is to define the unit of taxation. Either the individual or some definition of the family could be selected for personal income tax.[5] Although there may be socioeconomic reasons for choosing either the individual or the family, the present system is based predominantly on the individual, with certain adjustments relating to family size and structure. For this reason, the individual will be used as the tax unit for personal income tax purposes. As a result, we treat dependant-related provisions as tax expenditures. In addition, the non-refundable basic personal tax credit is not included as a tax expenditure, as it is considered part of the benchmark tax system.

Choice of the appropriate corporate tax unit also raises conceptual issues. Units from which to choose include an establishment or activity within an organization, a single legal corporate entity, and a consolidated group of related corporations. The existing system embodies elements of all three but is related most closely to the single corporate entity. For example, losses from one part of a business can be offset against other income within the same corporation, and losses by one corporation in a consolidated group generally cannot be deducted against the income of another unit in the group. For this reason, we use the single corporate entity as the benchmark unit.

A tax rate or rate structure is also part of the benchmark system. For personal income tax, the statutory rate structure is generally defined as part of the benchmark system, based on the idea that some element of progressivity is integral to the tax. For other taxes, the most common practice is to treat the standard rate as the benchmark and deviations from it as tax expenditures.

In income taxation, a year is usually the standard accounting period. Should business losses therefore be treated as tax expenditures? In addition to taking advantage of the current carry-forward and carry-back provisions, corporations can use certain losses from one activity to offset income from another. With a benchmark tax base, ability to use losses from one activity to offset income from another is considered a normal part of the tax system.

However, carry-forward and carry-back provisions may not ensure neutrality among taxpayers. Taxpayers with the same net income during a given year could be subject to different tax treatment depending on the source of any previous or future losses, the presence or absence of other income against which losses may be offset, and the timing of any previous or future positive income against which current losses can be offset. It is arguable that these differences among taxpayers should be considered tax expenditures. The alternative view, which we have adopted, is that these provisions are administrative conventions – albeit imperfect – to accommodate losses within a tax system based on annual accounting cycles. Therefore we do not treat these provisions as tax expenditures.

Tax neutrality implies that an income tax base should ideally reflect real income. As a result, the system should take into account the effects of inflation. For practical purposes, however, most sources of personal and corporate income have historically been based on nominal rather than real income. Certain adjustments for inflation can and have been introduced; the most common is indexing of credits and rate brackets based on movements in the consumer price index (CPI). Such arrangements should be viewed as a normal part of the income tax system; they adhere to our principles of neutrality and the definition of a comprehensive tax base.

In the case of capital gains, failure to adjust for inflation may increase a taxpayer's tax liability, based on nominal capital gains, even though real, inflation-adjusted gains are negative. Some have argued that partial exclusion of capital gains in calculation of taxable income adjusts approximately for inflation. However, we believe that preferential treatment of capital gains income should be treated as a tax expenditure. Its actual tax treatment bears no logical relationship to inflation; changes in the rate of inflation are not reflected in adjustment of the tax. Moreover, the preferential treatment has more often been justified as an incentive to investment, which clearly makes it a tax expenditure.

Finally, federal-provincial tax harmonization enters into the definition of the benchmark system in Canada. In Ontario, the personal income tax (PIT) is levied as a percentage of "basic federal tax" and is collected and administered by Revenue Canada on behalf of the province. This arrangement is set out in a formal tax collection agreement between Queen's Park and Ottawa. The other provinces, except Quebec, have similar agreements with Ottawa; Quebec administers its own personal income tax.

The agreements affect provincial PIT expenditures and benchmark systems. The requirement that each province levy its PIT as a percentage of federal tax means that it automatically adopts the federal tax base and tax brackets. As a result, the provinces parallel all federal tax expenditures incorporated in the calculation of "basic federal tax," including any income exclusions from the tax base, all tax deductions, and non-refundable tax credits. Below, we present estimates of all tax expenditures resulting in revenue costs to Ontario's treasury, whether their "origin" is federal or provincial.

Identifying Tax Expenditures

In principle, tax expenditures are simply deviations from the benchmark or normal tax system. Practice is, however, more complicated. Some measures are clearly tax expenditures, and others are just as clearly part of the normal tax system. What remains is a set of tax provisions that fall into a "grey area."

Tax provisions that are clearly tax expenditures are those that the government has publicly justified using criteria normally associated with direct spending programs. For example, when Queen's Park introduced the superallowance for research and development in the 1988 budget, it justified the tax expenditure on the basis that it would provide a powerful incentive to innovation and improvement in productivity. Tax provisions that are part of the normal tax system are those that are necessary to define a fair and adequate structure for the tax. For example, provisions that allow for deduction of expenses incurred to earn business income are needed to calculate net income and, therefore, should be characterized as a normal part of any system of business income tax, not as tax expenditures.

For most tax provisions, there will be little dispute over classification as tax expenditures or as part of the normal tax system. However, some fall into a grey area and could be characterized as either a standard part of the tax system or a tax expenditure, depending on the perspective taken.

We evaluate tax provisions that fall into the grey area using a very practical approach. First, we invoke the criterion of neutrality. This yardstick implies that a tax provision intended simply to raise revenue should not provide preferential treatment to any taxpayer on the basis of demographic characteristics, sources or uses of income, geographical location, or any other special circumstances. For example, it is generally accepted that tax provisions that define the benchmark income tax base should describe a comprehensive income measure. For individuals, this implies inclusion of income from all sources, less related expenses incurred to earn that income. For corporations, a comprehensive income tax base implies inclusion of all corporate revenues, less related current expenses and an amount representing the depreciation of the corporation's assets.[6] Similarly, the retail sales tax base is assumed to include final consumption of goods and services.

In some instances, this neutrality rule would imply a tax provision dramatically different from the existing tax provision. As a result, the information on tax expenditures identified strictly on the basis of neutrality may not always be appropriate for tax policy purposes. For example, it could be argued that the value of services provided by spouses at home or the value of imputed rents of owner-occupied homes should be included in the definition of income. However, despite any theoretical merit of characterizing these exclusions from income as tax expenditures, their inclusion would be such an extreme departure from the existing tax structure and prevailing public views that it would not make sense to characterize them as tax expenditures. In these cases, the benchmark tax rule is assumed to resemble the existing tax rule on the grounds of practicality, even though this may not satisfy the neutrality criterion.

Where there is doubt about a tax provision's being a tax expenditure, this paper errs on the side of inclusion. This is intended to increase the usefulness of the tax expenditure estimates as a source of information for evaluating the direction of government policy. Readers are, of course, free to disregard these arguable items when examining the estimates.

The approach used to identify the Ontario tax expenditures reported in this paper is similar to that used in various tax expenditure accounts or budgets prepared by other governments.[7] For example, the U.S. federal government defines tax expenditures as deviations from a "generally accepted structure of an income tax." This definition generally embraces the criteria of neutrality and practicality. However, some differences do arise. For example, the exemption for dependants, which is classified as a tax expenditure in this paper on the basis of non-neutrality, is treated by the United States as part of its "generally accepted tax structure." Hence, caution should be used when comparing respective tax expenditure accounts.

At the margins, there will always be disagreement about what is considered a normal part of the tax system and what is considered a tax expenditure. There are many borderline cases where it is debatable whether deduction of a certain business expenditure is part of the normal tax system or a tax expenditure. For example, depending on how the benchmark is defined, a business lunch can be viewed as either a legitimate business expense or a consumption expenditure. No matter how such an expenditure is treated under the prevailing tax laws (in Canada, 80 per cent deductibility), it will always appear on someone's tax expenditure list. According to some, denial of a total or partial deduction results in a negative tax expenditure; others see allowing of it as a positive tax expenditure. Similar controversy surround many expenditures that have both business and personal uses. Such debates do not, however, reduce the potential usefulness of a tax expenditure account. One of the objectives of this paper is to raise this subjectivity for discussion so that some level of consensus may be reached.

Identifying Grey Areas

When evaluating the provisions that fall into the grey area, a number of specific issues arise; they are discussed below.

Treatment of the Integration of the Corporate and
Personal Income Tax Systems

One of the major issues that tax expenditure accounting in Canada must address is the relationship between the corporate and the personal income tax systems. This issue is an element of a more general question related to definition of the primary tax unit – that is, whether corporations and individuals are separate units for income tax purposes. If one argues that the personal and corporate tax systems should be integrated, then taxes at the corporate level are essentially a withholding device for personal income tax. When evaluating the dividend tax credit to determine how it should be treated, it is useful to consider Canadian-controlled private corporations (CCPCs) separately from public corporations.

To compensate shareholders for the corporate income tax underlying dividend income, the existing tax system provides special treatment, through a dividend tax credit, to dividends paid to individuals by Canadian corporations. Individuals first "gross up" their dividend income by 25 per cent to the notional "pre-corporate income tax" earnings on which they are based. They calculate their individual tax on this amount and then apply a tax credit equal to two-thirds of the "gross-up." The credit is designed to recognize the taxes assumed to be paid by the corporation on behalf of the individual prior to distribution of the earnings in the form of dividends. Because it is intended to compensate shareholders for the corporate income tax paid on the dividend income, and thereby to address what would otherwise be double taxation of corporate-source income in an integrated tax system, the dividend tax credit in the personal income tax system could be regarded as part of the normal tax system and not as a tax expenditure. However, the credit bears no relation to the actual taxes paid at the corporate level. The assumed notional amount of corporate income tax used in determining the "gross-up" and tax credit is not the actual amount paid. In many cases, credit exceeds tax paid by corporations, particularly for those in a loss position for tax purposes.

In the case of CCPCs, the principle of neutrality suggests that tax treatment of business income should be the same for both incorporated and unincorporated businesses. Therefore dividend income earned from CCPCs should be taxed at the same rate as income earned through self-employment. The current corporate income tax operates as a withholding tax for income from CCPCs, which is immediately disbursed as dividends. However, retained earnings that remain in a CCPC receive a deferral of tax equal to the difference between personal and corporate income tax rates. The dividend tax credit is not adjusted for the timing of disbursement and is therefore a somewhat ad hoc adjustment. For consistency, the reduced tax rate for CCPCs is not included in the list of corporate tax expenditures. Consistent treatment suggests that the benchmark tax rate is that of personal income taxes, not the corporate tax rate on larger corporations.

For public corporations, the argument for integration is weak, as the current tax system usually treats individuals and corporations as distinct. The relationship between corporation and shareholders is likely to be remote, and ownership and control are probably quite separate. In addition, the relationship between corporate tax actually paid and the dividend tax credit is inexact. As a result, the credit can be characterized as a tax expenditure aimed at increasing investment in Canadian-controlled corporations. We therefore include it in the list of personal income tax expenditures.

Resource Allowance

The resource allowance in the corporate income tax system poses a similar difficulty. The resource allowance deduction is equal to 25 per cent of the amount by which resource profits exceed exploration and development overhead expenses. It is designed to offset partially the non-deductibility of rents and royalties on mining and oil and gas corporations. The inexact nature of the relationship between the resource allowance and actual royalties paid suggests that this provision can act as a tax incentive or a tax penalty.

Treatment of Deferrals

When a tax expenditure is a tax deferral rather than an exemption, calculation of forgone revenue should take into account, appropriately discounted, the amount of tax that will eventually be paid. This can be estimated only imperfectly. The recent federal tax expenditure account estimated deferrals on a cash-flow basis (Canada, Department of Finance, 1992, 8). The annual cost was calculated by estimating deductions for the current year and subtracting income inclusion from previous deferrals. The account argued that this method provides a reasonably accurate picture of the ongoing costs of maintaining a particular tax provision in a mature system. This method can be used for personal income tax measures such as registered retirement savings plans (RRSPs) and registered pension plans (RPPs). However, it cannot be used for the corporate income tax system for measures such as capital cost allowances (CCAs), where re-entry of income into the taxable stream cannot be identified. As a result, the estimates of corporate income tax expenditures reported below reflect only current revenue loss from tax deferrals without regard to future tax paid on the income when it becomes subject to tax. Therefore we overstate the estimated amount of tax revenue lost through such tax expenditures.

Treatment of UI and CPP Contributions

Because a comprehensive income tax base refers to net income rather than gross income, conceptual issues arise concerning the tax expenditure classification of contributions for unemployment insurance (UI) and to the Canada Pension Plan (CPP). For example, employee-paid UI contributions could be considered part of an insurance scheme or part of a government transfer program financed by a payroll tax. If the former, then a tax credit for UI contributions would be a tax expenditure, because it helps to offset the cost of a particular benefit. If the latter, then the tax credit is not a tax expenditure because payroll taxes are considered a cost incurred to earn income and, as a result, are deductible for income tax purposes. A similar argument could be made for CPP contributions. Because participation in both programs is mandatory and the link between contributions and benefits is weak, we followed the payroll approach, and the tax credits for UI and CPP contributions have not been included in the list of personal income tax expenditures.

Union and Professional Dues

The treatment of union and professional dues raise similar problems to UI and CPP contributions. These dues can be considered a cost incurred to earn income, in which case the deduction is part of the benchmark tax base. However, if they are considered employment-related expenses that would not ordinarily be deductible, then the tax treatment of these dues could be considered a tax expenditure. For completeness, they are included in the tax expenditure estimates.

Child-Care Expense Deduction

We can consider the child-care expense deduction an attempt to put mothers who work in the home and mothers who work outside the home on a more equal tax footing. The deduction has the effect of not taxing a mother who works outside the home on certain amounts that she pays for child-care services which a mother who stays at home provides tax free. Interpreted in this way, the deduction is a measure to ensure neutrality of the tax system and would not be considered a tax expenditure. However, two other views are more prevalent. One considers child care an expense incurred to earn income, which should receive the same tax treatment as other expenses and be fully deductible. The other considers the current tax treatment of child-care expenses as a subsidy to assist families with children in offsetting their child-care costs. Since this issue is not resolved, the cost of this measure is included in the estimates.

Interest Expense and Carrying Charges

Carrying charges and interest expenses can be characterized as either an incentive designed to encourage investment or a cost incurred to earn investment income. For completeness, we have included them in the estimates.

Treatment of Exceptions

Exceptions are exclusions that fall outside the province's taxing authority. For example, status Indians are exempted from the RST by federal legislation. Similarly, Queen's Park is prohibited from taxing federal agencies or federal crown corporations. To the extent that federal regulations prohibit the province from taxing a particular individual or corporation, the exclusion is not considered a tax expenditure.

Tax Expenditures v. Direct Expenditures

At one level, the essential difference between a tax expenditure and a similarly designated direct spending program appears to be only a matter of administration. If the measure were designed as a direct spending program, recipients would get cheques from the government directly. Alternatively, if the measure were designed as a tax expenditure, the recipients are allowed to offset their tax liabilities by amounts equal to the subsidies to which they are entitled.

However, the differences are more substantive. While there are clear similarities between tax expenditures and explicit subsidies, the two are by no means perfect substitutes for each other. The degree of substitutability is a function of numerous economic, financial, and political variables. Accordingly, as these parameters change, the balance between tax measures and direct spending measures will be altered. This section briefly looks at factors that influence this choice of instruments by governments.

Tax expenditures may be characterized as subsidy measures administered through the tax system. However, their link with broader objectives of the tax system distinguishes them from direct subsidies. Government decisions on revenue policy reflect the interaction between the tax base and rate, on the one hand, and the operation of tax expenditures on the other. As a result, decisions about tax expenditures carry revenue implications that direct subsidies do not. However, the extent to which government decision making relates to a net fiscal position (that is, deficit) rather than to revenue mutes this distinction.

Both tax expenditures and direct subsidies can influence market decisions and allocation of resources – precisely the point of many tax expenditures and direct grants. In fact, if this were not the case, then both types of programs would simply lead to windfall gains to the recipients without achieving any policy objective. Both tax expenditures and direct subsidies affect allocation of resources within the economy because they favour a defined group of individuals or corporations based on demographic characteristics (for example, disability and age), sources or uses of income (such as capital earnings and charitable donations), geographical location (for instance, regional investment incentives), or any other special circumstance.

Tax expenditures tend to complicate the tax system, but direct subsidies create even more complexity – not in taxes but in expenditures. However, tax complexity, besides being undesirable in itself, may also erode other desirable properties of the tax system, such as its credibility and the reliability of revenue flows generated by the affected tax bases.

Because tax expenditures reduce the liability of a taxpayer, they create the perception that the system is unfair. Many people view tax expenditures as "hidden" tax breaks given by government to favoured individuals and corporations. Therefore their use could lead to erosion of public trust in the overall integrity of the tax system. For example, tax expenditures structured as exclusions or deductions from the tax base can result in "upside-down equity" – a particular tax expenditure gives a larger marginal benefit to high-income taxpayers than to those with lower incomes. For example, suppose that the government decided to give a $2000 deduction to two taxpayers – a high-income earner who pays tax at a rate of 50 per cent and a lower-income person who pays 25 per cent.[8] The former would receive the equivalent of a $1000 benefit, and the latter, only $500. Although this upside-down effect could be eliminated with a non-refundable tax credit, it seems unlikely that a direct subsidy program would be structured in this way.

Critics argue that some tax expenditures are generally useful only if the recipient has enough income or tax liability to absorb the benefit. For example, if a taxpayer had only $1000 of income, he or she would not receive the total benefit from the $2000 deduction described above. As a result, the higher-income earner would receive more of a benefit than the person with the lower income. Other groups likely to fall outside the scope of tax expenditures are corporations incurring losses and tax-exempt private or government organizations. A refundable credit could, however, remedy this problem.

Depending upon circumstances, the lower visibility of tax expenditures as compared with direct ones may be an advantage or a disadvantage in the pursuit of policy objectives. For example, U.S. trade law makes tax expenditures more attractive as a method of furthering economic development. Because one of the determinants of a subsidy is generally availability, tax measures are less likely to attract counter-vailing duties.

Because the spending implications of tax expenditures are not always recognized, tax expenditures sometimes also attract support because of public perceptions that they do not involve government spending. Whereas direct spending programs in Canada are shown as line items in the budget, the costs of tax expenditures are simply absorbed in the overall revenue figures. This situation has led to calls for better disclosure of the costs associated with tax expenditures in the budgetary process.[9] In Ontario, initial information (for the first year or two of operation) on specific tax expenditures has traditionally been made available in the supplementary budget papers at the time the measures are introduced or when they are changed significantly. Ontario's Ministry of Treasury and Economics (MTE) produced its first general review of the matter in *Ontario Tax Expenditures* (MTE 1986).

Annual accounts appeared subsequently in the *Economic Outlook and Fiscal Review* (see MTE 1987–89.) Supporters have claimed that tax expenditures involve more private initiative or private decision mak-ing than do direct spending measures. Any difference, however, is only one of degree. Depending on how they are structured, direct subsidies can also rely on private initiatives. Generally speaking, more scope for private initiative means less ability for government to control spending (direct or indirect) in a public program. Therefore, to the extent that direct subsidies involve less private initiative, their costs are more controllable.

Direct subsidies will more probably result in better-targeted, more attainable program objectives. Typically, an applicant for a direct grant or subsidy is required to "jump through more hoops" to qualify than is the case with tax measures. Therefore windfall gains are less likely. Grants are often in the form of multi-year contractual arrangements, whereas tax expenditures are tied to the annual time frame of the tax system. Although carry-forward and carry-back tax provisions are common, they must still fit into the annual taxation cycle. Multi-year grants, in contrast, can be designed to meet the cycle of the primary program directly. However, the enhanced ability to monitor direct grants also reduces the flexibility and speed with which the treasurer can respond to developing problems. In addition, monitoring may discourage small businesses more than it does large ones.

Tax expenditures on occasion suffer from "leakages," because it is sometimes difficult, if not impossible, to write tax provisions to isolate the group of taxpayers for which the government assistance was intended. This impedes the ability of some tax expenditures to achieve a particular objective as cost-effectively as a similarly designed direct subsidy. It also limits the government's ability to ensure a socially optimal level of a particular activity.

Negative Expenditures (Tax Penalties)

Governments can also use the tax system to discourage certain activities by imposing on them higher-than-usual tax rates or additional taxes. The neutrality criterion implies that these tax penalties are departures from the generally accepted taxing provisions for a particular tax area and, thus, could be referred to as "negative tax expenditures."

Negative tax expenditures can serve various objectives. They can be used to penalize or discourage certain types of activities. For example, by disallowing what would otherwise be a legitimate expense incurred to earn income, the non-deductibility of advertising expenses in foreign media discourages Canadian businesses from using media abroad to advertise their products to Canadian consumers.

In cases where it is difficult to determine the appropriate amount of any taxpayer's deduction, negative tax expenditures may also result unintentionally from tax provisions intended to provide certainty, clarity, simplicity, and administrative feasibility for the tax system. For example, the resource allowance, to the extent that it undercompensates eligible corporations for the partial non-deductibility of rents and royalties paid to the crown for land use, could be considered such an expenditure.

Measuring the Cost of Tax Expenditures

There are three ways to measure tax expenditures. First, an "impact," or accounting method involves measuring the amount of "tax revenue loss" associated with a particular tax expenditure. This measure represents the difference between the amount of revenue that would have been raised by a particular statute in the absence of the tax expenditure and the amount of revenue raised by that statute under the existing rules. This method does not take into account behavioural changes by taxpayers that may result from removal of the tax expenditure. For example, the amount of revenue loss in Ontario associated with the reduced rate of the Employer Health Tax (EHT) for a small employer is measured by calculating, on the basis of the annual payroll, the amount of EHT payable at the top rate, 1.95 per cent, and then subtracting the actual amount of EHT paid. For example, with a payroll of $100,000 for a year, EHT payable, which would be $1950 at 1.95 per cent, is actually $980 (at 0.98 per cent), and so the tax expenditure is the difference ($970). This is the method used by the federal Department of Finance to calculate the cost of Ottawa's tax expenditures.

Second, an economic, or behavioural method estimates the amount of tax revenue that the government loses via a tax expenditure or gains if it eliminates a particular tax expenditure. But this method takes into account changes in taxpayers' behaviour that result from the tax expenditure. Consequently, the amount of tax revenue involved tends to be lower in the second method than in the first. For example, in the illustration used above, suppose removing the reduced EHT rate for small employers caused a small employer to let go one of its four employees, thereby reducing its payroll to $75,000. As a result, tax revenues gained from removal of the tax expenditure would not be $970, as in the case of tax revenue lost, but rather $482.50, which is the difference between the amount of EHT paid, given a payroll of $75,000 at the top rate of 1.95 per cent, and the amount of EHT previously paid, given a payroll of $100,000 and the reduced rates.

Third, one can express tax expenditures in terms of their "outlay equivalent" – the pre-tax dollar amount of a direct subsidy required to provide an equivalent after-tax incentive to a taxpayer as provided by a tax expenditure. (This is one of the methods used in the U.S. budget – see United States, various years.) In many cases, the outlay equivalent is greater than the tax revenue loss, because the subsidy would be included in taxable income. Again, considering the above illustration, suppose that the small employer was self-employed and paid income tax at a rate of 50 per cent. The outlay equivalent to the $970 tax expenditure that is received is a pre-tax direct subsidy of $1940, considerably more than the lost tax revenue (although the net fiscal position of the government remains unchanged). This example clearly demonstrates the importance of expressing the cost estimates of tax expenditures in terms of their outlay equivalents when comparing their cost-effectiveness with that of direct subsidy programs.

There are, nevertheless, some rather significant limitations to the outlay-equivalent approach. Most important, the amounts shown in the outlay-equivalent estimates depend crucially on the assumed income tax treatment of the comparable direct subsidy. For example, if the subsidy received is included in taxable income, then the revenue loss associated with a particular tax expenditure must be "grossed up" to reflect forgone taxes. As a result, the outlay equivalent would be more than the lost revenue. However, if the subsidy received is not taxable, as with a guaranteed loan, then the outlay equivalent is the same as the revenue loss. Moreover, the outlay-equivalent approach presupposes that each tax expenditure would be replaced by a comparable direct subsidy. Given the peculiar distribution that a progressive rate structure imposes on some tax expenditures, it is hard to imagine these tax expenditures being replaced by direct subsidies with similar upside-down equity traits.

The cost estimates of the tax expenditures reported in this paper are calculated using the impact (accounting) method of estimating and are based on the tax revenue loss associated with the particular tax expenditure. This choice reflects the theoretical and empirical difficulties associated with predicting changes in taxpayers' behaviour resulting from removal of a tax expenditure[10] and expressing some of the tax expenditures in terms of outlay equivalents. However, as illustrated above, accounting for changes in taxpayers' behaviour will generally reduce these estimates, while expressing them as outlay equivalents will increase them. In addition, except where otherwise stated, the estimates reported here have been measured at the margin – that is, while we hold all other aspects of the tax system constant, including other tax expenditures. This condition may affect the estimate of tax revenue loss associated with a particular tax expenditure. Because the tax system is interactive, tax expenditures in one tax area affect the amount of revenue raised in another and the revenue loss associated with other tax expenditures. For example, because the EHT is deductible against income tax, the reduced rates for smaller employers actually increase their taxable income for corporate income tax. This arrangement increases the government's revenues from corporate income tax.

The amount of lost revenue associated with a tax expenditure is affected also by the dynamic relationship between tax expenditures and the level of economic activity. For example, some tax expenditures may encourage job creation; by doing so, they increase government revenues from other taxes, particularly those on income and retail sales. This generally reduces the net revenue loss associated with a particular tax expenditure. However, taking these factors into account involves estimating behavioural responses. Therefore we have not included these feedback effects.[11]

This dynamic relationship also works in reverse. For example, the 1992–92 recession slowed capital investment in Ontario's manufacturing industry. As a result, the cost of the Ontario capital-cost adjustment (OCCA) should decrease for two reasons. First, the lower amount of capital investment directly reduces the amount of revenue forgone; second, firms may not have sufficient taxable income, as profits decline because of the recession, to deduct fully the OCCA. However, inflation could increase the cost of machinery and processing equipment and, in turn, increase the amount of forgone revenue associated with the OCCA. As a result, the tax expenditure estimate for the OCCA, as for any tax expenditure, may vary from year to year, depending on economic conditions.

Given the methodological issues described above, the estimates of tax expenditure costs presented in this paper should not be viewed as "hard" values in an accounting sense. Rather, they suggest "order of magnitude." They provide reliable, but not exact estimates of the revenue costs of the various tax expenditures. Also, it would be misleading simply to add together the cost estimates of each tax expenditure in order to calculate the total cost of all Ontario tax expenditures. To do so would in fact be to ignore the interactive effects that are discussed above.

We used several sources to estimate the tax expenditures reported here:

- for those made through *personal income tax*, 1989 tax returns made available by Ottawa to Queen's Park under terms of the tax collection agreements;
- for *corporate income tax* (unless otherwise stated), information from 1989 federal and Ontario corporate tax returns made available by the Ministry of Revenue of Ontario and by Revenue Canada Taxation;
- and for the *retail sales tax* and the *other commodity taxes*, data from Statistics Canada and Ontario's Ministry of Revenue and unpublished statistics supplied by a number of other provincial ministries.

Because statistics are based on the most recent available data, some estimates do not cover the same year, and some relate to the fiscal, rather than the calendar, year.

Revenue Costs for Tax Expenditures

Personal Income Tax Expenditures, 1989 (Table 1)

Shared with the Federal Government

INCOME EXCLUSIONS

Capital Gains Exclusion ($267 million). One-quarter of an individual's capital gains are exempt from income tax.

Government Transfer Payments and Worker's Compensation (not available). In addition to workers' compensation payments, some of the major forms of government transfer payments are excluded from the existing income tax base for the calculation of basic tax. These include welfare and other social assistance payments, guaranteed income supplements, war disability pensions, and spouses' allowances. (However, they are included in net income for the calculation of refundable tax credits.) Many of these transfer payments have implicit tax-back rates built into the program design.

Lotteries and Other Prize Winnings (not applicable). Lottery winnings, along with other gains resulting from prizes, gambling, and so on where chance is the determining factor, are not included in the income tax base.

DEDUCTIONS AND EXEMPTIONS

Registered Retirement Savings Plan Contributions ($[658 + 516 − 117] million). Contributions to a registered retirement savings plan (RRSP) are deductible from income up to prescribed limits (value $658 million), investment earnings on plan funds are not taxed as they accrue (value $516 million), and benefit payments or other withdrawals are fully subject to tax (value $117 million). For 1993, the maximum amount deductible for contributions to an RRSP by a tax filer enrolled in a registered pension plan (RPP) is the lesser of $12,500 minus a pension adjustment that includes both the employee's and the employer's RPP contributions or 18 per cent of earned income. For other tax filers, it is the lesser of $12,500 or 18 per cent of earned income. As of 1991, tax filers who do not use their allowed maximums in a given year may carry forward the unused portion for up to seven years.

TABLE 1
Personal Income Tax Expenditures: Estimates of Ontario
Revenue Forgone, Taxation Year 1989

Tax expenditures	Estimated revenue forgone ($ million)
SHARED WITH THE FEDERAL GOVERNMENT (pages 186–90)	
Income exclusions	
Capital gains exclusion	267
Government transfer payments and workers' compensation	n.a.
Lotteries and other prize winnings	n.a.
Deductions and exemptions	
Registered Retirement Savings Plans contributions	658
Non-taxation of investment income	516
Taxation of withdrawals	−117
Registered Pension Plan contributions (and non-taxation of employers' contributions	654
Non-taxation of investment income	872
Taxation of withdrawals	−603
Lifetime capital gains exemption	529
Carrying charges and interest expenses	188
Union and professional dues	68
Child-care expenses	57
Northern residents' deductions	9
Exploration and development expenses	20
Alimony and maintenance payments	35
Non-refundable tax credits	
Age credit	264
Married credit (including e-to-m)	219
Charitable donations	186
Credit for dependent children	81
Medical expenses	37
Pension income credit	59
Disability credit for self	31
Tuition fees	37
Education credit	9
Tuition fees transferred	n.a.
Dividend tax credit	162
SOLELY WITHIN ONTARIO'S JURISDICTION (pages 190–2)	
Ontario property and sales tax credits	407
Ontario tax reduction	40
OHOSP tax credit	21
Political contribution tax credit	3
Ontario investment and worker ownership program	n.a.

Source: Based on Revenue Canada's micro-database for Ontario (1989).

Registered Pension Plan Contributions ($[654 + 872 − 603] million). Employees' contributions as required under a registered pension plan (RPP) are deductible from income; contributions by employers to RPPs and deferred profit-sharing plans (DPSPs) are not considered taxable benefits and are therefore tax free to the employee (value $654 million). Investment earnings on plan funds are not taxed as they accrue (value $872 million), and benefit payments or other withdrawals are fully subject to tax (−$603 million).

Lifetime Capital Gains Exemption ($529 million). All taxpayers are permitted a cumulative lifetime capital gains exemption of $100,000. The 1992 federal budget imposed a restriction on qualifying property – the exemption would not apply to real estate purchased after February 1992. Moreover, for real estate bought before March 1992, the exemption would be prorated, based on the number of months during which the property was held before March 1992, against the total number of months held.

An additional $400,000 capital gains deduction is available on gains realized on the disposition of shares of qualified small business corporations, as well as dispositions of qualified farm properties.

Carrying Charges and Interest Expenses ($188 million). Individuals may deduct from income the interest cost on money borrowed to make investments, fees for investment counselling, and other investment-related expenses.

Union and Professional Dues ($68 million). Union and professional dues are fully deductible from income.

Child-Care Expenses ($57 million). Expenses paid for child-care services that enable single parents or both spouses in a two-parent family to earn income or to attend an educational or training program are deductible from income. In two-parent families, the lower-income spouse must claim the deduction. The maximum deduction in 1991 was $4000 for each child under the age of seven and $2000 for each child aged seven and over. The 1992 federal budget announced that the deduction limits would be increased for 1993 and subsequent tax years. For children under seven or those with documented disabilities, the new maximum deduction will be $5000 per child, and for children between 7 and 14, $3000 per child.

Northern Residents' Deductions ($9 million). To offset the relatively higher cost of living and travelling in the north, individuals living in a qualifying remote location in Canada for a continuous period of at least six months may be able to claim a deduction from income.

Exploration and Development Expenses ($20 million). Expenses associated with passive investments in petroleum, natural gas, or mining can be deducted from income.

Alimony and Maintenance Payments ($35 million). People paying alimony or maintenance deduct from taxable income the full amount of qualifying support payments, and recipients must report these payments as income, on which they are taxed. The amount of tax expenditure is equal to the difference between tax payable by the payee and that payable by the payer.

NON-REFUNDABLE TAX CREDITS[12]

Age Credit ($264 million). A tax credit of $3482 is available to all tax filers aged 65 and over. This provision results in an Ontario credit of $343 (value of federal credit times the Ontario tax note).

Married Credit (Including Equivalent-to-Married) ($219 million). A tax credit of $5380 is available to a tax filer with a dependent spouse or with an eligible dependant living with him or her. This provision results in an additional, Ontario credit of $530.

Charitable Donations ($186 million). A non-refundable tax credit is available for people making charitable donations and gifts to Canada or a province or gifts of cultural property. Eligible charitable donations are limited to 20 per cent of a tax filer's net income; the first $250 is eligible for a 17 per cent tax credit, and any amount in excess of $250 receives a 29 per cent credit.

Credit for Dependent Children ($81 million). Tax filers could claim $417 ($406 in 1991) for each of the first two dependent children under age 18. The amount doubles for additional children in the family. This provision results in an Ontario credit of $39 ($37 in 1991) for the first two children and $77 ($73 in 1991) for any others. This credit was replaced in 1992 with a new child tax benefit, which amalgamated federal family allowance payments, the child credit, and the refundable child tax credit.

Medical Expenses ($37 million). Individuals may claim eligible out-of-pocket medical expenses over $1614 not covered by a health plan, or 3 per cent of net income, whichever is less, in calculating this non-refundable tax credit.

Pension Income Credit ($59 million). Individuals may claim up to $1000 for certain types of pension income in calculating this non-refundable tax credit. This provision results in an Ontario credit of $99.

Disability Credit for Self ($31 million). Individuals with disabilities may claim $4233 in calculating this non-refundable tax credit. This provision results in an Ontario credit of $418.

Tuition Fees ($37 million). A student may claim a credit for eligible tuition fees. Any portion of the credit not claimed by the student is transferable to a supporting taxpayer (information not available).

Education Credit ($9 million). Student may claim $80 for each whole or part month that he or she is enrolled in a qualifying educational program at a designated institution. This provision results in an Ontario credit of about $8 per month of enrollment.

Tuition Fees Transferred (not available). Any portion of the credit not claimed by the student is transferable to a supporting taxpayer.

Dividend Tax Credit ($162 million). The dividend tax credit is part of a scheme of integration that provides relief from double taxation of income earned by corporations resident in Canada and passed on to individual shareholders.[13]

Solely within Ontario's Jurisdiction

ONTARIO PROPERTY AND SALES TAX CREDITS ($407 million)

Ontario provides refundable tax credits to help reduce the burden of property tax and sales tax on lower-income families. Benefits are based on the amount of property tax and/or rent paid, family composition, and family income.

"Occupancy cost" is defined as property tax paid and/or 20 per cent of rent paid; the basic property tax credit is the lesser of $500 or occupancy cost, plus 10 per cent of occupancy cost. The basic sales tax credit is $100 per adult, plus $50 for each dependent child. The Ontario tax credit is the basic property tax and sales tax credits added together and jointly reduced by 4 per cent of (combined) net income (of both spouses or supporting persons) in excess of $22,000.

The program was introduced in 1972 and has undergone numerous changes. The 1992 provincial budget replaced the Ontario tax grants for seniors with the Ontario tax credits for seniors.

ONTARIO TAX REDUCTION ($40 million)

This program reduces or eliminates the Ontario tax otherwise payable by lower-income tax filers. The taxpayer computes a "total personal amount" (we can call it TPA), equal to a basic amount of $205, plus $395 per child under 19 and $395 per disabled dependant. Taxpayers pay no provincial income tax if income is less than or equal to TPA; otherwise they can reduce such tax by an amount equal to three times TPA minus two times Ontario tax.

ONTARIO HOME OWNERSHIP SAVINGS PLAN (OHOSP) TAX CREDIT ($21 million)

This program provides refundable tax credits of up to $500 for individuals and $1000 for families saving to purchase a first home. Individuals with incomes of less than $40,000 and married couples with combined incomes of less than $80,000 are eligible. In addition to benefiting from the OHOSP tax credit, participants may receive a refund of the land transfer tax, with the amount depending on the purchase price of the eligible home.

POLITICAL CONTRIBUTION TAX CREDIT ($3 million)

A tax credit of up to $750 is available to offset a portion of contributions made to registered Ontario political parties. The tax credit is equal to 75 per cent of the first $200 in contributions, plus 50 per cent of the next $600, plus 33.3 per cent of the total amount exceeding $800.

ONTARIO INVESTMENT AND WORKER OWNERSHIP PROGRAM (not applicable)

This new program has two components. One operates very much like a mutual fund and provides tax credits to any Ontario resident who invests in registered funds. The maximum annual credit is 20 per cent on the first $5000 so invested. A matching federal credit is also available.

The other provides workers with tax credits on investments that they make in their own firm – 20 per cent on the first $3500 and 30 per cent on the incremental investments to a maximum of $15,000 per year and $150,000 for a lifetime. Workers as a group must acquire at least 40 per cent ownership of the business in acquisitions where an outside investor is also involved, and at least 50 per cent ownership where there is no outside investor.

Corporate Tax Expenditures (Income Tax, Capital Tax, EHT, and Mining Tax), 1989 (Table 2)

Corporate Income Tax (CIT) Expenditures

CAPITAL COST ALLOWANCE (CCA) V. ACCOUNTING DEPRECIATION ($460 million)

When a company acquires a capital asset – anything from a typewriter to an apartment building – it is allowed to deduct a portion of the cost of that asset as an expense incurred to earn income. For general accounting purposes, depreciation spreads the original capital cost over the economically useful life of the asset. However, for tax purposes, businesses are allowed to calculate depreciation according to prescribed capital cost allowance (CCA) provisions. Book depreciation does not necessarily reflect CCA provisions.[14] These differences occur for a number of reasons.

CCA provisions do not always reflect the estimated economically useful life of an asset. As a result, CCA often exceeds depreciation allowable for accounting purposes.[15] In particular, accelerated CCAs are available for certain assets employed in such activities as manufacturing and processing, mining, communications, drilling, rail transportation, pollution control, and energy conservation.

Under generally accepted accounting principles (GAAP), depreciation of assets over their useful life usually means that depreciation does not commence until the assets are actually being put to use in the business to earn income. Under CCA rules, however, claims may commence before that occurs. New "put-in-use" rules delay CCA until the capital is being used.

While accounting depreciation is generally claimed asset by asset,

TABLE 2
Corporate Tax Expenditures: Estimates of Ontario
Revenue Forgone, Taxation Year 1989

Tax expenditures	Estimated revenue forgone ($ million)
Corporate income tax (CIT) expenditures[a] (pages 192–6)	
Capital cost allowance (CCA) v. accounting depreciation	460
Capital gains exclusion	300
Reduced rate for specified sectors	50[b]
The Ontario current cost adjustment	75[b]
Research and development superallowance	50[b]
Exploration and development expenses	175
Resource allowance	25
Small business development corporations program	<5
Charitable donations	45
Corporations exempt from income tax	n.a.
Capital tax expenditures (page 196)	
Banks and trust companies	n.a.
Flat capital tax for small business	120[c]
Employer health tax (EHT) expenditures (page 196–7)	
Reduced rates for small employers	150[d]
Exemption for self-employed earnings	n.a.
Mining profits tax expenditures (pages 197–8)	
Three-year tax exemption for mining profits of new mines	10[e]
$500,000 tax exemption for mining profits	2
Charitable donations	n.a.
Operator's prescribed processing allowance	40[e]

Source: Taxation Policy Branch, Ontario Ministry of Finance
[a] Based on a detailed federal sample of corporations with taxable income allocated to Ontario.
[b] Special tabulation based on data from Ontario's Ministry of Finance.
[c] Deductible from corporate income taxes; therefore the cost of the tax expenditure is overstated.
[d] 1990.
[e] Rounded to the nearest $5 million.

CCA rules require similar assets to be pooled or grouped by classes. Since CCA rates and methods are usually more generous than those established by GAAP, pooling of assets can extend the period for tax deferral – sometimes indefinitely, as long as assets in the pool are continually replaced with equal- or higher-valued assets.

Since the accounting rate is based on estimated economically useful life, depreciation charges are made annually on a regular schedule. However, CCA rates specify the maximum available claim that may be made in a year; the corporate taxpayer can decide whether to use less.

CAPITAL GAINS EXCLUSION ($300 million)

Profits made on the sale of capital property, such as land or investments, owned by corporations are referred to as capital gains. Three-quarters of capital gains and capital losses are included in determining a corporation's taxable income. In 1988 and 1989, this figure was two-thirds, and previous to 1988 it was one-half. A reserve is allowed for capital gains to permit a corporation to bring a capital gain into income as its related proceeds are received. However, no reserves are permitted after five years, even if proceeds have not been fully received. This provides for a more equitable matching of receipt of proceeds of disposition and payment of taxes.

REDUCED RATE FOR SPECIFIED SECTORS ($50 million)

The usual Ontario corporate income tax (CIT) rate is reduced from 15.5 per cent to 14.5 per cent for income derived from manufacturing and processing, mining, logging, and farming and fishing to the extent that the qualifying income is not eligible for the small business deduction. Effective 1 January 1993, this tax rate was further reduced to 13.5 per cent. The purpose is to encourage such activities by providing a reduction in taxes, thus allowing companies to retain funds for investment.

Credit unions are eligible for a lower CIT rate of 10 per cent, instead of the statutory CIT rate of 15.5 per cent, on taxable income that falls below their reserve requirements. The lower rates are designed to allow credit unions to retain a greater share of their income to expand their capital base.

THE ONTARIO CURRENT COST ADJUSTMENT (OCCA) ($75 million)

The OCCA provides an additional deduction for Ontario CIT purposes for pollution-control equipment purchased for use in Ontario. It stipulates a 30 per cent tax deduction over and above the regular CCA that can be claimed in the first year of CCA.

RESEARCH AND DEVELOPMENT SUPERALLOWANCE ($50 million)

Ontario's research and development (R&D) superallowance provides an additional deduction against Ontario income for R&D expenditures incurred in the province. The superallowance gives corporations a 25 per cent deduction in addition to the immediate 100 per cent write-off otherwise available for R&D current and capital expenditures. For CCPCs, the deduction is increased from 25 to 35 per cent. For incremental R&D expenditures – the amount of R&D expenditures that exceeds average expenditures in the previous three taxation years – it is increased by 50 per cent (37.5 per cent and 52.5 per cent).

EXPLORATION AND DEVELOPMENT EXPENSES ($175 million)

A deduction for exploration and development expenses is available to corporations involved in oil and gas and the mining sectors. For CIT purposes, these expenses are grouped into specified pools and can be written off at yearly rates of 10 per cent, 30 per cent, or 100 per cent, depending on the pool. The tax deduction rates can result in accelerated write-offs of these expenditures (compared with accounting treatment).

RESOURCE ALLOWANCE ($25 million)

Oil and gas corporations are eligible for a resource allowance deduction in computing taxable income. This deduction is equal to 25 per cent of the amount by which resource profits exceed overhead expenses for exploration and development. Starting in 1989, mining corporations became eligible for the resource allowance, subject to a phase-in period.

SMALL BUSINESS DEVELOPMENT CORPORATIONS PROGRAM (less than $5 million)

This program entitles investors to receive an Ontario government grant (for individuals) or a tax credit (for corporations) based on an investment in eligible companies through an approved small business development corporation. Tax credits will normally be equal to 25 per cent of the amount invested, but 30 per cent if the investment is made in northern or eastern Ontario. The tax credits are a much smaller component of the program than the tax grants.

CHARITABLE DONATIONS ($45 million)

A deduction of up to 20 per cent of net income for tax purposes is permitted for charitable donations to specified registered organizations and charities.

CORPORATIONS EXEMPT FROM INCOME TAX (not available)

Under the existing income tax system, federal and provincial crown corporations, municipal corporations, agricultural organizations, registered charities, and other benevolent organizations are exempt from corporate income tax. However, according to the neutrality criterion, such corporations would be taxable under the generally accepted rules of the tax system to the extent that they had taxable income.

Capital Tax Expenditures

BANKS AND TRUST COMPANIES (not applicable)

A capital tax is levied on a corporation's taxable paid-up capital – capital stock, retained earnings, and surpluses and debt – reduced by an investment allowance. For banks and trust companies, only shareholders' equity is included in the base, for reasons of simplicity; however, their rate is higher to reflect their narrower tax base. As a result, the narrower base is not considered a tax expenditure in this paper.

FLAT CAPITAL TAX FOR SMALL BUSINESS ($120 million)

The general capital tax rate in Ontario is 3/10 of 1 per cent of taxable paid-up capital (in general terms, the capital invested in, or available for use in, the business operation at year's end). However, small corporations with total assets and gross revenues both less than or equal to $1 million are exempt. As well, corporations with paid-up capital less than or equal to $2 million generally pay reduced capital taxes. The actual amount payable in such cases depends on the corporation's size, and, in most cases, a flat capital tax of $100, $200, or $500 is payable. Credit unions and mortgage investment, family farm/fishing, and mutual insurance corporations are subject to a flat capital tax of $100.

Employer Health Tax (EHT) Expenditures

REDUCED RATES FOR SMALL EMPLOYERS ($150 million)

Employers having annual payrolls of $400,000 or less pay the employer health tax (EHT) at a rate between 0.98 per cent and the statutory rate of 1.95 per cent. Those with payrolls of $200,000 or less per year use the lowest rate, 0.98 per cent.

EXEMPTION FOR SELF-EMPLOYED EARNINGS (not applicable)

Effective for fiscal periods ending after 31 December 1992, self-employed individuals will pay the EHT on total net self-employment income as calculated for federal personal income tax. As announced in the 1992 Ontario budget, the first $40,000 of total net income from self-employment will be exempt. A tax credit of 22 per cent is provided against Ontario personal income tax.

Mining Profits Tax Expenditures

In addition to the mining profits tax expenditures that parallel corporate income tax expenditures (that is, exploration and development expenses, research and development expenses, and excess of tax depreciation versus book depreciation), the following could be described as mining profits tax expenditures.

THREE-YEAR TAX EXEMPTION FOR MINING PROFITS OF NEW MINES ($10 million)

New mines, major expansions, and rehabilitated mines are exempt from mining tax for three years of commercial production. The 1991 Ontario budget limits the exemption for new mines, major expansions to existing mines, and certain mine rehabilitations to either three years or $10 million of profit per mine, whichever is first. The limit provides a maximum benefit of $2 million per mine. This limitation applies to eligible profits earned after 30 April 1991.

$500,000 TAX EXEMPTION FOR MINING PROFITS ($2 million)

The first $500,000 of profit from an Ontario mine is tax exempt each year.

CHARITABLE DONATION DEDUCTION (not available)

Donations for charitable, educational, and benevolent purposes that are reasonably related to mining operations in Ontario are fully deductible in computing taxable mining profits.

OPERATOR'S PRESCRIBED PROCESSING ALLOWANCE ($40 million)

Mining operators may deduct from gross revenues a processing allowance in determining their taxable mining profits. The allowance is calculated as a percentage of the capital cost of processing assets and ranges from 8 to 20 per cent, depending on the type of processing activity, the location of the mine, and the source of the mineral input. A minimum amount available is set at 15 per cent of the operation's profits otherwise calculated; the maximum is 65 per cent.

Retail Sales Tax Expenditures, 1991 (Table 3)

For the purposes of this paper, the benchmark RST rate is assumed to be the statutory general rate of 8 per cent. One exception is the RST treatment of entertainment admissions, which were originally taxed under Ontario's Hospital Tax Act at a rate of 10 per cent. When admissions were brought under the Retail Sales Tax Act, the 10 per cent rate was maintained and is considered the benchmark rate for admissions.

Goods

ENERGY ($409 million)

Energy has never been subject to the RST. Some fuels, such as cigarette lighter fuel, fondue fuel, naphtha gas, varsol, and like products for cleaning purposes, are taxable under the RST.

MOTOR FUELS ($170 million)

Several forms of fuel, including motor fuels, are exempt from RST, and we consider all final consumption expenditures that are not in the base to be RST tax expenditures. Motor fuels are taxed instead under the province's Fuel Tax Act and Gasoline Tax Act.

TABLE 3
Retail Sales Tax Expenditures: Estimates of Ontario
Revenue Forgone, Taxation Year 1991

Tax expenditures	Estimated revenue forgone ($ million)*
Goods (pages 198–201)	
Energy	429
Motor fuels	170
Vehicles using alternative fuels	4
Basic groceries	1,188
Prepared food costing $4 or less	160
Reading material	61
Prescription drugs and medical equipment	169
Children's clothing	50
Footwear costing $30 or less	35
Feminine hygiene products	11
Housing and related goods (pages 201–2)	
Water charges	49
Housing purchases	636
Rent and board	656
Transient accommodation	26
Services (pages 202–3)	
Household services	240
Medical and health services	420
Transportation and related services	362
Recreational, educational, and other services	605
Personal services	148
Financial services	715
Accounting, legal, and other services	58
Admission fees	30
Purchaser specific (page 203)	
Items for people with physical disabilities	7

Source: Calculations based on Statistics Canada, System of National Accounts,
unpublished data; Taxation Policy Branch, Ontario Ministry of Finance
* Estimates are based on final consumption expenditures; for quasi-public goods, they
are based on costs minus subsidies. Motor fuels are subject to Ontario's Fuel and
Gasoline Tax acts.

VEHICLES USING ALTERNATIVE FUELS ($4 million)

Purchasers of vehicles that operate on electricity, propane, natural gas,
methanol, or manufactured gas or of dual-powered vehicles may
receive a sales tax refund to a maximum of $750 for propane vehicles

or $1000 for vehicles powered by alternative fuels. As part of the tax
to encourage fuel conservation, purchasers of cars that use less than
six litres of gasoline per 100 kilometres will be eligible for a $100 credit.
The gas-guzzler tax paid on fuel-inefficient cars is refundable when
the cars are converted to operate exclusively on an alternative fuel. The
tax paid on the purchase of conversion kits and installation labour is
refundable, and lessees of alternative-fuel vehicles leased on a long-
term basis also qualify for the tax rebate. Buses purchased to transport
people with physical disabilities qualify for rebate; also, buses are not
subject to the maximum rebate limits for alternative-fuel vehicles – in
both situations, the actual tax paid is refundable.

GROCERIES ($1,188 million)

The RST is not applied to grocery store food except for items of prepared
food priced over $4, soft drinks, snack food, and confections that are
subject to the 8 per cent rate. Chocolate for cooking is exempt, while
other chocolate is taxed. Vitamins are also exempt as food.

PREPARED FOOD COSTING $4 OR LESS ($160 million)

Ontario's Retail Sales Tax Act exempts prepared food costing $4 or less
purchased from eating establishments (such as restaurants, fast food
outlets, cafeterias, vending machines, and catering trucks).
   When the RST was introduced in 1961, prepared food costing $1.50
or less was exempt. The exemption was subsequently changed several
times and reached $6 by 1977. In 1982, the tax on prepared food was
expanded to include take-out food and the exemption was eliminated.
The exemption was reintroduced in 1985 at $1 and was increased in
steps to the current $4 threshold. The RST rate on prepared foods was
originally set at 10 per cent. After being changed several times, it was
set at the general rate in 1982.

READING MATERIAL ($61 million)

Magazines purchased on subscriptions, books, and newspapers; publications by religious, charitable, or benevolent organizations; and publications purchased by schools, school boards, community colleges,
universities, and public libraries are exempt from RST.

PRESCRIPTION DRUGS AND MEDICAL EQUIPMENT ($169 million)

Prescription drugs and medicines (prescribed by a doctor, dentist, or veterinarian) are exempt; over-the-counter drugs are taxed. Purchases of personal medical equipment such as dental appliances (for example, dentures), prescription optical appliances (eye glasses and contact lenses), and hearing aids are exempt. These exemptions date back to introduction of the RST in 1961.

CHILDREN'S CLOTHING ($50 million)

Children's clothing is exempt, based on clothing size. The exemption was part of the original RST legislation.

FOOTWEAR COSTING $30 OR LESS ($35 million)

Purchases of footwear costing $30 or less are exempt. The original exemption was intended for children's footwear, based on size and style. Since the current exemption threshold applies to all footwear, adult footwear also benefits, while children's priced in excess of $30 is no longer exempt.

FEMININE HYGIENE PRODUCTS ($11 million)

Tampons, sanitary pads, and sanitary belts have been exempt since 1986.

Housing and Related Goods

WATER CHARGES ($49 million)

There is no RST on the sale of natural water.

HOUSING PURCHASES ($636 million)

Since housing is real property and not tangible personal property, housing is not subject to RST. However, most building materials are taxed. Under a comprehensive value-added tax, purchases of new housing would be taxable.

RENT AND BOARD ($656 million)

Under a comprehensive value-added tax, rental accommodation and payments for lodging and board would be taxable as final consumption expenditures.

TRANSIENT ACCOMMODATION ($26 million)

Transient accommodation is taxed at a reduced rate of 5 per cent (i.e., three percentage points below the general rate of 8 per cent). Transient accommodation was first taxed in 1969 at the then general rate of 5 per cent. It was exempt from tax from 1978 until the end of 1981. On 1 January 1982, the exemption was removed and the general sales tax rate of 7 per cent was applied. Later that same year, however, the RST rate on transient accommodation was lowered to 5 per cent, where it remains today.

Services

HOUSEHOLD SERVICES ($240 million)

Household services such as laundry and dry cleaning, child-care, and domestic services are not included in the RST base. Given the base outlined in the text, we consider them tax expenditures.

MEDICAL AND HEALTH SERVICES ($420 million)

Medical and health services are not included in the RST base. Private expenditures on these services are tax expenditures, given the base outlined in the text.

TRANSPORTATION AND RELATED SERVICES ($362 million)

Transportation services such as air transport, inter-city and rural bus transit, railway transport, urban transit, and taxis are not in the RST base. A comprehensive tax on final consumption of all goods and services would include these services in the base.

RECREATIONAL, EDUCATIONAL, AND OTHER SERVICES ($605 million)

These services are not in the RST base. A comprehensive tax on final consumption of all goods and services would include these services in the base.

PERSONAL SERVICES ($148 million)

Personal services such as hairstyling, other personal care, and miscellaneous household services are not included in the RST base. They can be considered tax expenditures given our definition of the base.

FINANCIAL SERVICES ($715 million)

Financial services, including costs of services of financial institutions and interest charges, would be taxable under a comprehensive tax on final consumption of all goods and services. They are not in the RST base.

ACCOUNTING, LEGAL, AND OTHER SERVICES ($58 million)

These professional services are not included in the RST base and can be considered tax expenditures, given the base defined above.

ADMISSION FEES ($30 million)

Admission to a place of amusement is taxed at 10 per cent. However, the RST is not applied to admission prices of $4 or less, events sponsored by a charity, live theatrical performances, and performances with Canadian talent.

Purchaser Specific

PEOPLE WITH PHYSICAL DISABILITIES ($7 million)

A range of specific items used by people with physical disabilities, such as prosthetic and orthopaedic devices, is exempt from RST. Purchasers of vehicles for transporting people with physical disabilities are eligible for a refund of RST up to $1600 per car and up to $2400 per van.

Notes

1 The treasurer of Ontario asked the Fair Tax Commission (FTC) to evaluate Ontario's existing tax expenditures to ensure that they are achieving current policy objectives efficiently and effectively. The FTC has also been asked to suggest changes to specific tax expenditures that would increase the fairness of the tax system. It established an advisory group on tax expenditures to assist its work in this area. This paper benefited from extensive consultations with the advisory group. However, not all of its members necessarily endorse all aspects of the paper.

2 People often confuse the terms "tax loophole" and "tax expenditure." Tax loopholes are tax-reducing provisions that were not intended to be part of the tax system but have emerged, sometimes through court challenges of vaguely defined tax statutes, and hence are different from the law's original intent. Alternatively, they may develop through interaction of various tax measures in a fashion unforeseen when the provisions were introduced. Tax expenditures, as we have defined them, are spending provisions that are delivered through the tax system as a deliberate policy to achieve a specific objective.

3 The province's taxing power is restricted to direct taxation within the province; see Hog (1985).

4 The concept of negative tax expenditure is introduced below.

5 See Maloney (1994) for a more detailed discussion of the tax unit.

6 The tax base for corporate income tax differs from financial statement income, primarily as a result of the deductibility of prior years' losses, tax-free intercorporate dividends, the non-taxable portion of capital gains, accelerated deductions for capital expenditures, and other incentives that affect the corporate income tax base.

7 See, for example, Canada, Department of Finance (1992).

8 Tax expenditures tend to be conditional on the tax rate, without regard to the merits of individual programs. For example, suppose that the government decided to lower the tax rate from 50 per cent to 25 per cent but not to alter the value of a deduction that it was providing. As a result, the benefit received by the individual is decreased by half. In order to provide the same benefit that prevailed prior to lowering the tax rate, the government would have to double the amount of the deduction. Alternatively, raising tax rates would increase the benefit.

9 On tax expenditures and the budgetary process see Linquist (1994).

10 The commission is publishing a study on tax incidence (Block and Shillington 1994) that takes into account the behavioural effect of taxes. While the accounting approach used here is inconsistent with that of inci-

dence analysis, it is the standard method for tax expenditure inventories in Canada.

11 Public accounts' estimates for direct program expenditures also do not take into account the affect of such feedback.

12 We calculated the value of non-refundable tax credits in determining Ontario income tax payable by multiplying the maximum federal credit receivable by Ontario's 1993 basic tax rate of 58 per cent. The effect of the surtax is not taken into account.

13 A more detailed analysis of integration of the corporate and personal income tax systems and its implications for the tax expenditure classification of the dividend tax credit is included below.

14 It is generally accepted that accounting depreciation is a better allocation of the cost of the asset over its economically useful life than that permitted through the CCA.

15 The first stage of federal tax reform significantly reduced CCA rates as part of an initiative to broaden the base and reduce rates.

Bibliography

Block, Sheila M., and E. Richard Shillington. 1994 "Tax Incidence in Ontario 1991." In *Taxation and the Distribution of Income*, ed. Allan M. Maslove. Fair Tax Commission, Research Studies. Toronto: University of Toronto Press (forthcoming)

Canada. Department of Finance. 1992. *Government of Canada Personal Income Tax Expenditures*. Canada: Department of Finance

Hogg, Peter. 1985. *Constitutional Law of Canada* Toronto: Carswell

Lindquist, Evert A. 1994. "Improving the Scrutiny of Tax Expenditures in Ontario: Comparative Perspectives and Recommendations." In *Taxing and Spending: Issues of Process*, ed. Allan M. Maslove, 32–128. Fair Tax Commission, Research Studies. Toronto: University of Toronto Press

Maloney, Maureen. 1994. "What Is the Appropriate Tax Unit for the 1990s and Beyond?" In *Issues in the Taxation of Individuals*, ed. Allan M. Maslove. Fair Tax Commission, Research Studies. Toronto: University of Toronto Press (forthcoming)

Ontario. Ministry of Treasury and Economics (MTE). 1986. *Ontario Tax Expenditures*. Toronto: Queen's Printer for Ontario.

– 1987, 1988, 1989. *Economic Outlook and Fiscal Review*. Toronto: Queen's Printer for Ontario

United States. Various years. *The Budget of the United States Government*. Special Analysis G or H. Washington, DC: United States Government

Notes on Contributors

Mark Sproule-Jones is Victor K. Copps Professor, McMaster University. He is also author of a number of books on Canadian public policy and parliamentary federalism. Currently he is principal investigator of "Ecowise," a Tri-Council Eco-Research Program for Hamilton Harbour.

Morley Gunderson is director, Centre for Industrial Relations, as well as professor, Department of Economics, University of Toronto.

Wayne R. Thirsk is professor of economics at the University of Waterloo.

Arthur Donner is an economic consultant.

Fred Lazar is associate professor of economics in the Faculties of Arts and Administrative Studies, York University.

Sheila M. Block is assistant director of research for the Fair Tax Commission.

Allan M. Maslove is director of research of the Fair Tax Commission. He is also professor in the School of Public Administration at Carleton University, Ottawa.

Commission Organization

Chair**
Monica Townson

Vice-Chairs
Neil Brooks*
Robert Couzin*

Commissioners
Jayne Berman
William Blundell
Susan Giampietri
Brigitte Kitchen*
Gérard Lafrenière
Fiona Nelson
Satya Poddar*

Executive Director
Hugh Mackenzie

Director of Research
Allan M. Maslove

Assistant Director of Research
Sheila Block

Executive Assistant to Research Program
Moira Hutchinson

Editorial Assistant
Marguerite Martindale

*Member of the Research Subcommittee
**Chair of the Research Subcommittee

www.ingramcontent.com/pod-product-compliance
Lightning Source LLC
Chambersburg PA
CBHW032135020426
42334CB00016B/1169